The Reminiscences of
George Strother Gaines

Pioneer and Statesman of Early Alabama and Mississippi, 1805-1843

Edited with an Introduction
and Notes by **James P. Pate**

The University of Alabama Press
Tuscaloosa and London

"Gaines' Reminiscences" by George Strother Gaines was originally
published in *The Alabama Historical Quarterly* 26 (Fall–Winter 1964)
by the Alabama Department of Archives and History. "Gaines'
Reminiscences" and the material in the appendixes to this volume
are published with the permission of the Alabama Department
of Archives and History.

*Front Cover: Photograph of portrait of George Strother Gaines
from Gaineswood in Demopolis, Alabama. Photograph by Rob
Fleming. Courtesy of the Alabama Historical Commission.*

Text Designed by Lucinda Smith

∞

The paper on which this book is printed meets the minimum
requirements of American National Standard for Information
Science–Permanence of Paper for Printed Library Materials,
ANSI Z39.48-1984.

Library of Congress Cataloging-in-Publication Data

Gaines, George Strother, 1784–1873

The Reminiscences of George Strother Gaines: Pioneer and Statesman
of Early Alabama and Mississippi, 1805–1843 / edited with an
introduction and notes by James P. Pate.

p. cm. — (Library of Alabama Classics)
Includes bibliographical references (p.) and index.
ISBN 0-8173-0897-0 (alk. paper)

1. Gaines, George Strother, 1784–1873. 2. Pioneers—
Alabama—Biography. 3. Alabama—History—To 1819.
4. Alabama—History—1819–1950. 5. Alabama—Social life
and customs. 6. Choctaw Indians—Alabama—History—
19th century. I. Pate, James P. II. Title. III. Series.

F326.G28   1997
976.1'05'092—dc21   97-7084
[B]

British Library Cataloguing-in-Publication Data available

Contents

Gaines' Reminiscences

Illustrations

ℳote on the Text

The "Reminiscences" of George Strother Gaines and the three sup-
porting documents that follow in the appendixes are presented
here in cooperation with the Alabama Department of Archives and
History in Montgomery, Alabama. The "Introduction" and "Notes on the
Early Days of South Alabama" first appeared in the *Mobile Register* in five
issues between 19 June and 17 July 1872 and are generally referred to as
the "first series." They were subsequently republished along with the unpublished "Reminiscences of Early Times in Mississippi Territory," usually
called the "second series," in the *Alabama Historical Quarterly* in 1964.
Gaines' letter of 8 August 1857 to Anthony Winston Dillard, a Sumter
County, Alabama, lawyer and judge, provides additional reminiscences
about the Choctaw removal era. The two Gaines interviews conducted in
1847 and 1848 offer additional insights and corroborate the "Reminiscences" dictated by Gaines to Albert C. Coles nearly a quarter of a century
later. Together these documents trace Gaines' life from his arrival in the
Mississippi Territory in 1805 through his semiretirement in Spring Hill in
1843.

The present edition of the "Reminiscences" is based on the previously
published version in the *Alabama Historical Quarterly*, but the editor has
made some corrections based on the five issues of the *Mobile Register* and
the handwritten copy of the second series. The Dillard letter and Pickett
conversations are taken from copies of the original manuscripts, and mi-
nor changes have been made to punctuation, spelling and paragraph
breaks to assist the reader. Occasional editorial comment occurs within
the text when clarification is required. In each of the following original
documents, there is inconsistency in the spelling of proper names. The
Tombigbee and Ouachita Rivers, several Indian names, and some names
of European origin are spelled in several ways. It is important to remember that Gaines dictated both his "Reminiscences" and the 1857 letter to
Dillard, and the Pickett "conversations" are his uncorrected interview
notes.

James Gaines

George Strother Gaines
b. 5/1/1784 North Carolina
d. 1/21/1873 State Line, MS

Elizabeth Strother

The *Family* of George Strother Gaines

Young Gaines
b. 1760 South Carolina
d. 1829 Perry County,
    MS

Ann Lawrence Gaines
b. c.1795 Alabama
d. 1868 State Line, MS

Esther Lawrence
b. 1765 South Carolina
d. 1845 Perry County,
    MS

Elizabeth Ervin Gaines
b. 1813   d. 1813
Ft. St. Stephens, M.T.

George Washington Gaines
b. 7/4/1815 Mobile, AL
d. 1853

    Eliza Caroline Earle
    b. 7/17/1817
    d. 12/26/1878

    Darwin Bullock
    Capt., U.S. Army

Helen Elizabeth Gaines
b. 12/31/1819 St. Stephens, AL
d. 1/24/1897

James J. Gaines
b. 1821 St. Stephens, AL
d. c. 1876 Arkansas

    Rosa (?)

Mary Amelia Gaines
b. 1823 Demopolis, AL
d. 4/18/1893 State Line, MS
not md

Francis Young Gaines
b. 1825 Demopolis, AL
d. 1/26/1873 Tuscahoma, AL
not md

Henry Lawrence Gaines
b. 1827 Demopolis, AL
d. ?

    Mary Earle

Abner Strother Gaines
b. 1/20/1832 Demopolis, AL
d. 1905 State Line, MS

    Marion Viola Stark
    b. 8/10/1950 d. 8/10/1942

Jonathan Emanuel Gaines
b. 1835 Mobile, AL
d. c. 1884 State Line, MS
not md

Helen Mary Gaines
b. 6/9/1837 d. 9/29/1897
not md

Annie Rebecca Gaines
b. 11/25/1839 d. 4/5/ 1865
not md

Earle Gaines
b. 4/25/1842 d. 1870
    Mollie Pritchett

George Strother Gaines
b. 5/24/1845 d. infancy

Frank Young Gaines
b. 9/25/1848 d. infancy

Henry Lawrence Gaines
b. 4/9/1850 d. 12/22/1923
    Annie Eliza Tate
    b. 9/6/1851 d. 8/20/1930

Vivian Pendleton Gaines
b. 9/21/1852 d. 11/27/1923
    Margaret Caroline Tate
    b. 3/5/1855 d. 10/8/1924

Mary Elizabeth Bullock
    b. 1842
    d. 11/18/1918
    (1) William Merriwether
    (2) Archie M. Punch

Darwin Bullock, Jr. not md

Susan Earle Gaines
b. 9/9/1855   d. 9/9/1919
not md

Isabella Pendleton Gaines
b. 9/1/1859   d. 1930
    William Baskerville

George Stark Gaines
b. 12/31/1879 d. 1/15/1962
    (1) Mary Pillans
    b. 8/15/1885 d. 8/2/1916
    (2) Ann Stephenson
    b. 12/29/1892 d. ?

Abner Strother Gaines
b. 1883   d. infancy

Marion Viola Gaines
b. 7/14/1885   d. ?
not md

Edmund Pendleton Gaines
b. 9/13/1889 d. ?
not md

The Reminiscences of
George Strother Gaines

George Strother Gaines, 1784–1873 (Courtesy of Alabama Department of Archives and History, Montgomery, Alabama)

Introduction

JAMES P. PATE

In May 1805, George Strother Gaines rode into St. Stephens, Mississippi Territory, and into the history of Alabama and Mississippi for
the next six decades. Late in 1804 Gaines had accepted an appointment as assistant factor at the federal factory, the Choctaw Trading House,
at St. Stephens. When he left his Gallatin, Tennessee, home in March
1805, he could not have envisioned that his journey would link the next
sixty-eight years of his life to the states of Alabama and Mississippi. His
passage via the Cumberland, Ohio, and Mississippi Rivers brought him
on 10 April 1805 to Natchez, Mississippi Territory, where he met Colonel
Silas Dinsmoor, United States agent to the Choctaw Indians. Dinsmoor
was en route to New Orleans to purchase supplies for an approaching
Indian conference with the Choctaw Nation at St. Stephens. After learning
of a smallpox outbreak in New Orleans, Gaines was inoculated for smallpox the day after arriving in Natchez. However, despite the smallpox
threat, they remained in New Orleans for several days while Dinsmoor
completed his business transactions. Dinsmoor booked a small Spanish
schooner to haul his supplies, and they traveled to Spanish Mobile and up
the Mobile River to American territory at Fort Stoddert. From Fort Stoddert, Gaines and Dinsmoor traveled the final forty miles to St. Stephens
on the Tombigbee River by horseback. By the time Gaines arrived at St.
Stephens on 6 May 1805, he was duly impressed with the New England-
er's intellect and wit and was convinced that Dinsmoor was the "right man
in the right place" to conduct a "humane" government policy toward the
Choctaw.[1]

But George Strother Gaines was also the "right man in the right place."
Gaines played a pivotal role in events that shaped the early development
and history of Alabama and Mississippi prior to the Civil War. His per-

sonal "Reminiscences," dictated by the eighty-seven-year-old Gaines and recorded by his good friend and young business partner, Albert C. Coles of State Line, Mississippi, chronicle Gaines' private life and public service as factor, bank cashier, state senator, merchant, "exploring agent," "commissioner for treating with the Indians," superintendent for Choctaw removal, and state bond salesman and bank president. The first part of Gaines' "Reminiscences," referred to as the "first series," was originally published in five issues of the *Mobile Register* in 1872 as "Notes on the Early Days of South Alabama." Nearly a century later, in 1964, Peter Brannon, editor of the *Alabama Historical Quarterly,* published the first series along with the previously unpublished second series, "Reminiscences of Early Times in Mississippi Territory," as "Gaines' Reminiscences."[2]

Gaines had earlier shared his experiences and reminiscences with Albert James Pickett and Anthony Winston Dillard. Gaines and Pickett exchanged a series of letters in 1847, and Pickett interviewed Gaines at his home in Spring Hill, Alabama, in 1847 and 1848. Pickett used his "conversations" with Gaines to write his *History of Alabama,* published in 1851. Gaines and Dillard also exchanged correspondence, but only Gaines' lengthy letter of 8 August 1857 has survived. Dillard, a Sumter County, Alabama, lawyer and judge, used this letter to write a history of Sumter County and his "History of the Treaty of Dancing Rabbit," published in the *Transactions of the Alabama Historical Society* in 1899. Dillard notes in this publication that Gaines had agreed to assist him, but because of "defective vision" one of Gaines' sons had served as his secretary to dictate "such facts and events" as requested. Gaines' letter was later published in 1928 as "Removal of the Choctaws" in a pamphlet by the Alabama Department of Archives and History that includes Dillard's "Treaty of Dancing Rabbit" article. Unfortunately, the great bulk of Gaines' personal papers and correspondence has been lost or destroyed. However, some Gaines materials, letters, and reports can be found in a number of public collections and newspapers and are helpful in telling his unique story and validating his "Reminiscences."[3]

Gaines was the youngest son and the eleventh of thirteen children born to Captain James Gaines and his second wife, Elizabeth Strother Gaines. At his birth on 1 May 1784 in Surry County (later Stokes County), North Carolina, Gaines joined a distinguished family with a pedigree that included many of the prominent families of eighteenth-century Virginia. His father served as captain of the Culpepper County, Virginia, minutemen, and his cousins Henry and Nathaniel Pendleton, Jr., were also members. After the Revolutionary War, Captain Gaines moved his family over the

Virginia–North Carolina border into Surry County, where he was elected to the state legislature in 1787. He also served as a member of the North Carolina convention that was called for the ratification of the Constitution. Prior to removing his family to Sullivan County, Tennessee, in 1794, Captain Gaines served as a commissioner to divide Surry into two counties, Surry and Stokes.[4]

The Gaines family moved to Sullivan County to settle on lands bequeathed to Captain Gaines by his uncle Edward Pendleton, who presided over the Virginia convention that ratified the Constitution. Captain Gaines' family grew with the birth of two more children and prospered in the East Tennessee hill country. Little is known about George Strother Gaines' early life or education, but he had acquired some business acumen while working for the merchant brothers John and Robert Allen at Gallatin, Tennessee. Although Gaines reports in his "Reminiscences" that "Mr. Chambers" invited him to be his assistant, the record is not clear on how this twenty-year-old frontiersman received a federal appointment as assistant factor at the Choctaw Trading House. Perhaps there were strong Virginia–North Carolina political connections to the Jefferson administration, and obviously Gaines' family had ties to Joseph Chambers, a native of Salisbury, North Carolina, and the factor at the federal trading post. More recently, the Gaines family had developed important Tennessee political ties to Willie Blount, W. C. C. Claiborne, James Robertson, and Andrew Jackson that served Gaines well for many years.[5]

Choctaw Factor, Banker, and Merchant

When George Strother Gaines arrived at the Choctaw Trading House, located in buildings of the old Spanish Fort St. Stephens, he found his new employer, Joseph Chambers, burdened with official paperwork for three federal positions. Chambers was appointed factor by the Jefferson administration in 1802 and was subsequently appointed register of the federal land office in 1803 and postmaster in 1804. Overburdened by the demands of three federal positions, Chambers entrusted the day-to-day operations of the trading house to his new assistant factor. When Chambers resigned as factor in 1806 to return to North Carolina, he recommended that Gaines be appointed to replace him. Gaines' appointment as factor became official in 1807, and he was subsequently named postmaster at St. Stephens. Despite his youth, the twenty-three-year-old Gaines had established a solid reputation with the Indians, particularly the Choctaw, as well as with the settlers in the lower Tombigbee.[6]

At the Choctaw Trading House, Gaines and the Indians transacted most of their business through barter, with little cash involved. The Choctaw and other customers brought in otter, beaver, raccoon, fox, "cat," bear, wolf, and deer skins to exchange for all manner of manufactured goods. In addition to animal skins and furs, Gaines accepted beeswax, snakeroot, tallow, bear oil, corn, beef, bacon, venison, and other produce from his Indian and white customers. Gaines' customers purchased a large array of goods from the shelves of the trading house at St. Stephens and later at Fort Confederation, including blankets, strouds, calico, silver jewelry, knives, gunpowder, lead, vermilion, kettles, wool hats, salt, sugar, coffee, "corn hoes," cowbells, saddles, tools, and other items. The federal factories were expected to provide quality goods at fair prices while helping to "civilize" their Indian customers.[7] The following 10 May 1814 transaction is typical:[8]

Bartered with Indians

1/2 yd Blue cloth...	@.50	$1.75
1/4 # powder......	@ 1.00.	25
2/3 doz flints......	@ 1.00	12 1/2
2 British shawls	@ 87 1/2.	1.75
6 yds binding.		37 1/2
16 yds [ditto].		1.00
3 5/8 # powder	@ 1.00	3.37 1/2
19 yds binding.		1.18 3/4
2 1/2 # lead.......	@ 20	50
		$10.56

Received in Payment

24 deerskins	43 lbs @ 17.	$7.31
2 dressed deerskins .	@ 20	93 3/4
1 fox	@ 20	12 1/2
2 [dressed fox]....	@ 20	37 1/2
3 lbs Beeswax	@ 25	75
		$9.50
cash		1.06
		$10.56

Although the Choctaw were Gaines' principal customers, the trading house was visited by Chickasaw from the upper Tombigbee, Creeks living on the Black Warrior and Alabama Rivers, and white settlers from the lower Tombigbee and Tensaw settlements. While Indian customers and private traders leveled charges at the factory system generally for selling shoddy merchandise at high prices, the Choctaw Trading House was not guilty of this practice. Gaines took great care not to sell damaged goods to his Indian customers without pointing out the damage and reducing the price. Despite Gaines' good business sense, the trading house was continually plagued by the slow arrival of supplies, the payment of heavy import and export duties to the Spanish at Mobile, and the seizure of powder and lead for the Indian trade as "war material" by the Spanish. A depressed market for skins and furs, an unhealthy location, and the distance from the people it was intended to serve further hampered Gaines' efforts at the government trading house. Gaines' warehouse was filled with poor-quality skins, and the superintendent of Indian trade often ordered him not to send any peltry to New Orleans because of the large quantity there and the depressed market.[9]

A brief illness in February 1807 interrupted Gaines' routine at the trading house and caused him to seek the comfort of his older brother's quarters at Fort Stoddert. Lieutenant Edmund Pendleton Gaines had been assigned to Fort Stoddert in 1804 and had been serving as commander of the post since 1806. While his wife, Frances Toulmin Gaines, ministered to his sick brother, Lieutenant Gaines was alerted to the presence of Colonel Aaron Burr, former vice-president of the United States, in the territory. Burr was accused of conspiring to seize control of New Orleans and other American territory, and warrants had been issued for his arrest. Lieutenant Gaines and his mounted soldiers intercepted Burr on 19 February 1807 near Wakefield, the county seat of Washington County, and placed him under arrest. As George Strother Gaines relates in his 1847 "conversation" with Pickett, his older brother and his family treated Burr cordially at the fort, and he himself spent time in conversation with Burr discussing the Indians and their commerce. When not engaged in conversation with the Gaines brothers or other visitors, Burr played chess with Frances Toulmin Gaines. However, Lieutenant Gaines was anxious to deliver Burr to the proper authorities at "Washington City," and he dispatched his famous prisoner on 22 February 1807 under a party led by Nicholas Perkins. Subsequently, in April 1807 the War Department ordered Lieutenant Gaines to Richmond, Virginia, to serve as a witness in Burr's trial.[10]

With the "Burr conspiracy" over and a new trading season in the offing, George Strother Gaines and his superiors at the War Department attempted to find a solution to his supply problems by developing an overland route. In July 1807, Secretary of War Henry Dearborn ordered Gaines' older brother Edmund to explore the region between the Tennessee and Tombigbee Rivers and to discover the "botable waters of the Tombigby." Lieutenant Gaines, between December 1807 and January 1808, completed surveys from the Muscle Shoals of the Tennessee to Cotton Gin Port in the present Monroe County, Mississippi, on the Tombigbee and marked four possible routes between the two streams. Fearing the loss of revenue to his ferry over the Tennessee on the Natchez Trace, George Colbert of the Chickasaw Nation protested the proposed new wagon road and effectively blocked its development for several years. George Strother Gaines first made use of one route surveyed by his brother on the west bank of the Tombigbee between Colbert's Ferry and Major John Pitchlynn's home on Oktibbeha Creek in 1810, not as a wagon road but for packhorses conveying lead, powder, and other trade goods down to St. Stephens. Still later in 1813 Gaines built a barge at Pitchlynn's near the mouth of Oktibbeha Creek on the Tombigbee River and hauled trading house cargo down to St. Stephens. Despite the dangers of a flooded river and the growing hostility of the Creeks, Gaines' crew and cargo arrived safely. On several occasions prior to the American seizure of Mobile by General James Wilkinson in 1813, Gaines used the road to Pitchlynn's, the Tombigbee River route, and the overland route to Natchez to move supplies.[11]

Despite the demands of public service and the business problems associated with the trading house, Gaines found time to court and marry a distant cousin, Ann Gaines, in 1812. She was the seventeen-year-old daughter of Young Gaines, Sr., a prominent landowner and slave owner who lived about ten miles north of Wakefield near the mouth of Bassett's Creek on the west side of the Tombigbee River. Young Gaines and his wife, Esther, emigrated with their family from South Carolina, and he became a well-known and respected leader in the lower Tombigbee settlements. According to the Washington County tax records for 1808, Young Gaines owned twenty-three slaves and 2,400 acres of land—800 acres at the mouth of Bassett's Creek, 800 acres at McIntosh Bluff, and 800 acres at the mouth of the Alabama River. His new son-in-law was a more modest property owner who paid taxes on six slaves and 120 acres of land in 1811. However, Gaines and his father-in-law continued to buy and sell land and acquire slaves, Gaines added town lots in St. Stephens in 1813, and both purchased land in the present Perry County, Mississippi, between 1811 and 1817. Perry County tax records for 1827 show that Young Gaines owned 1,290 acres on the Leaf River, with forty-one slaves and several hundred cattle.[12]

While Gaines' family was very important to him and obviously influ-

Ann Gaines, 1795–1868. Wife of George Strother Gaines (Courtesy of Alabama Department of Archives and History, Montgomery, Alabama)

enced his long public service and business career, there are limited personal references to his family in his "Reminiscences," the Pickett interviews, and his limited personal papers and correspondence. Gaines does refer to Ann Gaines' "delicate health" in September 1813 before he traveled with Pushmataha, Choctaw chief of the Southern (or Six Towns) District, and Flood McCrew to seek the assistance of the Choctaw against the

Creeks. However, the birth of their first child, Elizabeth Ervin Gaines, generally given as 1813 at "Fort St. Stephens," and her death as an infant or in early childhood are not mentioned. While Gaines makes references to "my family" on several occasions, he makes no specific references to his other eight children, born between 1815 and 1835. He mentions his father-in-law's sending "a drove of cattle" to Fort Confederation in 1816 "for my family" and also mentions him in two other general references. References to "Mrs. Gaines" appear in several places in his "Reminiscences," and in May 1815, he reports, he made arrangements for the "comfortable traveling of my family and myself though the wilderness, to Tennessee." Gaines writes that he and his family encountered General and Mrs. Andrew Jackson on the Natchez Trace en route from New Orleans to Nashville, visited Nicholas Perkins at Franklin, and "spent a few days with John Allen at Gallatin" before traveling to his father's, where they spent several weeks "visiting relatives and friends." Yet there is no mention of George Washington Gaines, whose birth is generally given as 4 July 1815 in Mobile.[13]

After vacationing with family and friends in Tennessee, Gaines traveled on to Washington, where he met with John Mason, superintendent of Indian trade, at his office in Georgetown and with Secretary of War William H. Crawford. During these meetings, Gaines, Mason, and Crawford finalized a decision to move the trading house up the Tombigbee River to a location nearer the Choctaw and more convenient to the Chickasaw. Silas Dinsmoor had written to Crawford on 4 August 1813 urging that the trading house be moved into the "Chaktaw Country." Though the Creek War of 1813–14 delayed the removal, the postwar growth of settlements confirmed the wisdom of relocating the trading house near the people it was meant to serve. Crawford authorized Gaines to acquire "a cession of land, not exceeding two square miles, on the Tombigby river at or near fort confederation for the purpose of establishing a factory and a military post." Before Gaines left Washington, Mason and the War Department committed to sending a company of soldiers to assist with the construction of buildings at the new site.[14]

In November 1815, Gaines met with Pushmataha, who recommended that the trading house be located at the site of the old Spanish Fort Confederation at Jones' Bluff on the west bank of the Tombigbee near the present Epes, Sumter County, Alabama, upriver from the confluence of the Black Warrior and the Tombigbee. Gaines and John McKee, agent to the Choctaw who had replaced Dinsmoor, met at the Choctaw agency with the "mingoes, chiefs & warriors in full council" on 11–16 December 1815 to discuss the removal of the trading house "into the nation." Gaines addressed the council and presented a sketch of a "convention" or agreement for moving the trading house up the Tombigbee. After Gaines' address, several Choctaw leaders, including Pushmataha, expressed their support and agreed that the new trading house should be located "on the Tombigby at or near Fort Confederation." Pushmataha, in a short speech, requested that the prices of goods be fixed at a lower rate, acknowledged that the Choctaw and Americans were friends, and urged that they should always remain friends. Gaines selected a well-wooded site on the Old Box Maker's Creek, now Factory Creek, that his assistant factor, Thomas Malone, and several Choctaw surveyed. He paid Adam James, a half-blood Choctaw, $120 for the "cabins at James' Springs" and "for my claim to the section chosen for the factory buildings." The new factory was situated about two miles north and west of the remains of Fort Confederation. The fort site included trenches, a few scattered pickets, and a log house near the site occupied by Samuel Jones and his Indian family. Gaines reported to Mason that the chiefs had agreed to the president's wishes, and he returned to St. Stephens to gather a workforce to construct the new trading house.[15]

From December 1815 through December 1816, Gaines directed the construction of several buildings that became the new Choctaw Trading House. Mason had suggested the construction of a "dwelling house twenty by thirty," a store and warehouse of the same dimensions, and other small outhouses as necessary. Construction was slowed because of heavy rain in late January and February 1816 and the late arrival of the soldiers promised by Crawford. The troops arrived at St. Stephens on 4 February, and a few days later the twelve soldiers and a sergeant plus carpenters and other laborers from the lower Tombigbee settlements proceeded upriver with Gaines. Gaines complained that the soldiers were "old men and men incapable of doing much labour" and that completing the buildings was fraught with problems. Evidently, Gaines' residence was not completed until 30 December 1816, when John Cox Porter was paid $75 "for building two chimneys of two fireplaces each to the factors house and laying four harths." A plat of the trading house enclosed in a letter from Gaines to Mason on 25 July 1816 indicates that a stockade fence was erected to provide security to the trading house.[16]

Despite the slow progress on the new buildings, in late February 1816 Gaines began trading out of "an old house & accommodated such as come to trade." Two boatloads of cargo arrived on 22 February, and near the end of March, Gaines returned to St. Stephens "for the balance of goods,

my books, papers and family." Gaines wrote to Mason on 10 June, "I arrived here on the 11th May and have since opened all the goods and our
trade is becoming lively." The same spring Gaines directed the construction of two barges or keelboats, the *Young Chaktaw* and the *General
Pushmataha,* which hauled supplies and cargo between the factory and
Mobile. The factory barges were well equipped with "oars, socket poles,
hooks and jams" to move up and down the Tombigbee. While construction of or repairs to the factory barges and buildings continued through
1817, Gaines' new Choctaw Trading House quickly became a center of
economic and social activity. Choctaw, Chickasaw, "Indian countrymen,"
and a growing number of settlers from the Tombigbee and Black Warrior
settlements descended on the trading house.[17]

By the late fall of 1816, a small community had grown up around the
new trading house that included Gaines' family, Samuel Jones' family,
thirteen soldiers, trading house employees, craftsmen and other laborers,
several slaves, and visiting Indians. The trading house employees included
Thomas Malone, the assistant factor, and his family; Benjamin Everett,
the skinsman, and his wife; Joseph Pitchlynn, who assisted with the skins
and worked in the store; and William Y. Boykin, the interpreter. Everett,
Gaines' brother-in-law, was employed at St. Stephens in 1816 and became
"assistant agent" in 1817 and assistant factor in 1819 after Malone's resignation. The slave population included Malone's Isaac and three slaves
belonging to Gaines, including his trusted Dick. The population increased
seasonally with boat hands, freight haulers, traders, Indians, and settlers.
Even Postmaster General Josiah Meigs recognized the importance of
Gaines' frontier trading center by appointing Gaines postmaster at the
"Chactaw Tradinghouse" on 29 October 1816.[18]

Gaines' outpost on the Tombigbee hosted an important treaty conference in late October 1816. John McKee, the Choctaw agent, convened the
conference at the trading house at the direction of Secretary of War John
C. Calhoun. McKee was joined by John Rhea and John Coffee of Tennessee as commissioners for the United States. Choctaw from the three districts gathered at Gaines' settlement by the thousands to participate in the
treaty conference, the ball plays, the feasts of corn and beef, and the
nightly dances. The district chiefs—Pushmataha, Mushulatubbee, and
Puckshenubbee—and other leaders ate with the commissioners at the trading house with Gaines, Malone, Everett, and their families. The whole
atmosphere of the conference was one of friendship and respect, with a
great deal of reminiscing about the war with the Creeks. The treaty of
Fort Confederation contained two articles that provided that the Choctaw

agree to surrender "all their title and claim to lands" east of the Tombigbee River in exchange for an annuity of $6,000 for twenty years and $10,000 in merchandise. The treaty was signed on 24 October 1816 by the commissioners and thirteen Choctaw chiefs, and was witnessed by Thomas H. Williams, secretary to the commissioners.[19]

Gaines' isolated settlement and the nearby Choctaw towns were quickly deluged by emigrants, who flowed into the lands of the eastern Tombigbee River valley and the Black Warrior River basin. Settlers from Virginia, the Carolinas, Georgia, Tennessee, Kentucky, and more distant states were joined by Europeans—all searching for land, wealth, and a new life. Gaines had actively recruited family members in Tennessee and promoted the Alabama area in a letter to his brother James Taylor Gaines on 8 February 1814, when he declared, "Should the Alabama lands fall into the hands of the Gov't & I will not doubt it, you must come out & select you a tract of land & bring all our friends with you if possible. The Alabama will be a garden of America ere many years." In June 1817, Bonapartist exiles General Count Charles Lefebvre Desnouettes, Colonel Nicholas Simon Parmentier, and other French emigrants visited the outpost, seeking Gaines' advice about locating a settlement near the confluence of the Tombigbee and Black Warrior Rivers. Gaines advised the Frenchmen to establish their settlement at White Bluff (or "Ecor Blanc") on the Black Warrior, and they subsequently established a small town named Demopolis. Following this initial contact, Gaines became an important resource to the French, supplying them trade goods and on at least one occasion selling a pair of oxen to General Desnouettes. After the French settlers discovered that their original town site was outside their grant, they established a new settlement one mile east of Demopolis called Aigleville. In 1819 Gaines joined a group of businessmen from St. Stephens to establish the White Bluff Association, which purchased the Demopolis site and elected five commissioners to promote the development of their new town: James Childress, Walter Crenshaw, Lefebvre Desnouettes, Joseph B. Earle, and George Strother Gaines. One source claims that Gaines was the first mayor of Demopolis, but he probably only served as chairman of the association.[20]

Gaines submitted his resignation as factor of the Choctaw Trading House on 3 August 1818 to accept a position with the new Tombeckbe Bank in St. Stephens. He was elected secretary and cashier at the bank while Israel Pickens, a St. Stephens lawyer and register at the federal land office, was elected president. St. Stephens had become the temporary capital of the new Alabama Territory, and Gaines' bank was deeply involved in numerous land deals and other business transactions. He became active in the business and civic life of St. Stephens, renewing old friendships and making new ones that helped him to increase his property holdings and business activities. However, Thomas L. McKenney, superintendent of Indian affairs, delayed the acceptance of Gaines' resignation as factor and questioned Gaines' decision to accept the position as cashier: "Knowing as well as I do, the pressure that Banks feel; and the vexation that the Cashiers undergo now-a-days I am decidedly of the opinion the place of Factor is preferable." Gaines continued to make trips upriver to the trading house to examine the account books and transmit the required quarterly reports to Washington until John Hersey's appointment as the new factor in October 1819.[21]

Because of business and property interests in Demopolis as well as perhaps hard times for the bank, which were exacerbated by the panic of 1819, Gaines resigned his office in 1822. He had entered into a mercantile business in 1821 with Allen Glover, a wealthy planter and slave owner, who had moved from South Carolina to Demopolis in 1818. Glover owned more than one hundred slaves, and he became the town's wealthiest merchant and planter before his death in 1840. At least one source claims that Gaines opened the first store in Demopolis in 1818, and the new partnership with Glover may have been an outgrowth of that enterprise. Gaines purchased "several quarter sections" of land near Demopolis in 1819, and he sold a portion of these lands to Glover shortly after his arrival in Demopolis. Gaines moved his family to Demopolis in 1822, occupying cabins that he had built in 1821 on his property adjacent to the town. Gaines and Glover expanded their business in 1822 by purchasing the Choctaw Trading House from the federal government, and Gaines assumed responsibility for its operation. The Choctaw welcomed the return of their old friend, and the Northern and Southern Districts continued to receive their annuity goods at the old trading house until after the Treaty of Dancing Rabbit Creek.[22]

Gaines' years in Demopolis not only influenced his property and business interests but also affected his immediate and extended family. His family grew from three young children in 1822 to six children prior to their move to Mobile in 1832. The Gaines and Glover families became such good friends that the Glovers named their youngest daughter Ann Gaines Glover. Gaines' nephew Francis Strother Lyon moved from St. Stephens to Demopolis in 1821 and married Allen Glover's daughter Sarah Serena on 4 March 1824. Gaines' oldest son, George Washington Gaines, married Eliza Caroline Earle, a daughter of Dr. Joseph B. and Susan Sloan

Earle, in Demopolis in 1835. Dr. Earle later served as one of Gaines' assistants in conducting the first Choctaw removal party to the West in 1831. Several years later, on 31 October 1853, Henry Lawrence Gaines, Gaines' fourth-oldest son, married Mary Earle, the Earles' youngest daughter.[23]

While the Glover and Gaines business partnership flourished in the 1820s, Gaines entered into a brief political career. Although busily engaged at the Choctaw Trading House, as he acknowledges in his "Reminiscences," his "friends in Clark and Marengo" persuaded him to enter the race for state senator in 1825. Gaines remained occupied at the trading house, and two other candidates joined the race and began canvassing for votes. However, Gaines' many friends rallied sufficient support to elect him over his two opponents. His two-year term coincided with the relocation of the state capital from Cahaba to Tuscaloosa during Governor John Murphy's first term in office. Despite strong opposition, Gaines supported the move to Tuscaloosa and cast a "yea" in the close 11–10 decision during the 1825 session to move the capital. During his tenure he also had the opportunity to support his old friend and former governor Israel Pickens' interim appointment to the United States Senate, and he was one of two senators appointed to a joint committee with three house members to "inspect and examine such general accounts in the books of the Bank of the State of Alabama." His brief term in office allowed Gaines to develop important personal and political connections that proved useful in his second banking career in Mobile and in his lobbying efforts for the Mobile and Ohio Railroad.[24]

In the late summer of 1830, William Ward, federal agent to the Choctaw, notified Gaines of a treaty conference to be held on Dancing Rabbit Creek near Macon, Mississippi. Ward contracted with Glover and Gaines to provide beef, corn, and other supplies to feed several thousand participants. Gaines and his servant Dick established a camp near the treaty ground to manage the supplies and the cattle to be consumed at the conference. Secretary of War John H. Eaton and John Coffee from Florence, Alabama, were the federal commissioners who negotiated with the Choctaw from 15–30 September 1830. The Choctaw were bitterly divided— many opposed the surrender of their lands and removal to new lands west of the Mississippi. Several Choctaw leaders left the treaty grounds, and others sought Gaines' intercession and advice, but Eaton and Coffee— through harsh threats, bribery, and intimidation—ultimately gained acceptance of the removal treaty. While several Choctaw leaders vowed never to remove to the West, the three district chiefs—Greenwood LeFlore, Nitakechi, and Mushulatubbee—and 168 "Mingoes, chiefs, captains and warriors of the Choctaw Nation" made their "marks" on the Treaty of Dancing Rabbit Creek on 27 September. The treaty contained twenty-two articles filled with government promises that led to the sad demise of the Choctaw Nation in the state of Mississippi. The next day, several of the same signatories placed their "marks" on four supplemental articles that confirmed several additional "reservations," provided for an exploring party to the West, and granted two sections of land to Glover and Gaines to be sold to pay off accounts of "the poorest Indian first."[25]

The First Choctaw Removal, 1830–1832

Before the federal commissioners left the treaty grounds, Gaines agreed to Eaton's request that he accept an appointment as "exploring agent" for the Choctaw and a "commission for treating with the Indians." Jackson's administration was anxious to remove both the Choctaw and the Chickasaw from Mississippi and expected Gaines to convince the two tribes to share the Choctaw lands west of the Mississippi. As Gaines relates in his "Reminiscences," he cited his business and family obligations, but Eaton called on his patriotism and promised to appoint him "superintendent for the removal and subsistence of Indians." Gaines reluctantly accepted Eaton's request to lead a Choctaw party to explore their new lands and to convince a Chickasaw exploring party under Colonel Benjamin Reynolds to purchase a portion of the Choctaw lands. Before departing for home, Gaines called on the three district chiefs, requested that they select six or seven "captains for the exploring party," and promised to supply tents, packhorses, and "a new rifle for each man." Although Gaines notes in his "Reminiscences" that his partner, Glover, expressed dissatisfaction regarding his new federal appointments, he fails to share his family's reaction to his latest involvement "in the public service."[26]

Gaines and Dick left Demopolis on 14 October 1830 and journeyed into the Choctaw Nation to organize the Choctaw exploring party. They were joined by Nitakechi and "his six Captains" near the Sucarnochee River, and they rode west to the "Yazoo valley," where they were joined by captains from Mushulatubbee's and LeFlore's districts. With a party of twenty "on hardy Indian ponies," Gaines and his men traveled three days in rain as they crossed the swamps and backwaters of the Yalobusha, Yazoo, and "dead rivers" before reaching the Mississippi. They crossed the Mississippi into Arkansas Territory near the mouth of the Arkansas River and traveled up the north bank of the Arkansas, reaching Little Rock on 18 November. Gaines crossed over the river to pay his respects to Governor John Pope, and after a one-day delay Gaines' party resumed their journey up the Arkansas. Near Fort Smith in late November, the group encountered an independent Choctaw party led by George W. Harkins and Robert Folsom, who were returning to Mississippi after exploring the new lands on the Red River. On 28 November they crossed to the south bank of the Arkansas and camped for several days at Fort Smith. Gaines distributed new rifles and ammunition to each member of his party, and they took on supplies and packhorses. He reported to the Office of Indian Affairs from Fort Smith that the Choctaw captains were so poor and "so badly mounted and clad, that I have been compelled to aid them," and he purchased several horses, clothing, and blankets from the traders at Fort Smith.[27]

Rested and freshly supplied, Gaines' party continued their journey, ascending the north bank of the Arkansas to the Illinois. They camped near Bean's Salt Works on this stream while Gaines sent men to Fort Gibson to request supplies and an escort from Colonel Matthew Arbuckle as authorized by the War Department. The supplies from Colonel Arbuckle were delivered at Webbers Falls on 6 December 1830, and Gaines' party moved up the north bank of the Canadian until they ran out of forage for their horses above the South Fork. They then turned southwestward, where they soon encountered the Chickasaw exploring party under Colonel Reynolds. The weather had become severely cold, covering the cane with a thick coat of ice, threatening the parties with frostbite, and freezing the creeks with thick ice. On or about 20 December, Major James L. Dawson and his father-in-law, Assistant Surgeon James W. Baylor, and his troops united with the two exploring parties about eighty to one hundred miles above the forks of the Canadian. Gaines' party now numbered fifty-one men, and it had the added advantage of a Delaware guide hired by Major Dawson to help him find the Chickasaw and Choctaw parties. They traveled southwest across the headwaters of the Boggy and Blue Rivers to the Washita, with the Chickasaw complaining that they wished to cross over the Red River into Mexican territory. While the weather was "intensely cold" and "about 5 or 6 inches" of snow and sleet fell on the party between the Blue and the Washita, both parties were pleased with the lands near the Red River and expressed a desire to turn eastward for home. However, they were particularly impressed with the lands from the Blue River east into the Kiamichi River valley. Major Dawson's escort left the exploring parties near the Blue River on 10 January 1831, and Gaines and Reynolds led their delegations eastward along the north bank of the Red River into Arkansas Territory.[28]

After traveling in the Red River country for some two weeks, Gaines and his traveling companions arrived at Washington, Hempstead County, Arkansas Territory, on 29 January 1831. The party had been further reduced several days earlier when Major Levi Colbert and six other Chickasaw crossed over the Red River to visit the Caddo Indians and to explore the country from the Red to the Sabine River. The balance of Gaines' weary travelers arrived in Washington with few supplies, worn-out horses, and "without a dollar in our pocket." They spent several days resting and recruiting fresh horses for the return trip back to Mississippi. Gaines and Reynolds used their time to draft a joint report to Secretary of War Eaton, dated 7 February 1831, on the "Exploration of the Choctaw Country" and requested further instructions. They traveled a few days later to Little Rock, where Reynolds agreed to lead both delegations back to Mississippi, and Gaines and his servant returned in late February via steamboat to New Orleans and to Mobile. Gaines arrived in Mobile on 2 March and visited for several days before continuing his trip upriver to Demopolis. He was interviewed by the *Mobile Commercial Register*, which reported on 7 March that "Mr. Gaines returns in excellent health and spirits well pleased with his tour, and with the advantageous prospects that the country opens to the Choctaw, whose friend and benefactor he has long been regarded, and in whom, probably, they place more implicit confidence than in any other individual in this country."[29]

Upon his return to Demopolis, Gaines engaged in ending his business partnership with Glover and settling his accounts with the War Department. He sent his accounts, detailing expenses incurred as head of the 1830–31 Choctaw exploring expedition, to the War Department on 30 May 1831. When Secretary of War Eaton failed to respond to the 7 February 1831 report on the combined exploring parties or his subsequent correspondence, Gaines traveled to Mobile in June 1831 to open accounts and to purchase goods for a new mercantile business in Demopolis. While in Mobile he was offered a partnership by Jonathan Emanuel, who operated "a wholesale dry goods business." Gaines agreed to contact Emanuel during the latter's business trip to New York to confirm the agreement. He returned to Demopolis to discuss the new partnership proposal and a move to the port city with his wife and family.[30]

While Gaines turned his attention to family and business concerns, the federal effort to remove the Choctaw became entangled in politics and governmental bureaucracy. Eaton had resigned as secretary of war on 7 April 1831, followed closely by the resignation of Secretary of State Martin Van Buren and several other Jackson cabinet members because of the

"Peggy Eaton affair." Roger B. Taney replaced Eaton briefly as acting secretary before Lewis Cass was sworn in on 9 August. During the transition, Captain J. B. Clark was appointed removal agent for the Choctaw west of the Mississippi, and he proceeded to make arrangements for wagons and the necessary oxen and horses. While waiting for official instructions regarding his anticipated appointment to conduct the Choctaw removal, Gaines was visited in Demopolis by Major Francis W. Armstrong, who asked Gaines to introduce him as his friend "to some of the most influential chiefs." Gaines in his "Reminiscences" and in the 1857 letter to Dillard apparently misconstrued Armstrong's role with the Choctaw. Armstrong had received an appointment to conduct a census of the Choctaw in preparation for their removal to the West, and he was subsequently named Choctaw agent west of the Mississippi. Gaines spent several days in July 1831 in the Choctaw Nation introducing Armstrong as his friend and asking the Choctaw to assist Armstrong with his duties. From early July through the completion of the census on 7 September 1831, Armstrong encountered the Choctaw's strong and explicit support of Gaines as their removal agent. At about the same time, Gaines learned that William S. Colquhoun was in LeFlore's district "preparing for their removal." Finally in August 1831, Gaines received a letter from George Gibson, commissary general of subsistence, formally appointing Gaines "superintendent of the subsistence and removal of Indians" and giving Gaines, a civilian, complete authority and control over the removal of the Choctaw.[31]

By early September, Gaines had appointed a number of assistants to organize the Choctaw removal east of the Mississippi. Based on Armstrong's 1831 Choctaw census, which numbered 17,963 Indians, 151 whites, and 521 slaves, the federal government expected Gaines to remove approximately one-third of the Nation in 1831. While Dr. Joseph B. Earle and Sam Dale worked in Nitakechi's district, Thomas McGee recruited emigrants in Mushulatubbee's district and Robert M. Jones worked with Colquhoun in LeFlore's district. With his assistants and other agents gathering emigrant parties for the fall exodus, Gaines made arrangements to hire wagons, contract for supplies, open roads, and engage steamboats. As he traveled through Mississippi, Gaines witnessed the sadness and pain of the Choctaw as they were uprooted from their beloved country. He wrote from Vicksburg on 30 October 1831, "The feeling which many of them evince in separating, never to return again, from their long cherished hills, as poor as they are in this section of the country, is truly painful to witness; and would be more so to me, but for the conviction that removal is absolutely necessary for their preservation and future happiness."[32]

Gaines had selected Vicksburg as the primary embarkation point, and between late October and mid-November some 4,000 Choctaw had gathered at Vicksburg. Another group of approximately 400 of Mushulatubbee's followers arrived at Memphis under Peter Pitchlynn in November. Unfortunately, the steamboats necessary to ferry the emigrants via the Mississippi up the Arkansas River and up the Ouachita River via the Red River did not arrive in a timely manner. Before the steamboats arrived at Vicksburg, one party of Choctaw emigrants ferried up the Mississippi River to Lake Providence, Louisiana, and traveled overland to the Red River. About mid-November, Gaines dispatched some 2,000 Choctaw packed aboard the 200-ton *Walter Scott* and the 100-ton *Reindeer,* with a 170-ton keelboat in tow up the Mississippi to Arkansas Post on the north bank and near the mouth of the Arkansas River. Gaines and Dr. Joseph Earle joined the Choctaw aboard the *Walter Scott* for the journey upriver, but Gaines later transferred to a southbound steamboat. The Vicksburg emigrants were soon joined by Pitchlynn's emigrant party, which had left Memphis on 1 December 1831 aboard the 500-ton *Brandywine.* The horses belonging to Pitchlynn's party were transported downriver in flatboats. Gaines' last two emigrant parties left Vicksburg on 25 November 1831 on the 140-ton *Talma* and the 150-ton *Cleopatra* and traveled down the Mississippi, up the Red, and up the Ouachita to Ecore á Fabre, the present Camden, Arkansas. While suffering numerous hardships and a bitterly cold winter during their overland trek, the parties arrived in the new Choctaw lands in early March 1832. Lieutenant J. R. Stephenson reported issuing rations to 3,749 Choctaw on 30 April 1832 at four stations in the Red River country: Fort Towson, Horse Prairie, Mountain Fork, and Old Miller Court House. About the same time, 536 Choctaw received rations near Fort Smith, and stragglers from both government and self-emigrating parties continued their trek to the new lands west of the Mississippi throughout the spring of 1832.[33]

Despite the harsh conditions and poor coordination of supplies and transportation, Gaines was obviously pleased with his role as superintendent of the 1831 Choctaw emigration. He stopped briefly in Mobile on 16 December 1831 on his return to Demopolis, and the *Mobile Commercial Register* reported the successful "Choctaw Emigration" on 24 December: "In closing this account we cannot refrain from remarking that the parental care of the Government over these helpless sons of the forest, as well as its judicious policy, have been amply exemplified in the selection of the agent chosen by the Indians themselves, who has long been regarded by them as their most valuable friend and who was clothed with unrestricted authority to treat them in the manner his own benevolent feelings dictated." In his lengthy 1857 letter to Dillard, Gaines proudly proclaims, "I am satisfied that the same amount of work was never done in the way of subsisting & removing Indians by the Govt & never will be done hereafter at so little expense, as was incurred by me. . . . With money in hand, & my perfect knowledge of the resources of the country, my contracts were made on the very best terms to the Govt.:—add to this, the understanding between the Indians and Commissioners, when making the Treaty, that they were all to be removed by me, and you have the secret of my success."[34]

However, the War Department and Commissary General Gibson had a different perspective. Gibson's letter of 27 April 1832 notified Gaines of the decision to conduct all future Indian removals using military personnel to allow for more centralized control and to cut costs. The War Department considered the Choctaw removal of 1831 a failure because it cost nearly three times the original estimate. While cost and efficiency were legitimate concerns, there may have been other reasons for replacing Gaines. Francis W. Armstrong in 1832 complained that Gaines had spoiled and indulged the Choctaw in 1831. Perhaps the political connection between Armstrong and Cass, as noted by Gaines in his 1857 letter, was another factor in Gaines' removal. Meanwhile, Gibson urged Gaines to submit his final accounts and thanked him for his services. Gaines sent his accounts as superintendent for removal and subsistence forward to the War Department, but they met with the same fate as his previous expense accounts as "an exploring agent" and "commissioner." The government auditors either rejected or suspended numerous claims, and Gaines finally received a partial settlement of the accounts in 1843 under President John Tyler's administration.[35]

ALABAMA'S BOND SALESMAN, 1832–1833

It is difficult to understand how Gaines might have continued as removal superintendent in 1832, given his business partnership in Mobile and a new position with the state of Alabama. In October 1832 he had moved his family into rooms at White's Hotel in Mobile and shortly afterwards into a house at nearby Spring Hill. By his own admission, "my new business at Mobile, fully occupied my head and hands," and "the new firm of Emanuel & Gaines was doing a good business." When the Alabama legislature established branch banks of the State Bank of Alabama at Decatur, Montgomery, and Mobile in November, Gaines was elected president of the Mobile branch. However, before Gaines could begin his second banking career, Governor John Gayle appointed him as the state's agent to sell bonds to raise capital for the three new branch banks. Gaines quickly made arrangements to travel to New York to sell $3.5 million in state bonds.[36]

On his way to New York, Gaines made a brief visit to Washington, D.C., where he met with Secretary of War Lewis Cass to discuss his difficulties in settling his accounts while in the "public service." Gaines pointed out to Cass that the government auditors were requiring him to conform to guidelines and forms prescribed for "regular disbursing officers" and that Commissary General Gibson had relieved him of such government regulations for his service. Because Gaines was suspicious of Cass' character and his honesty, he had asked the Alabama congressional delegation to be present at his interview with Cass. The presence of Senator William Rufus King, who praised Gaines' public service, and other members of the Alabama delegation elicited a promise from Cass that Gaines' accounts would be settled before his return from New York. However, Gaines discovered on his return to Washington four months later that the status of his accounts had not changed, but because of pressing business, he returned to Alabama with his accounts unsettled.[37]

Gaines' brief visit to the nation's capital also included at least two meetings with an old friend, President Andrew Jackson. On one occasion, Gaines attended a dinner at the president's house with "members of the cabinet, foreign ministers, and members of Congress." Before leaving for New York, Gaines paid Jackson a second visit, and at this time Jackson praised Gaines' public service to Vice President Martin Van Buren, pointing out Gaines' efforts as factor of the Choctaw Trading House and his engaging the Choctaw as allies in the Creek War of 1813–14. In his 1857 letter to Dillard, Gaines declared that he expressed his gratitude to President Jackson and "told him that I desired no office, and had no favor to ask the Govt. on my own account. But in behalf of my Chaktaw friends I begged that the provisions of their late treaty might all be carried out by the Govt. in the spirit of kindness & liberality;—which he assured me should be done."[38]

After hobnobbing with the political elite of Washington, Gaines continued his journey to New York, stopping off for a week in Philadelphia. In New York, Gaines delivered his "letters of introduction," called on several "Bankers and Capitalists," and offered for sale the $3.5 million in Alabama bonds. He spent a week in Boston seeking bond buyers and then returned to New York, where he attempted to loosen the tight money market. He called on Albert Gallatin, former secretary of the treasury under Jefferson and Madison and current president of the National Bank of New York, to seek his advice on selling the Alabama bonds in Europe. Gaines also produced a brochure that included the Alabama acts chartering the three branch banks, letters by Governor John Gayle and others, and data about the availability of land and cotton production in the state. Gaines' bond "prospectus" did not produce quick results, but on 8 April 1833 the *Mobile Commercial Register and Patriot* reported that Gaines "had sold the state bonds for $3,500,000 to Beers and Company of New York."[39]

Gaines arrived back in Mobile on 5 May 1833 to report that he had sold one-half of the bonds for $1.75 million to J. D. Beers and Company of New York and Thomas Wilson and Company of London. The same buyers were given the option to purchase the remaining bonds, and they exercised this option between December 1833 and 4 September 1834. In contrast to his recent difficulties receiving payment from the federal government, Gaines was quickly remunerated for these services, receiving $5,000 as state agent and bond salesman. While Governor Gayle complimented Gaines for negotiating Alabama's first multimillion-dollar bond sale, the Alabama senate was not satisfied and demanded the sale documents. Gaines was criticized for selling the bonds at par and for failing to get a better price. However, the editor of the *Commercial Register and Patriot* responded to Gaines' critics and defended his actions.[40]

Mobile Banker and Public Servant, 1833–1846

Gaines, the officers, and the board of directors opened Mobile's newest banking house on 17 June 1833 in a rented building on Royal Street. Even the location of the new bank building, completed in 1835, on the northwest corner of Royal and St. Francis Streets was criticized by those who favored a site south of Dauphin Street. While the Mobile branch bank made sizable profits in 1834 and 1835, the annual reports by the state bank commissioners revealed that the officers and directors had incurred liabilities nearly equal to one-half the bank's capital. Gaines and his business partnership, Emanuel and Gaines, were listed with outstanding liabilities in excess of $149,000 in 1834 and $112,000 in 1835. The annual reports also noted that Gaines' Mobile branch bank had employed more officers than authorized and that they were being paid more than specified by the state legislature. Gaines defended his bank's policies by noting a net profit of over $99,000 for 1834, which exceeded that of the mother bank in Tuscaloosa by more than $23,000, and an even larger profit—in excess of $155,000—for 1835.[41]

Gaines' leadership and the branch bank's success were important to Mobile's emergence as the commercial and financial center of Alabama. The city had a population of about 6,500 in 1835, and it was proud of its commercial and financial leaders, who also greatly influenced the social life of the city. George Strother Gaines was one of the most prominent of Mobile's city leaders, and a grand reception for his brother, General Edmund Pendleton Gaines, on 26 March 1835, attended by "all the lights of Mobile," simply added to his growing prestige. General Gaines was "returning from the Florida war," and Mobile's elite celebrated the occasion with a banquet that featured twenty-nine toasts and lasted well into the night. While the record is not clear, it appears that Gaines had some contact with a second prominent visitor to Mobile in 1835 when the portrait painter George Catlin brought his famous Indian paintings to the city. One observer noted that "Mr. Catlin has reopened his exhibit of Indian portraits, costumes, etc. for 2 evenings at the Court House." Catlin and his wife spent the winter of 1834–35 in Pensacola, and his exhibit in Mobile was part of a national tour to promote his paintings and his book on the North American Indians, which would be published in 1841. While Gaines' contact with Catlin's work may be conjecture, his signature is prominently displayed along with those of other prominent Mobilians and Alabamians in the list of subscribers in volume three of Thomas L. McKenney and James Hall's *The Indian Tribes of North America; With Biographical Sketches and Anecdotes of the Principal Chiefs,* published between 1837 and 1844. He was also one of the sixteen prominent business and civic leaders listed as "Managers" who issued invitations to the "City Assemblies" to celebrate "the season at E. Murray's" in December 1835. These social and civic activities must have been welcome diversions to Gaines as criticism and controversy hounded his tenure as bank president.[42]

Despite the critical annual reports by state bank commissioners, Gaines' leadership and important political support allowed the Mobile branch bank to operate without outside interference until the panic of 1837. Gaines and the directors made loans in excess of $3.6 million in more than three-fourths of the state, including large loans in counties where other branch banks were located and loans to prominent members of the Alabama senate and house. Gaines was reelected president of the Mobile branch bank without opposition by the legislature each December from 1833 through 1836. In 1834 his bank was the only bank in Alabama and one of twenty-three in the nation designated by the secretary of the treasury to receive federal deposits that had formerly been deposited only in the Bank of the United States and its branches. Although there were criticisms of this "pet bank" status, the Mobile branch of the State Bank of Alabama continued to receive the greater share of federal deposits through 1836. Gaines was also one of twenty prominent Mobilians, each of whom had been an officer or director at one or more Mobile banks, who were named commissioners to manage the sale of stock in the new Planters and Merchants Bank. However, in April 1836 the United States Treasury withdrew $500,000 from the Mobile branch bank, and this action, along with reports of business failures in the Northeast and New Orleans, caused renewed attacks on Gaines and the Mobile branch bank. Mobile cotton prices were declining while unemployment was increasing, and the Bank of Mobile and Gaines' branch bank soon raised their rates of exchange.[43]

While the ill winds of financial crisis began to sweep the nation, Gaines' branch bank remained at the vortex of political and financial debates. During the 1836 legislative session, Governor Clement C. Clay attacked the directors of the Mobile branch bank for borrowing excessively from their funds, and the Alabama senate and house debated placing limits on the amount of money state bank directors could borrow. The *Mobile Register* reported, "Mismanagement and abuse were boldly charged, and incapacity or corruption more than hinted at." Despite the accusations and threats, Gaines was again reelected president without opposition, the newly passed law limiting loans to $35,000 was not offensive to Gaines' directors, and the state treasurer transferred nearly $1 million in specie to the Mobile branch bank. However, on 12 May 1837 the Mobile banks gave notice that they were suspending specie payments and locked their vaults. Other banks in the state took the same action within a matter of days, and by 25 May all banks in Alabama had suspended specie payments. By November, Gaines' bank was in deep trouble and could not meet its obligation of over $900,000 owed to the United States Treasury. The mood of the Alabama legislature had changed significantly by December 1837, when Gaines was reelected president of the Mobile branch bank over John B. Norris by a narrow 63–59 vote.[44]

While his bank and reputation had come under severe attack, Gaines was determined to persevere and to save the bank he had established in 1832. On 26 November 1838, D. D. Kane, president pro tem of the Mobile branch bank, transmitted the annual statement to the Alabama senate and wrote to the "President of the Senate" that the "President of this Branch is now in New York." As the financial crisis and political assaults mounted, Gaines traveled to New York to muster financial support for his bank and to get "Norris, Stodder & Co." and Jonathan Hunt to make payments on "$500,000 of Short Bonds" that they had contracted to purchase in May 1838. With a commitment of $491,858 and a "further increase" of $100,000, Gaines returned to Mobile, where the *Register* reported on 6 February 1839 that he had also "liquidated $645,000" and "deferred payment of $319,466.07." The same article noted that Gaines "obtained a credit for this bank in New York and Boston to the amount of $200,000." While Gaines was in New York, the Alabama legislature in December 1838 confirmed the election of John B. Norris as the new president of the Mobile branch of the State Bank of Alabama.[45]

Although Gaines was often criticized for his leadership of the Mobile branch bank, most Alabamians did not blame him for the abuses and excesses of the bank's directors or the state's financial crisis of 1837. Gaines was obviously proud of his role as a banking pioneer and innovator, although his comments on the six years he spent as president of the Mobile branch bank occupy only three brief paragraphs in his "Reminiscences." Citing that his "health was a good deal impaired," Gaines closed this important chapter of his long business career. However, William Garrett, writing in his *Reminiscences of Public Men in Alabama* in 1872, provides us with better closure on this topic than Gaines: "This year [1839] Mr. George S. Gaines, who had long filled the office of President of the Branch Bank of Mobile, retired on account of ill health and infirmities, from too close application to business. Mr. G. S. Gaines was extensively known and highly appreciated in business circles; was kind and amicable in his intercourse with men; too much so, it was said, to manage a bank, where it required the cold blood and iron to say 'no.' His integrity was unquestioned, and his honor unsullied during a long and eventful life."[46]

At this point in Gaines' "Reminiscences," we are confronted by an unexplained gap, which stretches from 1838 until 1843, when Gaines tells us again that his health was "much impaired." Although Gaines and his partner, Jonathan Emanuel, sold their dry goods business to their clerk, Henry Lazarus, in 1835, they continued a business partnership for several years. On 26 November 1835, Andrew Armstrong submitted "A List of the Liabilities of the President & Directors of the Branch Bank of the State of Alabama at Mobile" to the Alabama senate that listed "Emanuel & Gaines" with liabilities in excess of $105,000. However, the report of bank commissioners S. H. Garrow and Henry Goldthwaite dated 18 November 1835 lists a total amount of liabilities during 1835 for "Emanuel & Gaines" of $447,642 and unpaid liabilities of $91,540. The 1836 bank commissioners' report shows "Emanuel & Gaines" with total liabilities of $341,173.08. Yet an 1838 statement of liabilities of the directors of the

"Mobile Branch" lists George S. Gaines as president with a total personal liability of $19,545 and no outstanding partnership endorsements. While the 1840 census reports that three members of Gaines' household were employed in "commerce" and the 1850 census lists Emanuel as a merchant with real estate valued at $175,000, the record is silent on when their business partnership ended.[47]

Gaines closes his "Reminiscences" with a lengthy discourse about another visit to the nation's capital and his apparent final effort to settle his accounts with the federal government. Gaines and his wife left Mobile "in the early part of the summer 1843" and traveled to White Sulphur Springs, Virginia, now West Virginia, at the direction of his physician. By September the mountain air and mineral waters of Virginia had restored his health to the point where he decided to again pursue his outstanding claims against the federal government. Gaines tells us that he had been served a writ "for an alleged balance of about four hundred dollars due the government when in fact the government was indebted to me for several thousand dollars." With his health reinvigorated, Gaines sent a letter to Secretary of War James Madison Porter requesting the settlement of his old accounts. When Porter failed to respond, Gaines traveled to Washington determined to seek closure on a matter that had weighed on his mind and honor for more than a decade.[48]

Arriving in the fall of 1843, Gaines and his wife took a suite of rooms at Washington's finest hotel, Willard's Hotel on Pennsylvania Avenue, and Gaines started his round of visits to government offices the following day. Secretary Porter sent him to the "Indian Bureau," where Gaines learned that the accounts were closed and a "cold and crusty" clerk—Thomas Hartley Crawford, commissioner of Indian affairs—refused to reopen them. Undaunted, the fifty-nine-year-old Gaines visited Commissary General Gibson, who agreed to supply copies of correspondence and other documents regarding the removal and subsistence of the Choctaw by Gaines. After failing to meet with Porter to pursue his claims, Gaines petitioned President John Tyler, who met with him and assured him that Porter "would do what was right in the matter." Porter, who had left town briefly, met with Gaines some two weeks later and agreed to reexamine Gaines' accounts. The review was completed within a week, and Gaines reports that Porter "issued an order dismissing the suit against me, and allowing me about two thousand four hundred dollars." While Porter agreed that Gaines was entitled to more compensation "by the verbal promises of Secretary Eaton," there were no records to substantiate the "promises" made by Eaton in 1830 at the Dancing Rabbit Creek treaty grounds. Gaines submitted a petition to Congress requesting additional compensation for leading the Choctaw exploring expedition of 1830-31 and for his service "to quiet the discontented Indians and prevent bloodshed." Although Congress rejected his petition, Gaines' efforts to serve his government and his Choctaw friends did not end with his 1843 trip to Washington or with his "Reminiscences," which close at this point.[49]

Shortly after returning to Mobile, Gaines accepted what apparently was his final federal appointment in 1844, when he joined a three-member commission created to investigate Choctaw land patent claims. Under the Treaty of Dancing Rabbit Creek, Choctaw who chose to remain in Mississippi could claim individual allotments of 640 acres and an additional 320 acres for each child under age ten and 160 acres for dependent children over age ten. However, the Choctaw agent, William Ward, failed to register many of the land claims and turned away many legal claimants. The first Board of Choctaw Commissioners created in 1837 received 1,349 claims, but only 143 Choctaw claimants received land patents. A second commission, appointed by President Tyler in 1842, included J. F. H. Claiborne, Ralph Graves, and William Tyler and received an additional 1,093 claims. Claiborne, a congressman from Mississippi, became entangled in a controversy with Choctaw land speculators that led to his removal along with Graves. Gaines and Samuel Rush replaced Claiborne and Graves and joined William Tyler at Louisville, Mississippi, in April 1844.[50]

The second Choctaw commission was lobbied and criticized by local white citizens for meeting at Louisville and by the Choctaw for its slow progress. At the board's meeting on 22 April 1844, Colonel Charles Fisher's petition filed "last January" was read, which criticized the commission for meeting "at this place." In response to these criticisms, Gaines introduced the following resolutions on 30 April: "Resolved: That for the better progress of the business of the Board, it is expedient to change its location to a point more convenient to the Indians whose claims are to be examined [and] Resolved: That when this Board adjourns from this place it will adjourn to meet at *Philadelphia* in the county of *Neshoba*, on *Monday the 6th day of May next*, and that notice of said location be published in one or more papers printed in this state." Although the second commission validated 1,009 of the Choctaw claims, Congress eventually offered the Choctaw claimants scrip for half of their claims to open public lands in Mississippi, Alabama, or Louisiana, but the other half could be claimed only by removing to Indian Territory. Satisfied that they had acted fairly and impartially, Gaines, Rush, and Tyler "signed their final report to the

President of the U.S." and adjourned the commission "sine die" on 17 June 1845.[51]

Gaines returned to his family and home at Spring Hill outside Mobile, and he later became involved in Albert James Pickett's research and writing of *History of Alabama*. In two letters written to Gaines in the summer of 1847, Pickett asked Gaines to assist him with his *History* and to share his journals, correspondence, and other materials. Gaines responded to Pickett's requests in a letter of 27 July 1847 recommending that Pickett should consult the *Niles' Weekly Register* "from the 1st number to the end of the British & Indian [War of] 1815" for the early history of "this section of the country." He also mentioned the recent death of "my old friend Silas Dinsmore" at his home in Kentucky and noted that Dinsmoor had "kept a journal of daily events, interlined with curious traditions & historical sketches, during his Indian agency," and that he had also collected "statements of old white men, & manuscripts upon the same subject." Pickett responded with two additional letters on 3 August and 12 September pressing Gaines for more information, and Gaines answered on 28 September promising Pickett to sketch the events "which occurred during my agency of the Choctaw Trading House" and provide accounts of the Choctaw and Chickasaw "as soon as I am able." He again urged Pickett to contact the widow of the "late Col. Dinsmore" to acquire his papers, and he closed by explaining that the Choctaw had always claimed "the dividing ridge between the waters of the Alabama & Tombigbee rivers as [their] eastern boundary." Because Gaines wrote that he was "too feeble to use either body or mind with the labor of sketching a memorandum of events worthy of record," Pickett made the first of two trips to Spring Hill in the fall of 1847 to gather an oral record, which he transcribed as "Conversations with Mr. George S. Gaines." In a second visit to Spring Hill, in the spring of 1848, Pickett recorded his "2nd Conversation with Geo. S. Gaines," and he cited the Gaines conversations in his *History,* published in 1851.[52]

THE MISSISSIPPI YEARS

Despite repeated protestations to Pickett regarding his health in 1847 and 1848, the sixty-four-year-old Gaines became involved in another major venture and lent his name to the promotion of the Mobile and Ohio Railroad. At a public meeting on 11 February 1847, Marshall J. D. Baldwyn, Sidney Smith, Duke W. Goodman, and others heralded the concept of building a railroad from Mobile to the mouth of the Ohio River. "A committee of fifty six" prominent business leaders from Alabama and Mississippi formed to seek financial and political support, and the Alabama legislature passed an act on 3 February 1848 incorporating the Mobile and Ohio Railroad Company with a capital of $10 million and named a board of directors that included Gaines' former business partner Jonathan Emanuel. Gaines used his considerable business and political influence as the chief subscription agent for promoting the new railroad in Alabama and Mississippi. An unexpected visit by Stephen A. Douglas, United States senator from Illinois and an advocate for a north-south railroad connecting Chicago to the Gulf of Mexico, brought about an important alliance with the officers of the Mobile and Ohio and the Alabama congressional delegation led by William Rufus King. During the next session of Congress, King amended Douglas' stalled "Central Railroad" bill to extend from the Ohio River to the Gulf with federal land grants for right-of-way in Mississippi and Alabama. With the support of Alabama's King and Jefferson Davis of Mississippi, Douglas' bill passed the Senate by three votes and the House by a vote of 101 to 75 on 17 September 1850. At least one source credits Gaines for the successful completion of the Mobile and Ohio Railroad in April 1861 because of his subscription sales and his lobbying the Mississippi legislature "for two whole sessions."[53]

While the record is not clear about his mission, Gaines was back in the nation's capital in late 1849. There may be any number of reasons for his return to Washington: the unsettled claims with the War Department, promotional activities for the Mobile and Ohio Railroad, a political appointment, or a combination of these and other matters. At least one group of old friends knew about his trip to Washington, and in a letter from "One Hundred Red Men," dated 6 December 1849, the Choctaw of Newton and Jasper Counties in Mississippi asked their old trusted friend to seek the replacement of removal agents "who cheat us out of all they can, by use of fraud, duplicity, and even violence." We have every reason to believe that, during his visit with President Zachary Taylor, Gaines was as forthright and honest about his concern for his Choctaw friends in 1849 as he had been in 1832 when he visited Andrew Jackson. However, Gaines also discussed other issues with Taylor and probably expressed his interest in a diplomatic post. According to Gaines' old friend and former Alabama governor John Gayle, President Taylor had assured Gaines that on the occasion of the next vacancy the position would be his. Unfortunately, Taylor died unexpectedly on 9 July 1850, and when Gayle wrote Secretary of State Daniel Webster on 8 September 1850 to support Gaines' nomination as consul to Havana, Millard Fillmore had become president. Gayle assured Webster that Gaines was "one of the oldest citizens and, probably, the most popular man in the State."[54]

While Gaines seemingly disappears from the public record between 1850 and 1856, the evidence points to his removal to the state of Mississippi, first to Perry County and then to Wayne County. Gaines and his family appear on each federal census for Alabama until 1850, including 1820 in Washington County, 1830 in Marengo County, and 1840 in Mobile County, but they are not reported on the 1850 census for Mobile County. However, the tax rolls for Perry County, Mississippi, show Gaines paid taxes on slaves and cattle in 1846 and 1847, and Gaines' family is listed on the 1850 federal census for Perry County and the 1853 Mississippi state census for Perry County. The 1850 federal census listed the sixty-six-year-old Gaines, his fifty-five-year-old wife, Ann, two daughters, Helen Gaines Bullock at twenty-seven and Mary Gaines at twenty-five, and their youngest son, Jonathan, at fourteen years of age. The federal slave schedule for 1850 reports that Gaines owned twenty slaves, eight females between the ages of six and sixty-five and twelve males between the ages of three and sixty-one. Gaines' in-laws, Young and Esther Gaines, had removed to Perry County before the 1820 federal census, which lists their household with four adults and two children between age ten and sixteen. Young Gaines paid taxes on 1,290 acres and 20 slaves as late as 1829; his widow, Esther Gaines, paid taxes on 1,313 acres, 800 cattle, and 19 slaves in 1844, and the estate of Esther Gaines paid taxes on 750 cattle and 24 slaves in 1845. The Perry County lands on the Leaf River were apparently inherited by Ann Gaines from her mother in 1845, and the Gaineses moved to the Perry County property prior to the 1850 federal census and continued to raise cattle on this property. However, George Stark Gaines, writing on 2 August 1947, states that his grandfather, George Strother Gaines, had removed to his plantation near State Line, Mississippi, by 1856.[55]

Several contemporary sources document Gaines' residence in Wayne County, Mississippi, and at Peachwood near State Line, Mississippi. Willis Brewer, in his *Alabama: Her History, Resources, War Record, and Public Men*, published in 1872, states that Gaines, "having previously established a farm in southwest Mississippi, . . . removed to that State in 1856, and served in the legislature in 1861." While Brewer's geographical reference is erroneous, it appears that the other points in his statement have some degree of accuracy. *The Catalogue of Peachwood Nurseries, State Line, Wayne County, Mississippi* issued by the "Gaines, Coles & Co." in 1887 claims that the Peachwood Nurseries were established in 1856. There is

Peachwood (ca. 1900) by Marian Stark Gaines. Log house built (ca. 1856) by George Strother Gaines at State Line, Wayne County, Mississippi (Courtesy of Mrs. Chebie Gaines Bateman, Columbus, Mississippi)

also Gaines' letter to Dillard on 8 August 1857, which was written from Peachwood. Wayne County land records show that Gaines had purchased 40.12 acres at $2.50 per acre on 20 July 1860 in township 6, and the seventy-five-year-old Gaines and his family are listed on the 1860 federal census for Wayne County. Gaines is listed as a "nursery man" along with his sixty-five-year-old wife, Ann, their daughter Mary, who was thirty, and their son Jonathan Emanuel, who was twenty-five, but no value was noted for his real estate holdings. However, the 1860 federal slave schedule lists twenty-six slaves—ranging in age two to thirty and including ten males and sixteen females—and nine slave houses as Gaines' property in Wayne County.[56]

The sectional crises and the resulting disruption of the American Union were difficult times for Gaines and his generation, who had helped to build and expand the nation from thirteen states to thirty-three in 1860. Gaines in his 1857 letter to Dillard blamed the sectional crises on "the demon party spirit" and declared, "I am a firm believer in the ability of the people to govern themselves,—in the stability of this good Govt. of ours—& in the waking up of the people, although stupefied for a time by a party Press, party stump orators; and cheated out of their votes by party machinary." However, when secession came to Mississippi, Gaines cast his lot with the Confederacy. He was elected to the Mississippi house for a two-year term in 1861 and served through the end of the special session of 1862–63. The *Eastern Clarion,* in Paulding, Mississippi, hailed Gaines' candidacy in its 28 June 1861 issue, calling him "the patriarch of East Miss. and West Alabama" and closing with the assertion that "he ought to be elected unanimously." A later issue of the *Eastern Clarion* proposed that Gaines was "one of the best men in the world, let us honor him with the Speakership at the next legislature." Despite the *Clarion*'s glowing endorsement, Gaines' age and health limited his participation, and Henry Gray from Wayne County replaced him in 1863.[57]

Although Gaines' participation in the Confederate cause was limited by his advanced age and poor health, several members of his family became involved directly or indirectly in the war effort. A Wayne County volunteer infantry company was enrolled in October 1861 and named the "Gaines Invincibles" in honor of Gaines, and Ann Gaines ordered a flag of "stars and bars" to be made in Mobile to present to the company. A special flag presentation with speeches, an all-day picnic, and a barbecue was held at Peachwood on 15 October 1861, where Captain Angus Taylor received the flag from Mrs. Gaines. The Gaines Invincibles served throughout the war, and their flag was later adopted by the Forty-Sixth Confederate Regiment and survived the surrender at Vicksburg, but it was lost when part of the regiment surrendered on 1 April 1865 at Blakely near Pensacola, Florida. Several nephews and at least two sons, Frank Young Gaines and Abner Strother Gaines, served with distinction in the Confederate army. Frank Gaines, a graduate of West Point and veteran of the Mexican War, was commissioned a captain in the Third Alabama Dragoons, "Ruffin Dragoons," and advanced to major before resigning on 19 March 1863 because of poor health. His younger brother, Abner Gaines, served as a captain in the corps of engineers for the Confederate Army of Tennessee and was at the battles of Chickamauga and Missionary Ridge. The war came to Gaines' farm in September 1863, when 750 head of Texas cattle destined to feed Confederate soldiers were "penned on a five acre lot of our oldest peach orchard." When the war ended in 1865, Gaines turned his full attention to his family, to Peachwood, and to expanding his farming and nursery enterprises.[58]

The postwar era was a time of business growth and expansion for the old statesman and pioneer George Strother Gaines but also a time of sadness and reflection. The death of his wife and soul mate, Ann Gaines, at Peachwood in 1868 ended their fifty-six-year journey together and may have spurred Gaines to turn his attention to dictating his "Reminiscences." The success of his farming and nursery enterprises in the late 1860s led to his partnership with Albert C. Coles, who became his amanuensis during the summer of 1871. According to the federal census of 1870, Coles, a native of New Jersey, was a twenty-eight-year-old farmer with a talent for grafting trees and plants. The Wayne County agricultural census of 1870 lists Gaines' property as 60 acres "improved," 140 acres woodland, and 161 head of livestock. The 1870 federal census also lists the eighty-six-year-old Gaines and two sons—Abner, thirty-seven, and Emanuel, thirty-three—as farmers, and lists his forty-seven-year-old daughter Mary's occupation as "keeping house." Gaines' personal estate is valued at $10,000. Although the nursery had first developed around apple and peach trees, it expanded rapidly in the postwar era to include a large array of flowers, bedding plants, flowering shrubs, trees, fruit trees, and grapes. The postwar restoration of the nearby Mobile and Ohio Railroad allowed the Gaines and Coles nursery to market widely and to become one of the largest in the South. With the issue of the 1887–88 Gaines, Coles, & Co. *Catalogue of Peachwood Nurseries,* George Strother Gaines' last business venture was celebrating its "32nd year" of serving "our patrons . . . in the Gulf States."[59]

A journey begun in 1805 from the East Tennessee hills ended on the coastal plain of southeastern Mississippi when George Strother Gaines died on 21 January 1873. He was buried next to his wife, Ann, in the Peachwood cemetery, with a marker over his grave that heralds him as a "statesman and pioneer." But the casual passerby is not told of his legacy of service and commitment to Alabama and Mississippi, the nation, or the people, red and white. The documents that follow provide the reader with much of the factual history and a glimpse of the personality of this remarkable man. The "Reminiscences" are the recollections and reflections of a venerable and wise man in his eighty-eighth year, who, at the urging of his friend Percy Walker, attempts to share his journey. But his story is incomplete—he ignores such areas as his land speculating activities, his controversial years as a state bank president, and his role as a slave owner. In both the "Reminiscences" and the 1857 letter to Dillard, he reveals his courage and his willingness to meet any challenge, whether it is the removal of the Choctaw to the West or confrontations with politicians and bureaucrats in the nation's capital. His conversations with Pickett confirm his influence and leadership in Indian-white relations, and together these documents disclose a compassionate, persistent, and multitalented man who, through his energy and intellect, influenced the shape of his nine-teenth-century world. While there are gaps and unanswered questions, the story that follows is seldom dull or ordinary, and on occasion is truly fas-cinating.[60]

Gaines' Reminiscences

Introduction
from the *Mobile Register,* June 19, 1872

COL. GEORGE S. GAINES

In our issue of today our readers will find the Commencement of "Reminiscences of Early Times in the Mississippi Territory," written by the above named gentleman. We propose to follow this first installment in our Sunday paper until we lay before our readers the whole of the "Reminiscences" thus far written.[1]

They were prepared by Col. Gaines during the summer of last year, at the request of Percy Walker, Esq., and by him presented to the "Franklin Society."[2]

The manuscript consists of some sixty pages, and as they relate to this immediate section of county, and describe incidents and characters connected with the history of Mobile and the states of Alabama and Mississippi more than half a century ago, the "Reminiscences" cannot but be welcomed by our fellow citizens.[3]

The aged author has, we are pleased to hear, promised to continue them whenever his health will permit. This paper, of which we print the commencement this morning, embraces the period between 1805 and 1815, and the narrative will be found of interest, especially to those whose memories lead back to the times when Mobile was a Spanish dependency, and could boast no higher dignity than that of a village of fishermen.[4]

Let us say a few words about the author. In years agone, ere reverence for the truth, the inflexible integrity, the scorn of ill-gotten wealth and the almost equal contempt for undue fondness for self, combined with the high courtesy, the delicate consideration for others, which formed the standard of character of the Southern gentleman, had been crushed down with all their other ideals, it would not have been necessary to tell an Alabamian or a Mississippian who George Gaines was, the just, pure man, the friend and counsellor of the redman, the wise and faithful pioneer of civilization in Mississippi Territory—the patriarch of two States.[5]

Mr. Gaines is a North Carolinian by birth; but with the *salvo* said to be dear to every North Carolinian heart, he was born "close by the Virginia line"; by a comical chance a family of nine or ten children, all born in the same house, were about equally divided North Carolinian and Virginian, as they happened to be born at one or the other end of the house, for the parental dwelling stood midway on the State line.[6]

Col. Gaines unites in himself the bluest blood of old Virginia-Preston, Pendleton, Strother, etc.

At an early age he removed with his father to Tennessee, from thence he was appointed Indian Agent and Factor for the United States to the Indians in Mississippi Territory. From that time (then under 20 years of age), to the present, when in two or three months he will number eighty-nine years, his life has been one constant and unbroken series of kind deeds, wise council and active, enlarged thought for the good of his people. With remarkable and admirable business qualifications, he brought to his intercourse with the haughty and suspicious savages a consideration for their rights, a deference for their habits and feelings, and an unvarying politeness that won their entire confidence, their perfect trust, until his simple word became their law, and his sympathy and kindness their abiding reliance. The part Mr. Gaines acted in the early history of Mississippi Territory, and subsequently, upon its division into the States of Alabama and Mississippi, was one of untiring interest and of great advantage to the young communities in which he was equally at home. His position as Indian agent had brought him in contact with the leading men of both States; his influence was either directly or indirectly felt in every measure of public importance for a long term of years, in fact, until the bouleversement of the war so strangely and anomalously altered men's relations to the soil they claim as their own.[7]

Here in Mobile we are largely indebted to him for the accomplishment of the most important and gigantic work that has been achieved in the States of Mississippi and Alabama—the Mobile and Ohio Railroad. Originating in the active and far-seeing mind of one man, and persistently kept before the public by him until he made zealous converts to his scheme.[8] Among its most active and efficient champions was Mr. Gaines, who devoted time and means to its accomplishment; he not only canvassed the State of Mississippi at different times to that end, but he spent entire sessions of the Legislature in Jackson for the same purpose, urging it upon the members day after day, never absenting himself until his task was done. For several years he was President of the Branch of the State Bank at Mobile, and in that, as in his other public trusts, kept his hands clean, and no one ever questioned his integrity.[9]

Not the least remarkable thing about Mr. Gaines is his admirable style of composition, so Addisonian in its purity and finish, and replete with the grace and tender humor of Charles Lamb. One ponders and inquires whence is derived the charm and beauty of style in the composition of a frontiersman, actively and constantly engaged, now in sharp lookout for the pecuniary interest of Government (for large transactions involving great amounts of public property were entrusted to him); again military duty, guarding his home and his neighbors from the cruel and stealthy savage, and then off on a negotiation to some distant tribe to secure its adherence to the Government in a time of great peril and uncertainty.

Notes

on the Early Days of South Alabama

Not long since the venerable George S. Gaines, now verging on to 90 years of age, and who moved to St. Stephens in the year 1805, deposited with the Franklin Society of Mobile some notes on the early history of Mobile and its vicinity. Thus, in the deep twilight hours of his life, when no longer able to use his pen, Mr. Gaines has dictated to an amanuensis the notes in question. We have found these notes of so much interest that we begin today to give them serial publication in The Register. *We are indebted to the kind permission of the Franklin Society for the privilege of doing so:*[1]

Among the various means employed by the United States Government at the beginning of the present century to civilize and improve the condition of the Indian tribes within our borders was the establishment of trading houses for the accommodation of each of the large tribes, where the Indians could obtain necessary articles of merchandise, at reasonable prices, in exchange for their peltries, furs and other produce at full value.[2]

Joseph Chambers, Esq., of North Carolina, was appointed United States agent to the Choctaw Trading House, and established it at Fort St. Stephens on the Tombigbee river in 1803. Mr. Chambers was appointed a commissioner, with Robert C. Nicholas, of Virginia, to settle land claims in what was then called the "Tombigbee Settlement," in the Mississippi Territory.

In the latter part of 1804 I was invited by Mr. Chambers to come to Fort St. Stephens and take charge of the Trading House, as his Assistant, with the understanding that he would resign after I became thoroughly acquainted with the business, and recommend me as his successor. I was then residing at Gallatin, Tennessee, in the employment of Messrs. John and Robert Allen, merchants. I gave up my situation with them, notified Mr. Chambers of my acceptance, and arranged to leave for St. Stephens in

March, 1805, where I arrived by the slow routes of the Cumberland and Mississippi rivers to New Orleans, thence via Mobile, in a small Spanish schooner to Fort Stoddart—the balance of the distance by land. The day after my arrival at St. Stephens, being familiar with the business of a retail store, Mr. Chambers gave me charge of the Trading House, his time being occupied in the discharge of the duties of Register of the Land Office, and member of the Board of Commissioners for settling land claims.[3]

I fortunately met with Col. Silas Dinsmore, United States Agent of the Choctaws, at Natchez, Mississippi, on my way out. He was en route to New Orleans to purchase supplies for a treaty, which was to be held at St. Stephens, with the Choctaw Indians, in May or June. We travelled together to New Orleans, where we were detained several days, while Col. Dinsmore was making purchases for the accommodation of the treaty. He chartered a small Spanish schooner to transport his purchases to St. Stephens. We both took passage in it, and after a week's voyage reached Mobile. The delay was in part caused by getting aground at "Grant's Pass" (since named). From Mobile we continued our voyage to St. Stephens (Fort Stoddart), and from that place we travelled to St. Stephens on horseback. Col. Dinsmore was an Eastern man (from Massachusetts). He was a scholar, and had travelled a great deal; he was formally a purser in the navy; he possessed a large stock of useful knowledge, and his wit and humor appeared to be inexhaustible, which made him a general favorite; he was energetic and industrious in the discharge of his duties—in fact, he was the "right man in the right place" to aid in carrying out the humane policy of the Government toward the Indian tribes.[4]

In June, 1805, the Indians met at St. Stephens, according to appointment. Gen. Robertson, of Nashville, was associated with Col. Dinsmore as United States Commissioner to hold the treaty, the object of which was to purchase the Indian claim so as to connect the "Tombigbee settlement" with what was then called the "Natchez settlement." A very large number of the Indians attended at the time appointed; and the ample provision made for their accommodation rendered their encampment lively and gay with dances, ball plays, "hide the bullet" and other games of chance.[5]

The old Spanish fort St. Stephens, was located immediately on the bluff of the river; one of the block-houses was in a good state of preservation and was occupied as the store. There was an extensive frame war-house, a room which was used as the land-office; and a frame dwelling, which had been the officers quarters, all enclosed on three sides with pickets and a ditch, the river forming the defences on the fourth. The frame dwelling was occupied as a residence by the United States Factor. The officers of the two companies of United States infantry stationed at St. Stephens, Indian chiefs and their captains, were invited every day by the Treaty Commissioners to dine with them in the Factor's house while the negotiations were proceeding.[6]

Although the Indians seemed disposed to oblige their "Father," the President of the United States, they did not feel authorized to *sell,* but expressed a willingness to *talk* the matter over in the fall at Mount Dexter, near the present town of Macon, Mississippi.[7]

I saw much of the Indians during their stay at St. Stephens, which caused both surprise and admiration; they were not such savages as I had imagined. As I have mentioned before, Col. Dinsmore made arrangements for chiefs and their "right hand men," or captains, to dine every day with the Commissioners, officers of the army, and others. The table accommodated forty or fifty persons, half of whom were Indians. The bountiful supplies brought from New Orleans, and cooks furnished by the officers of the army, enabled the Colonel to offer a good dinner each day, with an abundance of wine, which the Indians greatly relished, participating freely in the wit and humor it brought forth. I remember an incident connected with one of those strange and pleasant festivities, which I will relate. A young lieutenant who sat by me became a little troublesome to the old chief, Mingo-Homa-stubbee, by asking a great many questions. It was so arranged that an interpreter sat by each chief for the convenience of conversation. The Lieutenant asked the old man "who was considered the greatest warrior among them?" (There were three great "Medal Chiefs"— Mingo-Homa-stubbee, Mingo-Puck-shennubee, and Push-matta-ha). The Chief answered, "I *was* considered the greatest warrior, but found it was not the case when returning from a visit we paid President Washington at Philadelphia." "How did you make the discovery?" enquired the Lieutenant. "The President sent us in a ship to New Orleans," said the Chief, "and when we were at sea, entirely out of sight of land, a storm came upon us. The waves were so high they seemed almost to kiss the clouds, and the ship rolled about among them until I thought that we would never see the beautiful hills and valleys, forests and streams of our beloved country; and our bones would lie scattered on the bottom of the strange waters instead of resting peacefully with our departed relations. All this alarmed me—I found that I had not the firmness in danger and the utter fearlessness of death of a great warrior, and concluded to go down in the cabin to see how my friend Puck-shennubbee was affected by this (to our party) new and strange danger. And what do you think he was doing?" The description of the storm attracted the attention of every one at the table. The

Lieutenant eagerly asked, "What was he doing?" "Why," said the old chief, with a very grave face but a humorous twinkle of the eyes, "Why, he was making love to an old squaw we took along as a cook for us, and he seemed to be as unconcerned about the danger as if he was at home in his own cabin sitting by the fire, and listening to the songs of the winds among the trees!" The roars of laughter that followed this "denouement" drowned Mingo-Puck-shennubbee's indignant denial of it. The Lieutenant did not attempt any further conversation.[8]

Puck-shennubbee was as remarkable for his modesty and simplicity of manner as Mingo-Homa-stubbee was for his wit and jolity.

The Indians met according to appointment in the autumn of 1805, and our commissioners were successful in the purchase of land to connect the Tombigbee and Natchez settlements. But the strip of land was narrower than was desired by the Government. It was bounded south by "Ellicott's line"; east by the ridge dividing the waters of the Alabama and Tombigbee; north by a line beginning at a point near the northeast corner of what is now called Clarke county, Ala., and crossing the Tombigbee at "Fallecta-brenna Oldfield," a few miles below Tuscahoma bluff; and crossing Chicka-sawha near the present northern boundary line of Wayne county, Miss., crossing Leaf River at or near the northern boundary line of Perry, thence running west to the Natchez settlement. "Ellicott's line" crossed Mobile River a few miles below Seymour's Bluff, striking the Mississippi above Baton Rouge.[9] The Tombigbee settlement in 1805 was composed mainly of a few planters on the river (who were generally owners of large stocks of cattle) and persons employed in the care of the cattle. There was also a small settlement east of the Alabama river, ten miles above its confluence with the Tombigbee, known as the "Tensaw settlement." Mr. Mimms, a man of considerable property, resided near Tensaw Lake, and was sur-rounded by a pleasant neighborhood composed of the Lingers, Duns, Thompsons, and others. William and John Peirce, merchants, had a store near Mimm's.[10] Of the original settlement I recollect Mr. Bates, who re-sided at Nanahubba Bluff; Mr. Hollinger, who resided a few miles above, and was one of the largest planters; his plantation was situated on the "Cut Off Island." McIntosh's Bluff was occupied by a Mr. Johnson. Some eight or ten miles above McIntosh's was the small village of New Wake-field, the seat of justice for Washington, the only county in the settlement. In the neighborhood of the village resided the Mungers, Hinsons, Wheats, Baldwins, and other families, names not recollected. Mr. Young Gaines resided about ten miles higher up the river. Major Frank Boykin, a Revo-lutionary officer, Thomas Bassett, Bowling, Brewers and Callers were Mr.

Gaines' neighbors. John McGrew lived near St. Stephens. He owned a plantation on the east side of the river, opposite St. Stephens. Mr. Baker resided on the first bluff above St. Stephens, Col. Bullock and Mr. Womack lived also in the neighborhood.[11]

I had considerable leisure during my first summer at St. Stephens, and wrote a good deal in the Land Office, recording claims, etc., which gave me an opportunity of becoming personally acquainted with most of the "settlers" while they were in attendance at the Land Office prosecuting their claims for land. The various classes of land claims, Spanish warrants of survey, donations by act of Congress to first settlers on public land, pre-emptions to more recent settlers, brought rich and poor to the Land Office. I remember there were British patents in the Land Office—whether for lands in this or other districts I do not remember, I have no recollection of their being recorded or acted upon by the Commissioners.

At this period our admirable system of State and general government worked well—each independently in its own sphere.

The Territories were treated as young States, and received aid and encouragement from the Federal parent during their minority. Washington county being cut off from the balance of the Territory by a wilderness of more than a hundred miles in width, was favored this year with a Territorial Judge—Harry Toulmin, formerly of Kentucky. He settled with his family at St. Stephens, organized his court, in the administration of which, and his examples of strict integrity, energy, and industry, exercised an improving influence in the settlement. The judge was a man of much learning, generous and hospitable almost to a fault.[12] Soon after the ratification of the treaty at Mount Dexter, in 1806, the eastern and northern boundary line of the "cession" was run by Col. Dinsmore. When the Colonel reached the Tombigbee, in running the northern boundary westward, he learned the "Captain" of Tuscahoma village threatened to prevent him from crossing. He suspended the survey and came down to St. Stephens and invited Young Gaines and myself to accompany him in a pirouge [pirogue] to Fallectabrenna Oldfield to quiet the Indians should they attempt to interfere with the survey. We accordingly went up with Col. Dinsmore; and upon arriving at Fallectabrenna, the Colonel gave orders to prepare a post and plant it on a mound he threw up. While this work was progressing the captain of the Tuscahoma village marched up with a number of warriors, all looking fierce and malignant. Seeing Young Gaines, the captain entered into a conversation with him, and the matter was soon amicably arranged. Mr. Gaines had influence with the Choctaws, owing to his kindness and fair dealing with them.[13]

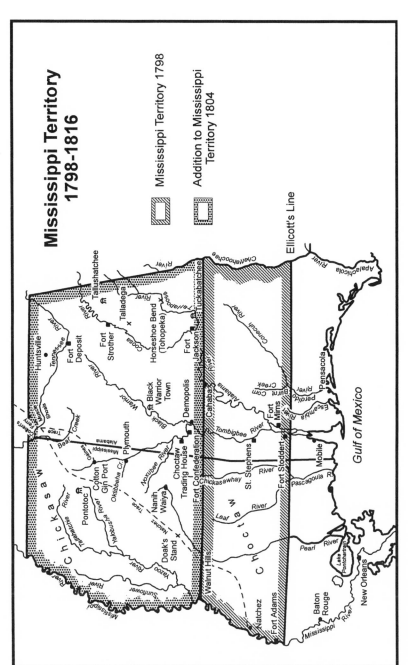

Mississippi Territory 1798-1816

▨ Mississippi Territory 1798

▦ Addition to Mississippi Territory 1804

Ellicott's Line

Chickasaw

Choctaw

Gulf of Mexico

Huntsville
Tallushatchee
Tennessee River
Talladega
Fort Deposit
Fort Strother
Horseshoe Bend (Tohopeka)
Fort Jackson
Coosa River
Tallapoosa River
Tuckabatchee
Chattahoochee River
Apalachicola R.
Pensacola
Black Warrior Town
Demopolis
Cahaba River
Warrior River
Coosa River
Alabama River
Conecuh River
Fort Mims
Burnt Corn Creek
Perdido River
Escambia River
Black River
Plymouth
Alabama
Bear Creek
Shoals
Colbert's Ferry
Gaines Trace
Cotton Gin Port
Oktibbeha Cr.
Tombigbee River
Fort Confederation
St. Stephens
Fort Stoddert
Mobile
Pascagoula R.
Choctaw Trading House
Chickasawhay River
Leaf River
Pontotoc
Tallahatchie River
Yakabusha River
Nanih Waiya
Natchez Trace
Doak's Stand
Yazoo River
Sunflower River
Mississippi River
Walnut Hills
Pearl River
Lake Pontchartrain
New Orleans
Baton Rouge
Natchez
Fort Adams
Mississippi River
Noxubee River

Mississippi Territory, 1798-1816

By this time I became pretty well acquainted with the manners and customs of the Choctaw Indians.[14] Polygamy was not forbidden. In some instances a very active hunter would have two wives: but one wife was generally the rule. Courtship was conducted in this wise: A young man becoming pleased with a maiden proposed for her to her maternal uncle (the eldest brother of her mother), often accompanying his proposal with presents before he could obtain the uncle's consent. When this was obtained the maiden was soon won. Such was the chastity and modesty of the females, jealousy on the part of husbands was rarely or [n]ever heard of. Instead of burying their dead the corpse was wrapped in a blanket and placed on a scaffold in the yard of the family. The scaffold was ten or twelve feet high. The body remained on the scaffold until the flesh became so much decayed as to separate easily from the bones, when a professional bone-picker was sent for to take down the body, separate the bones from the flesh, wash them clean, and lastly lay them in a small box made for the purpose. After this the box was deposited in the bone-house of the village. Every day while the corpse was lying on the scaffold the relatives near at hand seated themselves around, and covering their heads with a blanket or other garment, would weep and lament for half an hour. If any of the relatives were travelling, they would seat themselves by the pathside, cover their heads and weep at the same time of the day agreed upon with the mourners at home. The funeral ceremonies finished the relatives and friends enjoyed the feast prepared, thus ending the season of grief. Their amusements were ball plays, a few games of chance and dances. The ball plays by the men were enjoyed by both sexes. The dances were much enjoyed by the young people. Their rules of propriety were strictly observed generally. The eldest brother of the family was considered governor of the children of his sisters. The fathers of children seemed to have but little to do with their management. The mothers managed the children and appeared to take great pleasure in their well-doing; the girls assisted their mothers in their various duties, the boys amused themselves with blow-guns, bows and arrows, rarely ever being required to do any work. The mothers and their daughters cultivated their "truck patches," performed all the duties appertaining to the household, or camp, etc. The men were all hunters—that seemed to be considered their whole duty. They built the cabins. Beside the cabin in which they lived each family had another called "the hot house," to sleep in during cold weather. The walls were made of poles and mud, the whole structure made as air tight as possible, leaving one small door. The fire was built in the middle of the dirt floor, a small apperture was left in the roof for the escape of smoke,

a low scaffolding to sleep on was fixed to the walls all around. The "Choctaw Nation" was divided into three districts. Each district had its principal
chief. Mingo-Puckshennubbee ruled the western district situated west of
Pearl river. Mingo-homa-stubbee was chief of the northern district which
adjoined the Chickasaw country. Pushmataha ruled the southeastern district. His residence was near the present site of Meridian, Miss.[15] Major
John Pitchlyn resided in the northern district, near the mouth of the Oc-
tebbeha on the Tombigbee. I became acquainted with him soon after I
took charge of the Choctaw trading house in 1805. He appeared then to
be about thirty-five years of age—his face strikingly handsome denoting
mildness and firmness of purpose. I was proud of my position, and determined to make myself useful in the civilization of the Choctaws, and
availed myself of every opportunity of conversing with Major Pitchlyn on
the subject; and I was delighted to find he took a deep interest in it. I was
informed that he was "a self-made man"; that he was the son of a British
commissary, and accompanied his father, when quite a small boy, in a
journey the old gentleman was making through the Indian country from
South Carolina to the "Natchez settlement," on the Mississippi. His father
was seized with a sickness in the Choctaw Nation, and never reached his
destination. He died, leaving the boy to struggle for himself among the
Indians.[16]

Maj. Pitchlyn accumulated property, and took a wife when a young man
from a powerful family of the natives. He was appointed United States
Interpreter, and was highly respected by the Indian agents and officers of
the army. His property consisted mainly of horses and horned cattle. I was
told before I met him that he was a "natural gentleman," possessing the
material requisites belonging to that character. I found this opinion of him
true. He educated his children as thoroughly as practicable in those days.
Maj. Pitchlyn's influence in the northern district was considered by the
United States Agent so important in carrying out the views of the Government in the advancement of civilization that he was rarely called upon to
exercise his office as interpreter, except at treaties or the payment of Indian
annuities. Middleton Macky was also U.S. interpreter to the Choctaws.
Col. Dinsmore kept him at his residence, and when he travelled about
among the Indians, took this interpreter with him. Col. Dinsmore established his agency office in the valley of Chickasawha, near where Quitman, Miss., now stands. He removed in 1807 to the valley of Pearl river,
a few miles above the present site of Jackson. He seems to have inspired
his employees, blacksmiths, wheelwrights and others, with an ardent desire for the improvement of the Indians. Their "truck patches" were en-

larged, and now and then one was enclosed with fencing. Poultry began to enliven their yards; and the hog was now to be seen among them. To their patches of corn, potatoes, beans, pumpkins, etc., cotton began to be added. The white men among them introduced cows and horses, and many Indian families became owners of these useful animals. Col. Dinsmore rendered all the aid he could to the missionaries. That valuable institution known as the "Mayhew Mission," and several other schools were established in different parts of the nation and nothing occurred to check the progress of civilization and improvement of the domestic arts until 1812.[17] The Chickasaw country adjoined the Choctaws on the north. The language, manners, and customs of the two tribes were nearly alike. It is quite probable that they were originally of the same tribe. Everything that I have said about the manners and customs of the Choctaws will apply as well to the Chickasaws. There was a mildness and appearance of civility in these tribes which distinguished them from their neighbors the Creeks and Cherokees. Whether this was natural, or was owing to their former intercourse with the French people of Louisiana, I am unable to determine. The object of Mr. Chambers' mission to the South—that is, the establishment of the Choctaw trading house, a land office, and to aid in the adjudication of land claims in the Tombigbee settlement—having been accomplished, he resigned his appointment in the latter part of 1806, and returned to his native State, North Carolina. I was appointed his successor in the Choctaw trading house; and Thomas Malone my assistant. Thomas W. Maury, of Ablermarle, Virginia, was appointed Register of the Land Office and Lemuel Henry, Esq., Receiver of Public Moneys.[18]

The business of the trading house increased its popularity—brought hunters from all parts of the nation. Hunters of the Creek settlement at the falls of the Black Warrior came frequently to trade; and I had occasional visits from Creeks residing beyond the Alabama river. All appeared to be well pleased with our trade. My instructions from the Superintendent of Indian Trade made it my duty to be careful not to sell the Indians a damaged article of goods without pointing out the damage and reducing the price to what I considered its actual value; when blankets, shawls, or cotton and linen goods appeared to me to be lighter or more flimsy and less durable than they purported to be, to point out the defect and reduce the price also.[19]

In 1807 surveyors were put to work "running out" Clark and Washington counties, dividing into townships, etc.; surveying private claims, etc. Settlements began to extend higher up the river on both sides; also westward on Chickasawha, Leaf and Pearl Rivers. Wayne, Green, and Perry counties (now in the State of Mississippi), were organized in 1807. The counties were settled by emigrants principally from North and South Carolina and Georgia. Col. James Caller represented Washington county in the Territorial Legislature. The capital of the Territory was the village of Washington, a few miles above Natchez. Col. Caller was enthusiastic in the discharge of his duties. At this time the settlers were too much occupied in building cabins, and opening land for cultivation, to interest themselves with politics or elections. Members of the Legislature, however, were elected; and the militia was organized according to the laws of the Territory. Col. James Caller was the leading politician of the Tombigbee settlement.[20]

Nicholas Perkins, Lemuel Henry, R. H. Gilmore, J. P. Kenedy, Samuel Acee, Sallie and Joseph Carson were the lawyers of Washington county. The three first were living in the county when I came. We were almost entirely dependent on itinerant preachers for religious services.

The celebrated Lorenzo Dow was among them. I avoided taking any interest in the county or Territorial politics; I never attended any of the political gatherings, but ordinary civility compelled me to hear a good deal of what was going on from persons visiting the land office, which continued in the old Spanish Fort, St. Stephens.[21]

The country south of Ellicott's line, considered a part of the purchase of Louisiana from France, continued in the possession of Spain. Some difficulty had occurred in passing goods to the trading house by Mobile, where duties were exacted on Government goods, and on peltries and other produce received in exchange from the Indians, which caused the Government to forward supplies for the trading house via Pittsburg, thence down the Ohio and up the Tennessee to Colbert's Ferry.[22]

(The late Gen. Edmond P. Gaines, when a Lieutenant, was appointed Collector of Customs for the Mobile District, and kept his office at Fort Stoddart. He held office for five years.)[23]

In October, 1810, I received instructions from the Secretary of War to proceed to the Chickasaw Nation and endeavor to obtain permission of the Indians to open a wagon road from Colbert's Ferry to Cotton Gin Port, on the Tombigbee, and make arrangements to transport the goods thence to St. Stephens. I set out immediately, in obedience to my instructions; had an interview with the leading chiefs of the Chickasaws, who objected to opening the wagon road, but promised me facilities and safety for the transportation of the goods for the Choctaw trading house, on packhorses, at a very moderate expense. Lieut. Gaines, by order of the War Department, had, six or seven years before this time, surveyed and marked out the road I was instructed to open.[24]

I continued my journey to Smithland, at the mouth of the Cumberland, where I found the supplies in the charge of Wood Brothers, with the exception of lead, which I was instructed to purchase. Hearing that a boat load of lead had been sunk in the Ohio, below Fort Massac, I proceeded to the place, and, aided by the commanding officer at Massac, I purchased the quantity required, brought it up in a public barge to Smithland, engaged a careful bargeman and crew, with a good barge, to transport the goods found there, and with the lead I had purchased, to Colbert's Ferry, on the Tennessee. I then returned on horseback to Colbert's Ferry, made arrangements for receiving and "packing" the goods to Maj. Pitchlyn, at the mouth of the Octibbeha, below Cotton Gin Port. I proceeded to Maj. Pitchlyn's, and with his aid, arranged for transporting the goods down the Tombigbee to St. Stephens. It is a little remarkable that all my orders were carried out with precision and promptness, and the goods received at St. Stephens in good order without the loss of an article.[25]

In 1811 the quiet reigning in the Tombigbee settlement began to be somewhat disturbed by rumors of difficulties with England. Col. James Caller created some excitement in the settlement by his efforts to bring about a better organization of the militia. At this period we also received rumors of restlessness among the Creek Indians. Indeed it was apparent in the parties of the Creek who came to the trading house.[26]

A cunning Creek Chief named O-ce-o-che-mot-la obtained permission of the Choctaws to make a settlement at the falls of the Black Warrior, so that the hunters of each tribe might have a resting place when visiting each other. This settlement had increased to many families before I took charge of the Choctaw trading house, at St. Stephens, and traded largely with us. I was in the habit of extending a credit to the old Chief of about a hundred dollars, which he always paid off at his next visit, but expected the same indulgence after he finished bartering. He was in the habit of paying me a visit spring and fall coming down the river in a fleet of canoes. He came down as usual in the fall of 1811, with a large fleet of canoes and thirty or forty warriors bringing a cargo of peltries, furs, etc. There was a Mr. Tandy Walker, residing in the neighborhood of St. Stephens, who had lived many years before in the Creek Nation as a "Public Blacksmith." Walker had acquired their language and was a great favorite of the Indians. My Black Warrior "friend" always sent for Tandy Walker, when he came to trade with me, to act as an interpreter. On the present occasion I noticed that the old chief was exceedingly desirous to make me believe he was very much attached to me. He stated he had "took my talk," and had built a snug storehouse and brought down several hundred dollars' worth of furs, etc., to purchase a supply of goods for his store. I had offered him credit several times before to the amount of four or five hundred dollars, but he would never exceed one hundred dollars' debt. He stated to me he was ready to have his peltries, furs, etc., weighed and counted; and would first pay off his old debts, then barter the balance in his favor for blankets, etc. The first day was spent in receiving and taking account of his articles, which having been entered in my books, the chief renewed his friendly conversation about his storehouse and the advice I gave him. He said that the next morning he would barter out the value of his products, pay off his old debts, and would make his debt "an old hundred," (meaning a thousand dollars) this time. I answered that the times had changed—that the British Government had a misunderstanding with the President which might end in a war; and it would be unwise in me to permit him to contract so large a debt, and very imprudent in him to do so. He remarked that his friend Walker, who was a man of property, would be his security for "one or two hundreds." I noticed Walker was greatly troubled, and was endeavoring to appear calm. I reiterated I could only let him have one hundred dollars credit under the existing circumstances. But he was not to be put off so readily, and entered into an ingenious argument to overcome my objections. The sun went down and the store-house was crowded when I told the Chief it was time to prepare for sleep, and we would "tell each other our dreams in the morning." Bidding me good night he led his party off. In a short time Walker returned. Leaning over the counter he whispered to me, "I told the Chief I left my knife on the counter, for an excuse, so that I might come back to speak privately to you. Meet me at 'The Rock' at midnight. Let no one know, for both our lives will be in danger." Saying this, he hastened to follow the Indian party.[27]

At midnight I went cautiously to the "Hanging Rock," so called because it projected over the bluff of the river near the old Spanish fort. Walker was there; he said to me in a whisper, "let us go into the thicket." I followed into a dense thicket where we took seats. He then told me in a whisper that the Creeks had determined to join the British in the war soon to break out; that the Chief of the Black Warrior settlement of Creek Indians proposed to him to unite with him in obtaining all the goods they could possibly get from me; take his family and go up with him, and half an interest in the store, saying, "Before the time to pay for the goods there will be no one to demand it; the trading house will be one of the first objects to capture when the war commences." Walker said that he was obliged to consent to his proposition, but took care to impress O-ce-o-che-mot-la with the danger of offending me, as my brother was a great war-chief, very much beloved by the President. Walker remarked, "I see you are going to do right; I have told you all I know, and now I must return to camp, for if it is known that I have made this communication to you, or that I have been with you, I would not live to see my family." We separated in the thicket, and I returned home; went quietly to bed passing the balance of the night without sleep because of uneasiness. At this time there were no troops in St. Stephens and but very few men, not more than six or seven white men all told. The next morning the Chief with his warriors and interpreter all came smiling to the store. The Chief asked me what I dreamed. I said, "I dreamed there was a war. The English came over in their ships and engaged some of the northern tribes of the Indians to help them fight, but they were soon whipped by the President's warriors, and the English were driven back over the 'big water' in their ships. The Northern tribes suffered in the conflict. What did you dream?" O-ce-o-che-mot-la replied, "I dreamed that my good friend sold me all the goods I wanted for my new store; and I returned home with my canoes loaded. I placed the goods in my store, and my people all admired them, saying 'Mr. Gaines is a great man—was a man of his word, and our chief is a man of but one talk.'" I told the chief I was obliged to believe my own dream; and that we would not waste more time in idle words. We commenced bartering until the balance was exhausted, after paying his old debt. I then gave him credit for a hundred dollars, as usual, which consumed the second day of his visit. The next day the chief departed with this fleet, and that was the last I ever saw of him.[28] During this year, (1811) Lieut. Gaines tendered his resignation and commenced the practice of law. His resignation was not accepted, but a furlough was tendered him by the War Department. He was, however, soon afterwards ordered to Knoxville, Tennessee, on recruiting service. He had been promoted to a captaincy; and when he arrived at Knoxville he met with still further promotion as Major, and then as Colonel. Dennison Darling succeeded him in the Collector's office at Fort Stoddart. He continued in the office until after its removal to Mobile.

Gen. Wilkinson captured the Spanish Fort at Mobile soon after the events above mentioned, added the country south of "Ellicott's line" to the United States. This portion of country, as I said before, was claimed by our Government as a part of the purchase of Louisiana from the French.[29]

Rumors of the growing bad feeling of the Creek Indians rendered the settlers on the Mobile and Tombigbee rivers, and adjacent new settlements, a good deal uneasy during the year 1812, checking emigration to a great extent.

In the fall of this year Tandy Walker called at my house to tell me he had just learned from a Creek Indian, that a white woman had been brought from Tennessee as a prisoner to Tuskaloosa (falls of the Black Warrior) by a party of Creek Indians returning from a visit to the Shawnees on the Northern Lakes. Mrs. Gaines, who was present, suggested to Walker that he ought to endeavor to rescue the woman and bring her down to the settlement.[30] Walker said he could do so, but it would be at the risk of his life. He observed, he could walk up in pretense of paying a visit to his old friend O-ce-o-che-mot-la; whilst there could obtain a canoe, and buy or steal her and bring her down. Mrs. Gaines urged him to undertake the enterprise, and Tandy Walker being a brave, generous-hearted man, consented. He departed immediately on his mission of mercy, returning in about two weeks with the woman, in a canoe. She was in bad health, her mind a good deal impaired by her suffering; her limbs and feet were still in a wounded condition, caused by the brush, briars, etc., she was forced to walk through after she was captured by the Indians. Mrs. Gaines took charge of her, ordered a tepid bath, furnished her with comfortable clothing, etc. After a week's tender nursing her mind appeared to be restored. She then related her story. Her name was Crawley. She resided in a new settlement, near the mouth of the Tennessee river. One day, during the absence of her husband, a party of Creek Indians came to her house, murdered two of her children who were playing in the yard; and she had barely time to shut and bolt the door, hastily raising a "puncheon" over a small potato cellar and place her two youngest children there, before the Indians broke down the door, dragged her out of the house and compelled her to keep up with them in their retreat.

Several families were massacred at the same time in that neighborhood. They compelled her to cook for them on the march, but offered her no other violence. She thought she would die after reaching the village, and doubtless would soon have died but for Mr. Walker's kindness and humanity in rescuing her and bringing her down to St. Stephens.[31] It was several weeks before she was able to undertake the journey home. A party of gentlemen, friends of mine, were going through the wilderness to Tennessee, and consented to take her with them. Col. Haynes and Mr. Malone aided me in purchasing a horse, saddle and bridle for her, and Mrs. Gaines furnished her with suitable clothing, shawls, etc., to render her journey comfortable. When she reached home she was delighted to find her husband, and two children she hid in the potato cellar, alive. The Legislature voted money to Tandy Walker for his noble agency in this affair.

I promptly communicated to the War Department the conduct of the Chief Oceochematla on his last visit to the trading house; also Mrs. Crawley's capture and rescue, and her return to her family. But the policy of Mr. Jefferson's and Mr. Madison's administrations towards the Indians was so humane as to overlook their faults in the hope and expectation of their ultimate civilization.

The old building of Fort St. Stephens, in which the goods of the Choctaw Trading House and the land office were kept since their establishment, became leaky and untenable, the goods of the trading house, and also the land office, were removed in the early part of 1812 to a new brick building which I had erected in 1811, a few hundred yards west of the old Fort; perhaps the first brick building in the present State of Alabama, unless at Huntsville.

Having received advices from the Superintendent of Indian trade, that my supplies for the ensuing winter, spring and summer would be forwarded as the last, via Pittsburgh, Colbert's Ferry, on the Tennessee, to Major John Pitchlyn, near the mouth of the Oktibbeha, on the Tombigbee, I caused a barge to be built at Major Pitchlyn's to bring the goods down. About the same time the barge was finished and the goods arrived at Major Pitchlyn's, several small settlements of Choctaws on the Tombigbee, below the mouth of the Black Warrior, were understood to have become dupes of the Creeks, whose unfriendly demeanor to the white people seemed to be increasing; I therefore deemed it necessary to obtain a Sergeant's command and go up myself for the goods.[32]

I caused the barge to be boxed, as usual in those days. This was meant not only for the safety of the goods but for the protection of the rowers and steersman. I had the sides and top well lined with heavy beef hides, so as to make them entirely bullet-proof. Both ends of the "boxing" were open, so that the steersman could see how to guide the barge. I found my contrivance was a clumsy one for descending the river, which was out of its banks in many places with an unusually high freshet. The second day of our voyage—a very cold evening, just before sunset—the boat was drawn to one side of the river by a rapid current which overflowed the land, drifted sideways against a tree standing on the margin, having more than twenty feet of water pressing against it. The barge became entangled in the branches. I ran up on deck, and saw that the tree was vibrating, and each vibration appeared to turn the boat on one side. I immediately requested the Sergeant to order the men on deck and have the tree cut off.

The Sergeant and his men quickly appeared, when my faithful servant, Dick, (Dick is still living in Greene county, Mississippi,) whose judgement on several occasions I had found very good, said to the Sergeant, "Tell your men to put their shoulders to the strongest limbs and the body of the tree and push with all their might, or the boat will be turned over before the tree can be cut down; the water is up to the oar-holes." I directed the Sergeant to do so. Each vibration of the tree, with the aid of the men, brought the boat up a little, and in ten minutes it was finally extricated and worked out in the stream. Had it upset the public goods would have been lost and many of us drowned.[33]

We were not attacked, but we noticed, after we passed the mouth of the Black Warrior, all the Indian settlements deserted. Some of the inhabitants went over to the Creeks, and others toward the interior of the Choctaw nation.

We arrived all safe at St. Stephens. Upon opening the goods they were found in good condition, with not a single article missing. These goods were greatly needed, and the trade was active during February, 1813, and the ensuing spring months.

After the summer opened upon us we had notice from the Creek nation of hostile preparation.

The Tombigbee settlement was now increased by new settlements in Clarke on the east, in Greene, Wayne and Perry on the west, and Mobile county, south of Ellicott's Line. All were uneasy for their safety.

Col. Caller received reliable information in July that a large number of Creeks had gone to Pensacola to receive offered supplies of arms and ammunition to enable them to commence war on the settlements, as allies of the British army. This information came chiefly through Sam Dale, Sam Manac, a half-breed Indian, and John E. Miles.[34]

He hastily collected as much of his militia force as he could, and marched to the frontier to meet the expected invaders; crossed the Alabama, and proceeded in the direction of Pensacola; met a considerable force at Burnt Corn Creek and a battle occurred. This celebrated battle, although somewhat disastrous on our part, delayed the attack on the settlements, and deranged the plans of the Indians. Col. Caller's force consisted of about one hundred and eighty men, the principal officers being Maj. Wood, Capts. Ben Smoot, Bailey Dix (half-breed), Bailey Heard, David Cartwright, Lieuts. Creagh, Pat May, Wm. Bradbury, Bob Caller, Zach Philipi, Jourdan McFarlane and others. Sam Dale distinguished himself during the battle and retreat. So did many others.[35]

Measures of safety were now the order of the day throughout the settlement. Stockade forts were commenced at Mimms' Tensaw settlement; Fort Madison, eastern border of Clark county; Fort Easley, on the northern border of Clark county, at St. Stephens, and many other points not remembered.[36]

Gen. Claiborne was on the march from the Mississippi settlements with his militia forces, arriving at Fort Stoddart about August first. He made a judicious distribution of his forces among the works commenced by the citizens.[37]

I commenced a stockading around the trading house and was furnished with a lieutenant and forty men to assist in the work.

Great numbers of citizens from Clark county fled to St. Stephens and constructed a stockade fort with my neighbors on Mount Republic, a hill in the village. A very worthy member of the Methodist Church—Mr. Hand—superintended this work, and volunteered the construction of a "hut" in it for my family, and also for Mr. Malone's. This courtesy was accepted, but we built the huts ourselves, as there was no provision for accommodation for ladies in my fort. Capt. Hand was elected captain of "Fort Republic." He was a grand uncle of Vanderbilt. The day after the massacre of Fort Mimms a letter was brought to me by a young man named Slay—I think from William Pierce—giving a somewhat detailed account of the massacre. The messenger belonged to a squad of militia that happened to be at or near Pierce's Mills when the massacre took place.[38]

It was late in the evening when I received the letter. I was in the citizen's fort at the time; and read the letter aloud for the information of those around me. I saw it created a panic, and remarked that if we could get Gen. Jackson down with his "Brigade of Mounted Volunteers," the Creek Indians could soon be quieted.

A young man named Edmondson, who was a guest in my family, was standing near, and looking at him, I remarked: "If I could induce a cheerful man to go as express to Nashville, Tennessee, I have a fine horse ready, and can manage, by writing to persons I know on the path, to have a fresh horse for him every day." He said that he was willing to go.[39]

Mrs. Gaines said that she would prepare provisions for him. I immediately sat down and wrote letters to General Jackson and Governor Blount, communicating the massacre of Fort Mimms and the defenseless condition of our frontier, appealing to Gen. Jackson to march down with his brigade of mounted men and save the Tombigbee settlements and the public property in my charge.[40]

I was personally acquainted with the General, also with Gov. Blount. I wrote a letter to Charles Juzant and William Starner at Oaknoxubee, John Pitchlyn, mouth of Oktibbeha, George James, residing at or near the present site of Egypt (M. & O. R. R.,) Jim Brown, Natchez road, George Colbert, Chief of the Chickasaws, Colbert's Ferry, and others beyond the Tennessee river, requesting them on the arrival of Mr. Edmondson to furnish him with their best horse and take care of the horse he would leave until his return from Nashville; then bring or send me their bills for payment. (Each of the persons named was in the habit of visiting the trading house for supplies of salt, sugar, coffee, etc.)[41]

This task occupied me nearly all night. In the morning Mr. Edmondson, with provisions, a well filled purse, etc., set out for Nashville.

Pushmataha learned from Mr. Juzant, where Edmondson obtained a fresh horse, (Pushmataha lived only a few miles from Juzant's), of the massacre of Fort Mimms, and came down to St. Stephens at once to offer his services in defense of the Tombigbee settlements. I informed him I was not a "war chief," but would gladly accompany him to Mobile and introduce him to Gen. Flournoy, who, I had no doubt, would accept his services. I accordingly had my horse saddled and proceeded with the chief to Mobile, to wait upon Gen. Flournoy, whose headquarters was in the old Spanish fort. I introduced the chief, and told the General the object of his visit. An interpreter was at hand. Pushmataha told the General that, upon his hearing of the massacre of Fort Mimms, he at once set out for St. Stephens and Mobile, to offer his services, with his young men, to assist in the protection of the Tombigbee frontier.[42]

The General answered that he was not authorized to accept. The chief then addressed to him a very handsome speech. He said, in conclusion, he had three objects in view in offering his services: one was the protection of the settlement; another was to be avenged on an ancient enemy for the massacre of a number of personal friends at Fort Mimms, some of whom played ball with him when a young man; but more especially to engage his warriors on the right side in the war, as many of his young men were becoming excited, and were desirous to be engaged in the war.[43]

But the eloquence of the old chief appeared to make no impression upon the General.

I ventured to inquire whether he considered his force sufficient for the protection of the frontier? He replied that he could not say.

I ventured the opinion that if he felt any doubt about it, certainly it was his duty to obtain such additional force as the chief offered.

I did not receive a very civil reply, and remarked that I would hasten back to St. Stephens and do the best I could to prevent the public property from falling into the hands of the Creeks. I remarked to the chief that we had better return to St. Stephens as soon as possible; that I had sent an express to Gen. Jackson, and that we would soon hear from him.

When we arrived at St. Stephens we rode up to the gate of the "Citizens' Fort," and before we could alight from our horses we were surrounded by a dense crowd which came pouring out of the fort to hear the result of our trip to Mobile.

While relating the conversation between Pushmataha and Gen. Flournoy, a horseman was seen making his way toward us—the crowd opening to let him pass when they learned that he had dispatches for me. He rode up and handed me a package, saying that it was from General Flournoy. I tore off the envelope and read the contents aloud. The General stated that after we left him he reflected seriously upon the object of our mission to him, and determined to accept the services of the chief and all the warriors he could bring into the field; and begged me to accompany the chief to the Nation and aid him to bring out as many men as could come at once, drawing upon his Quartermaster for necessary expenses.

Captain Hand said to me, "You will go, of course, Mr. Gaines." It was nearly sundown, and I replied that I would at least alight and visit my family, at the same time inviting the chief into the fort. We dismounted, turning our horses over to my man Dick; Captain Hand and several of the citizens following to my hut.

I read Gen. Flournoy's dispatch over again.

The captain repeated the inquiry, will you go, Mr. Gaines? stating that Mrs. Hand and the ladies of the fort would take care of Mrs. Gaines, who was in delicate health.[44]

I replied that it was my first duty to take care of the public property placed in my charge.

Mrs. Gaines, after hearing Gen. Flournoy's letter read said, "you will have to go, Mr. Gaines. Mr. Malone will take care of the public goods, and I will rest safely in the care of Mrs. Hand and the ladies of the fort."

Col. Dinsmore's absence from his agency at this critical moment rendered the situation more alarming, in my opinion. I therefore felt it my duty to comply with Gen. Flournoy's request. I told Capt. Hand I would go. Mr. Flood McGrew, one of our most worthy citizens, volunteered to accompany me.[45]

The following morning, after an early breakfast, we set out for the Nation, with Pushmataha. The second day, when near Charles Juzant's, the chief left us, after appointing a day for a council with his people, near the present site of Quitman, Mississippi, which I promised to attend. Mr.

McGrew and I proceeded on our way to Major Pitchlyn's two days travel further north.

Col. John McKee reached Major Pitchlyn's from Nashville the same hour we arrived.[46]

Col. McKee informed me that my messenger, Mr. Edmondson, arrived at Nashville in a remarkably short time, delivered my letters to Gen. Jackson and Gov. Blount, and the General had sent him (McKee) to "get out" as many Chickasaw and Choctaw warriors as practicable, and then march against the Creek towns at the falls of the Black Warrior. The General had issued orders to his mounted brigade to rendezvous, and would march immediately on the Creek settlements on the headwaters of the Alabama.[47]

Colonel McKee was a gentleman of great worth. He served as United States Agent of Choctaws during the administration of John Adams. He was very much respected by the Indian chiefs and the whites living in the nation; he stood high also among the Chickasaws.

It was agreed between us that he should operate in the northern district and the adjacent Chickasaw country, aided by Maj. Pitchlyn; and that I should return to the southern district and attend the meeting appointed by Pushmataha. Accordingly next morning Mr. McGrew and myself departed southward, on our return to Pushmataha's "Council Ground." Several thousand Indians were collected when we arrived. The chief himself soon rode up accompanied by his wife, and alighted under a spreading oak tree. He unsaddled the horses, hobbled them out, piled the saddles, etc., at the foot of the tree, and threw himself on a bear skin in the shade, his wife meanwhile mixing with the women on the outskirts of the crowd.[48]

McGrew and I were seated on a log some twenty or thirty feet from the oak, where Mrs. Nail, a half-breed, wife of a white man and the old acquaintance of Mr. McGrew's joined us and sit beside. She was a good interpreter.[49]

Pushmataha laid fully a quarter of an hour without speaking to any one. McGrew said, "Mr. Gaines you ought to go and shake hands with him." I replied, "I am a visitor and the chief ought to come and shake hands with me." McGrew said, "I think you ought to salute him." Mrs. Nail said, "Never mind, Flood; although you have been raised with the Choctaws, Mr. Gaines understands how to treat the chief better than you do."

At this moment the chief raised his head, and in a low voice said something to his speaker (the speaker was a sort of Secretary of State), who got up, and loud tones informed the audience that the chief was about to deliver an address.[50]

Men and boys immediately crowded about the tree, and seated themselves on the grass in circles. The chief arose to his feet, and commenced his speech by reminding his audience that he was a member of the delegation sent by his nation to visit Gen. Washington some years before. He stated that it was a long journey, but was made pleasant by the kind treatment of their white friends everywhere on the route. Arriving at Philadelphia, the delegation was quartered at a pleasant hotel and their horses at a livery stable.

"The delegation was received by Gen. Washington as a father would receive his sons who had been a long time absent. He inquired into the wants of our people at home, telling us he would send us blacksmiths and wheelrights to make for us implements of husbandry, spinning wheels, looms, and other necessary articles, for it would not do for us to rely much longer upon the game of the woods for support; it would become scarcer and scarcer every year. He advised us to pay more attention to our truck-patches—to enlarge them into fields of corn, potatoes, garden vegetables and cotton patches; and to encourage our women to spin and weave, and make clothing for their families.[51]

"We visited the President for a few hours almost every day during our stay in Philadelphia.

"He was a man, to be sure, but not like other men: he rarely opened his lips to speak without saying something useful, to be remembered for the good of mankind, and especially for his red children."

During this part of his speech Pushmataha held a long string of white beads in his hands; he put them in his shot-pouch, and continued:[52]

"The English people across the big water have provoked a war with our good father, the President; and the English agents have for many moon poisoned the minds of the Northern Indians, persuading most of the tribes to aid in the war against our Virginia friends." (The Indians called the whites "Virginians.") "Emissaries from the Northern tribes have been among us, but have made little impression. They have, however, succeeded in persuading the Creeks to join the strangers in the war, and many of our friends in the Tombigbee settlements have been massacred by them. Fort Mimms, over the river, where a number of our friends had collected for safety, has been destroyed, and several hundred persons killed.[53]

"President Washington advised us not to engage in war—one tribe with another—and even if he should happen to be engaged in war he advised us to remain quietly at home attending to our peaceful occupations, as he would always be able to fight his own battles. But who, that is a man and a warrior, can be idle at home and hear of his friends being butchered around him? I am a man and a warrior."

Saying this he drew his sword, using it in his gesticulations.

"I will not advise you to act contrary to the advice of our good father, but I will go and help my friends. If any of you think proper to follow me voluntarily, I will lead you to victory and glory."

Almost every man and boy sprang to their feet, shouting "I, too, am a man and a warrior, and will follow the chief." The chief concluded by saying, "I see our beloved factor from St. Stephens. He never deceived you in anything. He will speak to you."[54]

He walked to the log where we were sitting and shook hands with each of us cordially, inviting me to the tree to speak to the people.

I said to them the chief had left but little for me to say. "He has told you truly all about the war, I have only to say, all that think proper to follow him may organize themselves into companies, elect their officers and report as soon as possible at St. Stephens for duty, where you will be armed and equipped for the 'war path,' and will receive the same pay of our own officers and men. If you deem proper you may collect at St. Stephens and be organized there."[55]

I then remarked that I would sleep at Mrs. Nail's, and would be glad to see the chief and his captains in the morning before I set out for St. Stephens. Mrs. Nail remarked to the chief that she would take care to have an early dinner, so that Mr. McGrew and I could have the latter part of the day to travel home.

Accordingly, next morning the chief and his captains called upon me. The chief agreed to follow me in a day or two, with as many of his young men as could be got ready for the march, and would advise others to follow as they could get ready.

Mrs. Nail was as good as her word. She was so delighted with the result of the council that, after returning home her daughters and some squaws were put to pounding meal. I could hear the sound of the pestles whenever I awoke at night, and before day in the morning her husband, a very worthy man, making preparations for butchering pigs and a beef for the promised feast, which was served up about 12 o'clock. The meats were barbecued. The heartiness with which it was enjoyed proved its excellence. Some of the Nails' descendants live in Choctaw county, Ala. They are much respected.[56]

McGrew and self took leave of the chief Pushmataha, his captains, our host and his family, and set out on our journey home; travelling all night, and reaching St. Stephens the following night.

The next morning after our arrival there was a collection of nearly all the men of the two forts at the door of my "hut," to hear the news, and I never saw a collection of happier faces. For several weeks previous they had been expecting an attack from the Creeks, but the news from Tennessee and from the Choctaw nation seemed to dispel the panic and to fill every heart with a sense of safety and rejoicing.[57]

It was deemed very fortunate that Mr. Edmondson was sent to Nashville so promptly. I was praised for what I considered merely the discharge of my duty under the then existing circumstances. It is quite probable that no other man could, at the time, have controlled the facilities which enabled Mr. Edmondson to perform the journey to Nashville in so short a time.[58]

Gen. Claiborne was so busily engaged at the time in making preparations for the defence of the frontier, and to carry the war into the Creek Nation, although he knew I had sent an express to Nashville, looked to Gen. Flournoy and the War Department for the necessary aid to accomplish his purposes, and was doubtless surprised to hear of Gen. Jackson's movements, and of his first battles on the upper waters of the Alabama, about the same time.[59]

Mr. Edmondson's return from Nashville gave us later accounts of General Jackson's movements. The General had taken up the line of his march with his brigade of mounted men toward the head waters of the Alabama. Mr. Edmondson said that he was greatly fatigued when he arrived at Nashville, but he lost no time in finding Gov. Blount and General Jackson. Upon enquiry he learned they were both in the State-house, and immediately called upon them, found them in a room together and delivered my letters. The General, after reading his, arose and walked rapidly backward and forwards across the room. The Governor, after reading his letter, was the first to speak, although he was much longer in getting through with it. He said to the General, "My letter is from Geo. S. Gaines, United States factor at St. Stephens, Tombigbee river, and gives us bad news," handed the letter to the General. "I know Mr. Gaines also and we may rely upon his statements." The General handed the Governor the letter, saying, "mine is from Mr. Gaines also—I am personally acquainted with him, and there can be no doubt about the massacre and the perilous situation of the Tombigbee settlements." Edmondson said that he had not been noticed—was still standing, almost ready to sink with fatigue. The Governor now asked him to take a seat.[60] He made many inquiries about the state of settlements and the apparent feeling of the Choctaws and Chickasaws; and how he managed to perform the journey in so short a time. He then remarked to Gen. Jackson "I am very sorry General that you are not able to take the field at once." The General had his arm in a sling and appeared to be suffering with pain. He replied, "I shall take the field at once." The Governor then said to him, "make your arrangements, General, as you think best. You know from my correspondence with the War Department, which you have read, there will be no trouble about money for your outfit; and the Legislature will pass any law that you may recommend to facilitate your movements."[61]

The General then sat by a table remarking, "my brigade is scattered but I will soon have it together." He then wrote an order instructing it to rendezvous for the purpose of marching southward.[62]

Pushmataha soon made his appearance at St. Stephens, with such of his warriors as were ready to come with him. He stated that others would follow every day until he would have a good force in the field. Gen. Claiborne lost no time in having them armed and equipped as they arrived at St. Stephens, and then placed on the frontier.[63]

Families began to leave the forts and return to their homes except those residing on the frontier, but the men of the latter returned to look after their stock and gather their corn.

Mingo Homastubbee died two or three years after the treaty of Mt. Dexter, and was succeeded by his son Mushalatubbee as Mingo, or principal Chief of the Northern District. He was a man of sense, but had not much of his father's energy and versatility of character. He came down to the trading house soon after his father's death, and told me that his father directed that he should come to the trading house after his death and assume his debt and pay it as soon as he could. He requested me to carry the balance of his father's account to him on the books of the trading house, which was accordingly done. His residence was near that of Maj. Pitchlyn, in whose society he acquired much useful information, both in regard to the government of his people and the relations of the Indian tribes with the Government of the United States.[64]

Col. McKee found no difficulty in raising, with the aid of Maj. Pitchlyn, all the warriors necessary for this projected expedition to the Creek village at the falls of the Black Warrior, and took up his line of march within less than a week after his arrival from Nashville. On his arrival at the falls of the Black Warrior he found that the Chief Oceochemotla, with his villagers, had made his escape, and there was nothing left for the Choctaw and Chickasaw warriors to do but burn the deserted cabins and return home.[65]

This slight foretaste of war hurried Mushalatubbee and a great number of his warriors to St. Stephens, where they were organized, armed, equipped, and sent to the frontier.

The war spirit about this time began to spread among Puckshennubbee's warriors, and parties began to arrive at St. Stephens from that district. And although the war was going on satisfactorily, a great deal of excitement prevailed.[66]

Col. McGrew, a much-esteemed militia officer, who had been raised in the neighborhood of St. Stephens, was killed in a battle by a party of Creeks, in the northern portion of Clarke county, who had with them a few renegade Choctaws. Col. McGrew commanded the militia of the Tombigbee settlement in this battle. Mr. Bradbury, a young lawyer, was wounded and brought to St. Stephens, where he died soon after. Several other of our citizens were killed and wounded.[67]

About this time a party of Creek Indians were overtaken by some of our militia at the very moment they entered the house of a settler in Clarke county. They found the Indians tomahawking and scalping a woman and two children, but were in such haste to escape, the "tomahawking" was ineffectually done. The woman and children survived; and were brought to St. Stephens and nursed in a hut in my yard.

Dale's celebrated "Canoe Battle" took place about this period. My worthy friend, Jere Austill distinguished himself in this engagement.[68]

A dispatch was received at the post office, addressed to Gen. Claiborne, with a request that I would forward it immediately by an express. I could find no one, owner of a horse, who would agree to carry it for any price.

My friend, Tandy Walker, was then wounded and lying at Fort Madison. He was shot during one of his scouts on the Alabama river. I determined to carry it myself. Bailey Heard and another young friend of mine offered to accompany me. We set out late in the evening, crossed the Tombigbee at Jackson after dark, and slept at the village; proceeding on next morning, we called at Fort Madison, where we found Tandy Walker, who was greatly rejoiced to see us and hear from home.[69]

From Fort Madison to Fort Claiborne there was no road, and the "blind path" had many forks. We took one of them, leading us out of the way, and it was dark before we reached the Alabama river, opposite Fort Claiborne. This section was infested with Creek spies, therefore we kept a pretty sharp lookout, and when about midway between Forts Madison and Claiborne we saw two Indians, with guns in their hands, emerge from behind, and run with great swiftness. My young friends proposed we should pursue; each of us armed with rifles and pistols; but this I objected to, reminding them that I had a dispatch for Gen. Claiborne, which was probably of great importance, and if we pursued, it might be lost, for it was possible these Indians belonged to a party near at hand, which they might reach before we could overtake them. After having convinced them that we had better move on and let the Indians alone, we continued our journey in a rather livelier trot.[70]

It was some time after reaching the Alabama before we could make ourselves heard across the river at the new fort and a flat could be sent for us. Some dogs came to where we were, which we supposed might have belonged to the Indians killed in Dale's canoe engagement.

Thinking the noise we made might attract hostile Indians in the neighborhood, we were impatient at the delay. After the boat from the other side pushed off the men continued to halloo, so that our replies might enable them to land in the right place; consequently the questions and answers continued until the boat actually landed. Two or three men got out, I suppose, to look for a suitable place to take our horses aboard, when Mr. Heard cocked his rifle and whispered to me, "There are Indians down on the bar." I said, "No, they are some of the men from the flat." He said, "No, they are not." "The boat hasn't reached the shore," I said to him, "don't shoot, they are our own men." And just then the sergeant, who was the steersman, called to us—"Come on; we are ready for you." We were soon ferried over, and received at Gen. Claiborne's headquarters. "Mingo" Pushmataha happened to be with him, and appeared delighted to see me. We had a pleasant night of it, and spent the next day at the fort, to give Gen. Claiborne time to prepare his dispatches. We returned to St. Stephens without any adventure worth relating.[71]

We began to hear of Gen. Jackson's first battle with the Creeks, on the upper waters of the Alabama.

Gen. Claiborne having completed the stockade, Fort Claiborne, the 3d Regiment U.S. Infantry, commanded by Col. Russel, reached that place about the last of the month (November).[72]

The settlers became quieter; and having gathered as much of their crops as escaped devastation while they were enforted, resumed their winter occupation, believing Gen. Jackson would soon conquer the Indians.

I saw but little of Col. Dinsmore after he removed his agency west of Pearl river. He purchased a number of Africans, and with them opened a large plantation at the Agency. He married a most estimable Philadelphian lady a few years before this time.[73]

He seemed to rely upon Maj. Pitchlyn to carry out his plans in the eastern part of the nation, whilst he applied himself, as heretofore, with his characteristic energy to the improvement of Puckshennubbee's district, and to the task of breaking up the remnants of a notorious gang of rob-bers, (Murrell's clan,) who were supposed to find shelter in the western part of the nation.[74]

Their depredations in the white settlements below, stealing horses and negroes, were loudly complained of to the War Department, which caused instructions to be issued to Col. Dinsmore to require passports from travellers going through the "Nation"; and to use every means in his power to detect and bring to justice all marauders found in his district. Some gentlemen, citizens of Tennessee and Kentucky, of high standing complained to the War Department of the trouble and annoyance they underwent in obtaining passports and reporting to the agency office, which some enemies of Col. Dinsmore's took advantage of, and petitioned the War Department to remove him from office. This rendered it necessary for the Colonel to visit Washington in his defense, such were the rumors afloat. I have no recollection of ever having had any conversation with him on the subject. I remember he informed me after the treaty of Mt. Dexter that in the settlement of his accounts of expenses at St. Stephens and Mt. Dexter, several large items were suspended by the Auditor, Peter Hagner, and several smaller items were absolutely rejected. He showed me his correspondence with the Auditor on the subject, in which he was lectured for having purchased *anchovies* and *condiments,* as these articles were not considered requisite for the tables of Indian treaty commissioners and their guests. Col. Dinsmore, being familiar with the requisite supplies of a man of war, seemed to regard it very unreasonable in the accounting officers to complain of his purchases for Indian treaties. These difficulties in the settlement of his accounts *may have* taken him to Washington several times before the present year. But it is probable the rumors before mentioned may have taken him there in 1813, detained him some time.[75]

This year, 1814, the war with Great Britain and with the Indian tribes (British allies) became so familiar as to be much less alarming, and the people talked of it as drawing nearer a successful termination.

General Jackson was looked upon as the savior of the Tombigbee settlements and probably the whole of the Mississippi Territory.

The Mississippi militia and Choctaw volunteers, under General Claiborne, had given universal satisfaction.

General Jackson's operations on the upper waters of the Alabama drew off from our frontier a great number of Creek warriors, who were making preparations to overrun the settlements. This deprived General Claiborne's forces of many of the laurels they would otherwise have obtained; but as all did their duty, I never heard any complaints. After General Claiborne's battle of the "Holy Ground," on the Alabama river, he returned to the Tombigbee frontier with his militia and Indians, as it was not deemed necessary for him to penetrate the Creek nation any farther; and General Jackson, after he had taken measures to secure and perpetuate the benefits of his victories on the upper waters of the Alabama, also came down in the latter part of the winter or early in the spring of 1814.[76]

While Jackson was at Fort Claiborne he addressed an order to me, as U.S. Factor, St. Stephens, for blankets, strouds and shirting for our Indian warriors. I sent the goods, enclosing a bill requesting a draft on the War Department in payment. A friend of mine was present when he received my letter, and he told me that the General appeared vexed at my request for payment. He remarked, "What does Gaines mean? I knew him when he was a boy—all right." My friend said, "The goods are for the Indian trade, General, and probably Mr. Gaines had no instructions to furnish any of them to the army."[77]

The General's face relaxed in a smile, and as he handed the bill to a member of his staff, he said: "It's all right; prepare the draft."

This was General Flournoy's District, but his name was rarely mentioned in connection with the movements of the army or the public service.[78]

I could hear of General Jackson speaking of the Spanish authorities at Pensacola as aiding the British in the war, and of his preparations for an expedition to Pensacola to punish the authorities for furnishing arms and munitions to the Creeks, and encouraging them to make war on our settlements. The hanging of Ambrister and Arbuthnot, agents of the British army, who it was proved had been supplying munitions of war and encouraging the Creek Indians, seemed to be regretted by some Northern editors, whose papers occasionally reached us; but the fate of these two desperate men excited no sympathy in our settlements, which had suffered so much from the depredations of the Creeks.[79] In the fall of this year Gen. Coffee's brigade of mounted men came down through the Choctaw and Chickasaw Nations from Tennessee, where they had been resting after their services upon the upper waters of the Alabama. The General halted a day at St. Stephens to rest his horses, and then proceeded to Mobile to join Gen. Jackson, who it was believed expected the British to land troops at Mobile from several war vessels known to be lying off Mobile Point.[80]

While his headquarters were at Mobile, Gen. Jackson wrote me, enclosing an anonymous letter, which had been mailed at my post office, charging a friend of mine, one of our most prominent citizens, with being in secret correspondence with the English vessels lying off Mobile Point, requesting me to ascertain who was the author and let him know. I replied that I did not know the hand-writing, nor who dropped the letter in my letter box; assuring the General that there could not be the slightest ground for these charges, that my friend was one of the best men I ever knew, and had done everything in his power for the security of the settlements against the savage allies of the English. The mail rider was waiting for my hastily written letter and departed as soon as it was put in the bag.[81]

I happened to mention the matter to Mrs. Gaines, who remarked, "You had better go to Mobile and have a conversation with Gen. Jackson, for fear some enemy of our friend has prejudiced the General against him." I accordingly ordered my horse and set out for Mobile with the expectation of overtaking the mail rider before night, but was mistaken, and the night being dark, after crossing Bates' creek I slept at Mr. Bates'.[82] It was late in the evening of the next day when I reached Alvarez's Ferry, on the Chickasawbogue, and learned that the mail rider had crossed an hour before, and the ferryman had gone off with the flat and would not return until after night. I passed the night at Alvarez's and was ferried over Chickasawbogue early in the morning, and on reaching Mobile obtained directions to Gen. Jackson's headquarters, and rode up to the gate, dismounted, opened the gate and found Gen. Jackson standing in the piazza reading an open letter.[83]

The General knew me the moment he saw me, although it had been nine years since our last meeting. He held out his hand and said: "I think this is Mr. Gaines? I was just reading your letter; you seem to have misunderstood me. I know your friend very well; he was a man of high standing. I knew him well before he moved to Tombigbee. I only wanted to know the scoundrel that dared to practice such an imposition upon me."

I expressed my pleasure in seeing him well, and hearing what he said of my friend, as my letter was written in so much haste that I deemed it proper to follow it.[84]

We conversed about mutual friends in Tennessee, over the breakfast table; and then about the war and Indian tribes. He made many inquiries about the character of the Choctaws and Chickasaws who had withstood the evil machinations of the Shawnee Prophet which were so potent in seducing the Creeks to their ruin. He seemed to be doubtful when the British troops would land, and remarked that he would endeavor to give them a warm reception.[85]

After dinner with the General I set out on my return home. I recollect nothing of interest occurring until we heard of Gen. Jackson's rapid march, with his available force, in December, toward New Orleans.

Peace followed Gen. Jackson's battle of the 8 of January.[86]

———————

I have deemed it proper to suspend my Reminiscences of the Early Times in Mississippi Territory, intending to continue them during the present summer should my health permit, and at least bring them down to the time when the Territory was divided into the present States of Alabama and Mississippi, and to the removal of the Choctaw and Chickasaw tribes west.

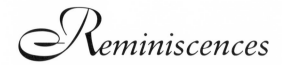

Reminiscences

of Early Times in Mississippi Territory

 War is horrible, whether between two nations of people speaking different languages, and with different forms of Government, or between two nations of people speaking the same language, professing the same religion and of kindred blood. The war recently terminated was rendered intensely horrible in this section of country by the stealthy raids of the Creek Indians, the massacre of Fort Mimms; & of unprotected families of women and children until Gen. Jackson, with his volunteers, reached the northern border of the Creek Nation; and the Chief Pushmataha, with his warriors, reinforced Gen. Claiborne on our Eastern border. And, although a feeling of personal safety soon followed these events, it was not until after the Battle of New Orleans, and the news of peace reached us, in the latter part of January, that the inhabitants seemed to emerge from the stupor occasioned by the war, and to enter spiritedly upon the preparation of their grounds to plant. The militia began to make their way homeward including the Choctaw and Chickasaw warriors.[1]

I applied for a furlough to visit my aged parents, residing in East Tennessee, which was promptly granted.

Col. Silas Dinsmore, for many years past U.S. Agent to the Choctaws, and who had been so successful in their improvement, removed his family this spring to St. Stephens. Col. John McKee succeeded him as U.S. Agent to the Choctaws.[2]

In April I perfected my arrangements to visit my parents, with my family. I turned over the Choctaw trading house to my worthy assistant Thomas Malone. I was relieved of all care of official duty and devoted myself to making preparations for the comfortable travelling of my family and myself through the wilderness, to Tennessee. This wilderness commenced one day's travel from St. Stephens and extended beyond the Tennessee River and within one or two days' travel of Columbia, Maury County, Tennessee.[3]

There was nothing but a "trading path" for the first three hundred miles—yet our journey was rendered delightful by the fine May weather, and the kind attentions of the Indians whilst we were "moving" about every day.[4]

It so happened that at the moment we reached what was called the "Natchez Trace" Gen. Jackson was travelling with his family homeward and we had the pleasure of their company to the neighborhood of Columbia,* they treated us with much kindness which rendered the balance of our journey through the wilderness still more delightful. I had promised my friend, Mr. McGee, who resided in the neighborhood of Columbia, that we would call and rest at his house, which promise I felt it a duty to fulfill notwithstanding the pressing invitation of the General and his good lady, to go home with them and visit at the Hermitage.[5]

We remained several days at Mr. McGee's then proceeded on our journey stopping a week at Franklin with my friend Nicholas Perkins through whose agency I exchanged my horse and gig for a pair of fine horses and a good travelling carriage.** We spent a few days with John Allen of Gallatin; and few days with my friends in the neighborhood of Dixon Springs—then travelled without unnecessary delay to my father's, where after spending several weeks visiting relatives and friends, I proceeded to Washington City where my stay was longer than intended, having been confined there by sickness (contracted on the journey) for three or four weeks. I was cheered during this confinement by the visits of our brother Edmond's friends, and several officers of the Government.[6]

Before I left Washington it was determined by the Government to remove the Choctaw Trading House from St. Stephens to the interior of the Nation. I was instructed by the Sect'y of War to select a suitable site and erect buildings.[7] I was also furnished with an order upon the Commanding Officer at New Orleans for a company of U.S. Infantry to aid in constructing the new buildings; and to protect the establishment until there was no further danger from wandering Creek Indians. I returned home with my family about the end of October, and in November returned to the interior of the nation horseback. I consulted Pushmataha about a desirable location for the trading house, and was recommended to examine Fort Confederation Bluff.[8] A creek known as Etomba-igabee runs into the

*The General was returning home from New Orleans. Mrs. Jackson joined him there after peace was declared.
**Maj. Perkins caused the capture of Aaron Burr.

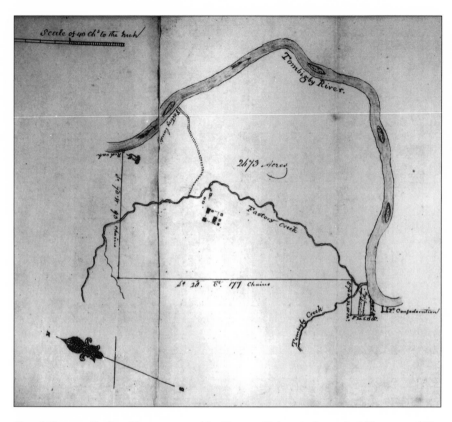

Plat of Choctaw Trading House, surveyed by Thomas Malone in June 1816 (Courtesy of National Archives)

River at the upper end of the Bluff. This creek & bluff, Pushmataha told me, was familiar to the Choctaws, not only on account of the old Spanish Fort, but of a celebrated box maker, who resided on the creek, from whom the Choctaws obtained boxes for the bones of their dead. I visited the Fort or rather its remains. I found the ditch which surrounded three sides of the fortifications. Many of the pickets were standing inside the line of the ditch, but there was nothing to be seen of the block-house, officers and soldiers quarters.[9]

Samuel Jones, a white man with an Indian family, resided in an old house, which he told me was built by the Spaniards, about a hundred yards from the site of the fort.* I spent several days with him, to examine the

*This place is now known as Jones' Bluff. The Ala. and Chattanooga RR crosses the river there.

surrounding country. There was another creek which united with the Etomba-igabee, near the river. I determined to erect the buildings of the trading house near a fine spring, which ran into the last mentioned creek.[10]

I then set out for home by way of Mr. Juzant's, whose residence was but a few miles from what is now known as Lauderdale Springs. Mr. Juzant's was quite a favorite of Mingo Pushmataha, who often visited him. I found him there and during the conversation upon the object of my journey he told me that the Choctaws all knew the paths to the "Old Box Makers" and would be pleased to travel them "for blankets for the living instead of boxes for the dead." I inquired what was the Choctaw name of the Tombigbee river? Pushmataha answered—"Hatchie." (Hatchie is river) I turned to Mr. Juzant's and asked, "Have the Choctaws no name for the river?" "Not until the whites came among them," he replied. "The Indian Country men"** hearing the Indians speaking of their journeys to Etomba-igabee (The Box Maker), before the stream was much known to the whites, supposed it was the name of the river, and it was called by them "Tombigbee"—[11]

I forwarded the order from the Secretary of War upon the Commanding officer at New Orleans to furnish me with a company of infantry to aid in putting up the buildings of the new trading house. I received only a sergeant and twelve men, as more could not be spared from that military district. I employed carpenters and several choppers & proceeded to the place selected, with everything necessary to carry on the work, which was prosecuted so industriously that it was so nearly completed in May, I chartered a barge to carry up the public goods with my furniture and family. We had a pleasant trip. The goods were opened in the new store house, where an active trade with the Indians commenced.[12]

Late in the season as it was to begin gardening and to plant a crop of corn, potatoes, etc. this work had to be done, requiring the active co-operation not only of every individual belonging to the establishment, but also my own servants. My father-in-law sent us a drove of cattle. A few days after they reached us the second grade chief, who considered himself Governor of the Shu-qua-noochee country, called upon me, and with a grave face told me that strangers had driven upon his lands a great number of cattle, and asked me if I knew about it. I told Hopia-skitteena (Little Leader) that my wife was a daughter of Young Gaines, and the old gentleman had sent the cattle to me that I might have beef, butter & milk for my family. He said, "It is all right then. I knew Young Gaines—he is a

---

**White men living among the Indians were so called.

good and sensible man. I will see that your cattle eat my grass in safety."[13] Some time afterward, he came to the Factory & told me that one of his men had killed a two year old steer of mine. The man was out hunting, with his family at his camp; but failed to kill a deer, until his wife and children were almost starving, which was the cause of his killing my steer; adding that the U.S. Government owed him for services and he would see that I should be paid. Col. McKee, U.S. Agent to the Choctaws, invited me to accompany him to the Little Leader's to witness the payment of his people for services in the war, for which purpose, the Little Leader had summoned them to be at his house on a certain day. I acted as Clerk for Col. McKee. Whilst the payment was going on the Little Leader brought me ten silver dollars saying "This is for your steer my man killed." I said, "Never mind—the man did well in reporting the act, and his family was near starving at the time, you may give him back the money." He said, "No, that won't do. Put the money in your pocket. If it is returned to him he will very likely kill another one of your steers. Thinking he has done no harm. When a man does wrong he ought to be made to feel it."[14]

Col. McKee received orders from the War Department to provide for a treaty to be held at the trading house. The Commissioners for holding the treaty were the Hon. John Rhea of Tennessee, Gen. John Coffee and Col. McKee. They arrived at the trading house early in October 1817. The Indians began to assemble soon after from every part of the nation. Beef of the best quality and corn were issued in abundance to the assembled thousands. The Chiefs and their principal Captains took their meals with the Commissioners at the trading house. Ball plays and other games enlivened the encampment during the day, and the dances of the young folks at night. The Chiefs and the Commissioners "talked" over the objects of the meeting in the meantime. Several days passed in this way when the business was submitted to a formal council of the parties and thoroughly discussed on both sides, resulting in the purchase of the Choctaw claim to all lands lying east of the Tombigbee river. The treaty proved satisfactory to the Choctaws as there were few resident members of the tribe east of the river; and it was duly ratified by Congress at the ensuing session.[15]

The survey of the lands was soon commenced with great activity. Emigrants from Virginia, the Carolinas, Georgia, Tennessee, and Kentucky poured into the valleys of the Alabama and the Tombigbee without waiting for the sales of the lands. Among them were the Pickens, Winstons, Bibbs, Murphys, Lewis, Saffolds, Gayles, Glovers, Bagbys, Kings, Crawfords, Meeks, Herndons, Alstons, Starks, Hunters, Turners, and many others whose good names "are as familiar as household words" in Alabama. Mr. J. Hancock, father of Hon. Wm. H. Hancock of Mississippi, settled about this time in Clarke County not far from Coffeeville. Mr. Hancock is one of the few early settlers of Alabama now living. He has been for many years past a citizen of Lauderdale County, Miss., well and favorably known in that and surrounding counties. Wm. Murrell purchased land in the neighborhood of Coffeeville. Messrs. Thompson, Love, Malone, Turner and several other worthy men also settled in the vicinity.[16]

It is now more than fifty years ago since Coffeeville was first settled by Col. Haynes G. Taylor and others whose names I do not now remember. Some of these families were endeared to me by friendships formed before the war and strengthened by our association and suffering during that period. I remember a circumstance showing that the citizens of the village and vicinity were warm, fast friends of mine. It was some ten years after the close of the war, while I was a citizen of Demopolis, that I was solicited by friends in Clark and Marengo to become a candidate for the Senatorial branch of the Legislature. I consented reluctantly because much of my time was required at the Choctaw trading house to superintend that branch of the business of Glover & Gaines; but it was urged that I was so well known there would be no necessity of my canvassing the counties before election; and that I owed it to my friends to become a candidate. I had been spending two or three weeks at the trading house, and returned home on Sunday, only a week before the election, when I was informed two competitors were in the field, who had been canvassing several weeks, and it was apprehended would prevent my election. I found letters from the Tax Collectors of Marengo and Clark informing me that they had advertised meetings to collect taxes so that I might attend one of them every day, during the week, to address the people I thought proper. Next morning (Monday) I began by attending a meeting in Marengo. On Thursday when I reached Coffeeville I found a large number of persons on the street, among them several old friends who received me warmly. One of them remarked, "We regret we did not know you would be a candidate. Several of your old friends solicited your friend Mr. Shields to offer, not having heard you were a candidate." I said, "Well, you'll have to vote for him. He is better qualified to discharge the duties of the office than either of the candidates."[17]

The tax paying proceeded, meanwhile I had a pleasant time with old friends. In the evening, a gentleman who resided on the road to the Court House, invited me to go home with him saying that he would accompany me to the Court House in the morning. When I was going to bed that night he remarked, "We will start early and breakfast at Mr. Calhoun's, a good, old Scotchman." Accordingly we went to Mr. Calhoun's in the morning, and a very excellent breakfast was soon served us. During the meal I asked Mr. C. from which part of Scotland he came, & conversed with him about the localities, and matters and customs of the people. As we were leaving table he inquired how I happened to know so much of Scotland. I told him my mother was of a Scotch family. Just then a boy came in and reported one of our horses loose, and was going off. I looked out and saw it was mine and followed, caught him and returned to the gate where I found my host and friend. The latter said, "We have no time to spare, Mr. Gaines. It is late and we have a long ride before us." "I'll first step in the house," said I, "and take leave of the family." My host said, "Never mind that, gang yer way. I'll deliver your farewell." I inquired of my friend why he hurried me off so suddenly. He told me that after I left the house the old man remarked, "The boy's Scotch blood shall help him at the polls. There are nineteen boys who always vote with me, and we'll give him every one of them." He knew then that I had gained the old man and fearing that if I prolonged the visit I might say something that would do away with the good impression made, he thought it best to hurry me off. Although Mr. Shields stated in the short address he made to the tax-payers that if he had known I would have become a candidate he would not have consented to have run, but for my old friends of Coffeeville and the neighborhood I would have been beaten. They gave me one hundred out of the one hundred and five votes polled which elected me by a small majority over both my competitors.[18]

The trade became very active and satisfactory to the Indians at the new establishment.

Previous to the late war the ancient custom of scaffolding their dead, until decomposition had progressed to the point where the services of the professional Bone Picker was required, unanimously prevailed. But the services of the Choctaw volunteers with our troops on the eastern frontier seemed to convince them that burying the dead was better than scaffolding, etc. They relinquished their ancient custom and buried, though they did not believe this mode as respectful to the memory of the deceased. They were gradually adopting the dress of the white people. Some of them seemed to have a more favorable disposition to work, during the intervals of the chase, accumulating a little property.[19]

My friend, the Little Leader (Hopia-skitteena) caused "a Rain Maker" to be put to death; and the friends of the deceased threatened to kill him.

I rode out to his residence on Shuquanoochie, some twenty miles distant, taking with me the public Interpreter, to inquire into the circumstances, and offer my services in bringing about an amicable settlement. He received us with great politeness, ordered dinner to be prepared for us, and the horses tended. Upon stating the object of my visit he thanked me for my kindness, but stated he was in no sort of danger from the rumored threats. "The late drought," he said, "checked the growth of our corn. My people, were greatly alarmed, fearing their corn and beans would be destroyed, I sent for a great rain maker and employed him to make it rain on my lands. He went to work, boiled his strongest medicine; went on the top of my house with it, and would stir the medicine, which caused dark clouds to appear day after day, but the rain maker I caused to be killed would draw them from over my land. My rain maker told me that his opponent boasted of possessing stronger medicine, and threatened to prevent him from making it rain for my people. I sent a party to put him to death, and the day after my rain maker brought up dark clouds, as before, with thunder and lightening, which spread over my lands & gave us an abundance of rain. Cast your eyes over my corn field. See what a fine prospect for a crop the rains have brought about. Was it not better that I should have the hostile rain maker put to death than my women and children should starve? Give yourself no uneasiness about my safety—even my enemies must acknowledge that I have done my duty to my people, therefore no one ought to complain." I saw that it would be useless to reason with him about the skill and power of the rain makers. The next day I received a visit from my ancient neighbor Mr. Samuel Jones, of Jones Bluff, I told him of my visit to Little Leader, and was surprised to find that he also believed in the power of Rain Makers, though a man of good common sense. I remarked, "Mr. Jones, do you really believe any man can cause rain to fall?" He replied, "Of course I must believe what I have seen with my eyes. A long drought was killing my corn. I employed a rain maker; he prepared his medicine and told me rain would fall next day. Sure enough he mounted my house top, pot in hand, next morning, and began to stir the contents vigorously—very soon clouds began to move towards us, and when over my land poured down torrents of rain."[20]

The schools established during Col. Dinsmore's agency, and fostered by him with so much care, and encouraged by Col. McKee, were since the war looked upon by the common Indians with favor. The schools were now doing well every where they were established. The Mayhew establishment, conducted by Rev. Mr. Kingsbury was doing much good intellectually and physically. The boys were taught farm work and the more useful and simple branches of machinism. The girls were taught in the female department, housework, sewing knitting, spinning, weaving, &c.

The influence which the school at Mayhew exercised in the surrounding country proved the superiority of the Rev. Mr. Kingsbury's mode of
civilization. It is believed Maj. John Pitchlyn's influence in behalf of the
schools, especially the boarding school at Mayhew, as well as the substantial aid he rendered, contributed very much to its success.[21]

About this time I received a letter from Judge Toulmin asking my opinion whether a line drawn from Pascagoula Bay to the mouth of Bear Creek,
Tennessee River, would include on the East the rich valley of the Tombigbee, as the Territory of Mississippi was about to be divided—the eastern
portion would be named Alabama Territory. I had no maps, but had travelled several times a path from St. Stephens leading to Colbert's Ferry not
far above the mouth of Bear Creek. Knowing that Judge Toulmin had travelled the same path, I replied that I thought such a line would not run far
from the path to Colbert's Ferry. This line was agreed upon in the division
of Mississippi Territory; and when surveyed left a choice part of the Tombigbee valley to the Territory of Mississippi.[22]

The Indian families living in the neighborhood of the new government
establishment were pretty good neighbors. The men brought us game, and
the women poultry, etc. The women were always ready to work in the
garden, or fields for a very reasonable compensation.

The Government made a grant of four townships of land, located above
the mouth of the Black Warrior, in favor of French Refugees which they
commenced to settle in 1817.[23] General [Desnouettes,] Col. Raoul, with
others of Napoleon's distinguished officers arrived and commenced settlements near the mouth of the Black Warrior, extending up on the east side
of the river above the mouth of Prairie Creek.[24]

Before I removed my family to St. Stephens I became acquainted with
Gen. [Desnouettes] and several of his companions. Also with several families from Philadelphia, friends of the Refugees, who had been persuaded
to unite with them in their venture in a strange land.[25]

The General's first visit to me was one of business. He wished to purchase oxen. He was accompanied by a gentleman who was formerly an
Engineer in the French army. Upon their arrival the General told me his
business. I replied that my oxen were in the woods but would soon come
home with the milch cows, as it was then late in the evening, and he could
see them in the morning. The Engineer, while we were conversing, began
to sketch the store and warehouses. Before dark he had the dwelling and
surroundings sketched with remarkable accuracy. I had some good, old
french brandy and excellent claret which, with the supper, my visitors
seemed to enjoy very much.

Next morning the oxen were examined and a pair selected. The General inquired the price. I answered that it was fifty dollars. Remarking he had bought some before for the same price but they were much inferior to mine he handed me a hundred dollar bank note. He said, "Fifty dollars for one and fifty dollars for the other." Returning the note I said, "I only ask you fifty dollars for the pair, General." He seemed well pleased with his visit so far and consented to remain until the next morning.

It so happened that morning a hunter brought me a venison and turkey so the dinner was very good. After an early breakfast next morning the General and the Engineer set out to drive the oxen home. One of my servants accustomed to the management of oxen went with them several miles enabling them to reach home before night without much trouble. This was the beginning of a warm friendship, which afterward grew up between Gen. [Desnouettes] and myself. Sometime after the events related before, he wrote me that a number of friends would dine with him on a certain day; and that he would be much gratified if I would be one of the party. I accordingly attended.[26]

The dinner was excellent, cooked in french style of course; and the wine was very good. The General and several others spoke english. All appeared to enjoy themselves. I consented to spend the night with my kind host. After we were left alone, all of the other guests having departed before dark, the conversation was very interesting to me. During the evening I made some remark about the dinner and the wine. The General informed me that he had written to a countryman of his in Philadelphia for a few necessary groceries, and also a few luxuries so as to enable him to give a dinner now and then. "He took advantage of my confidence," continued the General. "He sent me wine and other luxuries to the amount of two thousand and five hundred dollars."[27]

When the time for retiring arrived he said, "It is bed time. I will accompany you to your chamber." It was a small cabin in the yard built of cedar logs and finished off with great neatness. The walls of the room were nearly concealed by the colors of France and several other nations. Some of them were trophies of the battle field. On one side of the room was a comfortable single bed, on the other a table. In the middle of the floor stood a cedar block about ten feet high with a bust of Napoleon on top. Ranged around the foot of the block were a dozen or more pistols of different sizes and patterns, with a number of swords and daggers stacked around the sides.[28]

On the table was a fine silver mounted travelling case which he opened to show me. In the case there was a silver pitcher, basin, and cup. He

informed me that it was a present from the Emperor Napoleon. Upon remarking there were a great many conveniences in the case, he touched a
secret spring on the inside and small drawer protruded. In this drawer, he
informed me, he formerly kept his money when travelling. My attention
was attracted to the miniature of a beautiful woman, and I took it out to
examine. "That is the picture of my wife," said the General. Something in
the voice caused me to look at him attentively. I noticed his eyes were full
of unshed tears. I returned the miniature to the drawer, the case was
closed, and he bid me good night.[29]

The new Territory of Alabama, comprising the eastern division of Mississippi Territory, was organized and the first seat of government established at St. Stephens in 1818.[30]

The village of St. Stephens increased rapidly in population. Many
wealthy families from North Carolina, South Carolina, Georgia and other
states settled in the town and vicinity awaiting the sale of the rich lands
in the valleys of the Tombigbee and Alabama. Merchants and traders
seemed to overlook the objects of these settlements; and went actively to
work building stores and substantial dwellings. There were not less than
twenty good stores in the place.

Among the prominent merchants I recollect Capt. J. F. Ross, father of
Maj. W. H. and Dr. F. A. Ross of Mobile, Wm. D. Gaines, father of Dr.
E. P. Gaines of Mobile, Thos. H. Herndon, Esq., father of Col. T. H. Herndon of Mobile, Messrs. Dearing, John Morrisett, Jas. Lyon and others,
who, like many of their posterity, were celebrated for their integrity and
public spirit.[31]

The Bar was remarkably well represented by Judge A. L. Lipscomb,
Wm. Crawford, Henry Hitchcock,* Reuben Saffold, John Gayle (afterward governor of Alabama) and G. F. Sallee, the only one now living. He
resides in Washington County, Ala.[32]

The physicians were Drs. Buchanan, Meeker, Strong and Bonner. A
weekly newspaper was published by Mr. Thomas Easton.[33] My old friend
Micajah McGee became a citizen in 1817. He is yet living, and is now
residing in Enterprise, Miss., respected and beloved. It was before this period the Hon. F. S. Lyon of Demopolis, Ala., then a youth, came to St.
Stephens.[34]

The citizens of St. Stephens and vicinity obtained a charter for a bank.
I was invited to become its cashier. I resigned my appointment as United
States Factor but my resignation was not accepted. I was urged by the

*Major Crawford and Hitchcock were judges some years after.

Superintendent of Indian Trade to relinquish my cashiership and continue in the public service.[35]

Nearly a year expired before my successor in the Factory was appointed. In the meantime the trading house was conducted by my assistant Benj. Everett, and clerk Wm. Boykin. I visited the factory at the end of each quarter year to examine the books, quarterly accounts and transmit the latter to the government.[36]

The proprietors of the land at St. Stephens laid off the town, before anything was known of steamboats, believing McGrew's Shoals was the head of sloop and schooner navigation. About the time (1819) steamboats and the navigation of the Tombigbee with them, began to excite an interest. The Messrs. Deerings built one obtaining the machinery at the North. It was thought the river might be navigated as high up as the mouth of the Black Warrior. At the sales of the public lands the fractions, including the first bluff below the mouth of the Black Warrior, were purchased by a company believing that place would be the head of steamboat navigation. The town was laid off and the lots sold on credit at enormous prices.[37]

Some of the French refugees and their friends who came with them from Philadelphia were among the purchasers, and the first who built houses. A lovely little village was soon formed named Demopolis.[38]

The first steamboat that passed up the river to Demopolis went up the Black Warrior as high as Tuskaloosa. Not long after one descended the Tombigbee as far as the present site of Columbus.

St. Stephens began to decline more rapidly than it went up.[39]

The purchasers of lots in Demopolis being disappointed in the belief that the mouth of the Black Warrior would be the head of steamboat navigation refused to pay for them. Indeed, Congress granted to the purchasers of public lands on the credit system, at high prices, an act of relief, which the "Demopolis Town Company" adopted; and a few of the purchasers of lots availed themselves of it, relinquishing a portion of their purchases and obtaining these for the lots they had improved.[40] I purchased at the land sales several quarter sections, two of which adjoined the Town Company's land, with a view of removing to Demopolis. I sold a portion of these lands to Mr. Allen Glover, who had moved from South Carolina, and had established a store in Demopolis. I became associated in the store with him in 1821.[41]

Gen. Lefebre Desnouettes this year visited me at St. Stephens. He informed me that he had received letters from France assuring him that he would soon be pardoned by the existing government, which induced him to set out for Philadelphia, where, if he did not meet the expected pardon he would proceed to Belgium where his family would meet him, and return with him to this country, if he was not in the meantime pardoned. But he felt almost certain he would meet the pardon at Philadelphia in which event he would sail direct to France and would probably remain there. He asked the favor of me to act, under a power of attorney he would leave for me, for the sale and transfer of his real estate, under written directions he would transfer me from Paris. His personal property, he said, he loaned to some friends, who would relieve me of all trouble but the execution of title deeds.[42]

My neighbor Col. Dinsmore expressed to me a wish to have an opportunity of conversing with Gen. Desnouettes about the retreat of the French army from Moscow.[43] Finding that the General would spend the next day with me, I invited Col. Dinsmore and family to dine with us. After the ladies left the table Col. Dinsmore introduced the subject of the famous retreat. The General detailed the sufferings of the army which were much greater than we had conceived from the accounts published. I think none of us had dry eyes when the interesting and patriotic story of the disastrous retreat was completed. Next day, Gen. Desnouettes departed for Philadelphia. Sometime after I heard he was on board of a vessel, bound for a German port, which was wrecked on the coast of Ireland and he was lost.

I resigned my cashiership early in 1822 and removed my family to Demopolis, having had comfortable cabins built the year before, on the site since called "Gaineswood" by the purchaser, Gen. Whitfield.[44]

I made my first trip to New York in the summer of this year, accompanied by the son of Mr. Glover, a youth sixteen or seventeen years old, to purchase goods. After our return in the fall Mr. Glover and I purchased from a special agent sent out from Washington to sell the goods and other public property on hand at the Choctaw trading house,—the U.S. Indian trading house having been discontinued by act of Congress. Our new goods arrived from New York enabling us to spare from Demopolis store goods enough to make a handsome stock at the trading house, with the goods purchased from the Government. We determined to continue the business of the trading house precisely as it had been carried on by the Government agents, which required much of my personal attention.[45]

The establishment soon regained its old popularity. The chiefs and head men applied to me to purchase annuity goods, which we agreed to do for the commissions merely to compensate our risks. Their agent was instructed to settle with us accordingly. We ordered the annuity goods from the English manufacturers, giving the lengths, breadths and weights, as

well as the quality of the wool of the various blankets so that each member
of a family would have a blanket suited to his age and pursuits. Blankets
and strouds were the leading articles required. "Strouds" was a stout fab-
ric of wool one and a half yards in width, colored blue and scarlet. A yard
and a half of this cloth made a favorite shawl for a woman, or two petti-
coats.[46]

Col. John McKee resigned his appointment of Choctaw Agent in 1823.
Col. Wm. Ward, of Kentucky was appointed his successor.[47]

Puckshenubbee, chief of the Western District, died and was succeeded
by Greenwood Lafleur. The annuity goods of that District were ordered
through other parties after 1823, but we purchased the goods for the
other districts until 1830.[48]

The Treaty of Doak's Stand took place in the year 18—. In fixing the
western line of the tract of country exchanged with the Choctaws for that
part of their country, including what is now the city of Vicksburg, there
was some mistake. Some of the settlers of the Arkansas Territory settled
above the line on the Red river rendering it necessary to the Government
to have a treaty with the tribe to correct the mistake. The delegation of
Chiefs were invited to Washington by the War Department to adjust the
matter. The celebrated Pushmattaha was a member of this committee. Before he started on his journey he came to Demopolis to ask the favor of
Glover & Gaines, in event of his death before his return, to present a keg
of gunpowder to his nephew that he might pay proper respect to his memory.[49]

Col. McKee was at Washington when the delegation arrived; and was
present at the first conference with the Secretary of War. He related to me
an interesting circumstance which I repeat:—At night, after the conference, Col. McKee paid a visit to the delegation at their quarters. He remarked during a lively conversation with Pushmattaha, "Mingo, I have
known you a great many years and never until to day have I heard you
deviate one hair's breadth from the truth!" The chief with some anger said,
"What do you mean?" Col. McKee replied, "You know I was present at
the Treaty of Doak's Stand and heard you describe the country west of
Arkansas Territory, between the Canadian fork of the Arkansas and Red
Rivers, as a prairie country so barren of wood and scarce of water as to
be unfit for settlements—that when you were hunting buffalo and deer you
frequently had to make fire of buffalo droppings to cook your meals. To
day you described that portion of the tract which the Government wanted
you to surrender to the Territory of Arkansas, to correct the mistake in
the Treaty of Doak's Stand, as being fertile, well wooded and watered,

therefore being desirable for settlement." The Chief's face relaxed into a smile. "I was buying then," he said, "but I am selling now, which you know, Colonel, makes a difference. I learned that from the white people. But to be serious the corner of the tract in question is really suitable for settlements." The matter was satisfactorily settled soon after.[50]

Pushmattaha died at Washington from an attack of croup.[51] In a biography of his life the following account of his death is given:—

He seemed to feel a presentiment of his death. In a few days he was no more. He was taken sick at Washington and died in a strange land. When he found his end approaching he called his companions around him and desired them to raise him up, to bring his arms and decorate him with all his ornaments that his death might be that of a man. He was particularly anxious that his interment be accompanied with military honors, and when a promise was kindly given that his wishes should be fulfilled he became cheerful and conversed with composure until the moment when he expired without a groan. In conversation with his Indian friends, shortly before his death, he said,—"I shall die, but you will return to our brethern. As you go along the paths you will see the flowers and hear the birds sing but Pushmattaha will see them and hear them no more. When you shall come to your home they will ask you, 'Where is Pushmattaha?' and you will say to them, 'He is no more.' They will hear the tidings like the sound of the fall of a mighty oak in the stillness of the woods."

The celebrated John Randolph in a speech upon the floor of the Senate alluded thus to the forest chieftain—[52]

Sir, in a late visit to the public grave yard my attention was arrested by a simple monument of the Choctaw Chief Pushmattaha. He was, I have been told by those who knew him, one of nature's nobility; a man who would have adorned any society. He lies quietly by the side of our statesmen and high magistrates in the region—for there is one such— where the red man and the white man are on a level. On the sides of the plain shaft that marks his place of burial I read these words:—"Pushmattaha, a Choctaw chief lies here. This monument to his memory is erected by his brother chiefs who were associated with him in a delegation from their Nation in the year 1824 to the Government of the United States. Pushmattaha was a warrior of great distinction, and under all circumstances the white man's friend. He died in Washington on

Pushmataha, "The Sapling Is Ready for Him," 1760-1824, by Charles Bird
King in 1824. Choctaw chief of the Southern District (Courtesy of The Warner
Collection of Gulf States Paper Corporation, Tuscaloosa, Alabama)

the 24th of December 1824 of the croup in the sixtieth year of his age."
Among his last words were, "Let the big guns be fired over me" and they
were fired. The ceremonies of the funeral were very imposing. Besides
the firing of cannon, minute guns were discharged on Capitol Hill, and
from the grounds contiguous to the place of interment—there was an
immense concourse of citizens, a long train of carriages, calvary, military, bands of music the whole procession extending at least a mile in
length; and thousands lined the ways & filled doors and windows.

His nephew came for the promised keg of powder in paying proper respect to the memory of the departed Chieftain by his district.

The nephew quietly assumed the chiefship as successor. Such was the respect for Pushmattaha no objection was made. But the habits of the young man and his want of ability to govern the district caused the leading men and the chief's relatives to advise him to withdraw into private life. He did so.[53]

Netuckijah succeeded by appointment. He proved to be well qualified and became popular in the Nation. His character was a good deal like that of Pushmattaha.[54]

The following incident occurred about this time:—Mr. Glover and I were in the Demopolis store one day when a young Choctaw man came in and stated that he was going to die that day. He said they were digging his grave over the river and he came to bid us "good bye," and also to ask us to present him with a black silk handkerchief, some beads ribbons, etc., to dress him for the occasion. He had promised to cross the river and be ready to die as soon as the grave was finished—to stand by it and be shot by the friends of the man he killed the night before in a drunken quarrel. F. S. Lyon, Esq. happened to step in the store at this time. He told the Indian that if he had killed the man in defending himself against an attack with a butcher knife, as appeared to be the case from the statement he made to us, he ought not to die for it. Mr. Glover was a good deal attached to the young man and offered to furnish him with a horse to ride to Cahaba (then the seat of government) and in the meantime we would negotiate with the friends of the dead man for an amicable settlement of the affair. I urged the young man to accept Mr. Glover's offer at once. He replied, "Mr. Gaines you hurt my feelings—you know the Indian laws and customs, Mr. Glover and your nephew do not. I can only feel grateful kindness but your talk distresses me. You know that I would be branded as a coward if I was to attempt to escape from the penalty of my deed."

He was furnished with the articles he desired, shook hands warmly with us then walked forth calmly to his fate. Not long after the departure we heard the report of rifles from over the river and we knew that our hapless friend had passed from earth.[55]

Col. John McKee, while agent of the Choctaws, induced a talented young man, then a clerk in one of the departments at Washington, to come home with him and assist him in his public duties. After the Colonel resigned his Indian Agency he accepted the office of Register of land at Tuskaloosa, probably for the benefit of his young friend Gold who afterward married the daughter of one of his old friends.[56]

Col. McKee became a candidate for Congress in the Tuskaloosa district and was elected. He purchased land for a settlement four or five miles from the Indian trading house. He commenced a settlement upon an eminence, which he called the "Hill of Hoath." Mr. Gold with his interesting young wife resided there as the Colonel's adopted children. The appointment as Register of the Land Office was of course relinquished when the Colonel became a candidate for Congress; and the Hill of Hoath became celebrated for its refined hospitality.[57]

In the fall of the year Mr. Glover and I were at the Indian trading house aiding the Chiefs Netuckijah and Mushalatubba, and their Captains, in dividing annuity goods for distribution. As the people from the district were collecting to receive the goods, a messenger made his appearance stating that the chief Greenwood Lafleur with eight hundred armed men was on the march to the trading house to force Mushalatubba to relinquish his office as Chief. This was astounding news to all of us. Netuckijah remarked to Mushalatubba, "I'll stand by you. The Captains must see that the guns of the men are in good condition. Those who have not guns must use their knives [and] tomahawks and clubs should this matter have to be decided by battle."[58]

We sent to the "Hill of Hoath" for Col. McKee. Our work of dividing goods was suspended and the rooms containing them locked. All was excitement and preparation.

Lafleur and his army arrived in the neighborhood that evening and camped within two miles of us. Next morning Col. McKee and I rode out to his encampment where we were received with much apparent satisfaction by the chief and his Captains. Col. McKee made a pointed and brief address to them. He said, "I am always glad to see you, my friends, but I am very sorry that you should have visited our friends here in hostile array. I trust that you will upon reflection consider yourselves among friends. If there be any misunderstanding between the Western and Northern Districts I advise them to meet in council, without arms in their hands, and settle the matter amicably. The conduct of the Choctaw tribe in the late war has placed it in high and good opinion and friendship of the President and Government of the United States, as a beloved and respected member of the National family and the President will be deeply grieved to hear of any misunderstanding between you unless it be settled in a friendly manner." To which Lafleur replied, "Mingo Mushalatubba began to interfere several months ago in the public affairs of our Western District. He has caused several of our churches and schoolhouses to be burned. He is an enemy to civilization and religion. We have come to force him to resign that we may enjoy the benefits of our schools and churches unmolested. That is what we came for and intend to accomplish this day before the sun goes down. We have no cause of complaint against Mingo Netuckijah and the people of the Eastern District. We greet them as friends and brothers. You are answered."[59]

Col. McKee then held a private conversation with the chief's venerable father, Monsieur Lafleur.[60] After this Col. McKee said to me, "Let us return." He shook hands with the chief earnestly requesting him to reflect upon his words. We mounted and rode back to the store.

There was a lane leading west from the store. We found it lined with men and boys armed with guns, hatchets, clubs, etc., evidently ready and anxious for the battle to begin. Mushalatubba appeared utterly astonished when Col. McKee related his conversation with Lafleur. Netuckijah and his captains were present. Col. McKee advised them to do everything in their power to have an amicable settlement of the difficulty, that it would grieve the President of the United States to hear that his Choctaw children were quarrelling among themselves, and could not settle their difficulties with[out] bloodshed. Netuckijah promised me that he would do everything in his power to allay the excitement. He assured me that Mushalatubba's people, although prepared for the worst, had promised him to act only on the defensive; and suggested to me that it might have a good effect if I would ride out to Lafleur's camp and obtain a like promise from him and his people; and also insist that the matter should be settled without bloodshed. Accordingly I rode out to the camp and told Lafleur that Mushalatubba denied the charges made against him and that he was willing to meet him and his people in friendly council.

I told Lafleur that I had come to him as a friend at the suggestion of his friend Netuckijah. He replied that he had great respect for me and for my advice. "Col. McKee," he continued, "has become a stranger to the Indians and cannot be expected to feel as much interest in their well doing as you feel. I shall be happy to converse with you further on the subject. I ordered my people before you came to form in line to march to the trading house, and you see that they are now ready. If you will have the kindness to ride with me to the front our friendly conversation can be continued."

He gave the command to march placing himself at the head of the line. His forces had neither drum or fife, but there was some kind of music nevertheless. As they marched with slow steps, Lafleur commenced singing a hymn in which all his people united. My young horse did not like it, attempting to leave the vicinity several times. Lafleur requested me to dismount and walk with him, adding that one of his men would lead the horse. Accordingly I dismounted. We had nearly two miles to go, and I took advantage of the slow march to advise the chief not to be too exacting; and to meet Mushalatubba and Netuckijah in peace, and consent to go into a friendly council. I did not doubt that he would be satisfied Mushalatubba was innocent of the charges against him. I added that Netuckijah would act as umpire between them if requested. Hymns and spiritual songs succeeded each other at short intervals until we reached the entrance of the lane, which, as I have said before, was filled with Mushalatubba's and Netuckijah's people.[61] Lafleur halted. Netuckijah walked forward to meet him. He proposed that Lafleur should continue his march to Gaines' yard, stack [arms] and Mushalatubba's people should do the same. Then both parties should proceed to friendly council. This was consented to, when the crowd in the lane fell back followed by the other party. Entering my yard, Mushalatubba's party stacked arms which example was soon followed by Lafleur's warriors. The Council of the Chiefs and Captains was immediately formed in the middle of the yard. Lafleur repeated the charges. Mushalatubba replied, "You have been deceived and imposed upon by bad men. I never meddled in the affairs of the Western District. I am incapable of wronging you and your people. I am a friend to religion and education, and defy any man to say that I ever uttered a word discouraging either. That all may be satisfied I resign my office; and my Captains and warriors are requested to make a new appointment." Whereupon the Captains and warriors of the district unanimously re-elected him.[62]

Lafleur and his captains acknowledged themselves satisfied. Netuckijah and his Captains rejoiced at the fortunate result of the council. A general hand shaking ensued. As the sun was nearly down all of the Indians departed to their encampments.

The next morning as soon as the store was opened, it was crowded with Lafleur's people, and we had an active trade with them during that day. Next morning they departed for their homes.

Netuckijah, Mushalatubba and their people waited quietly until their western friends completed their purchases, when the rooms containing the annuity goods were unlocked; and dividing the goods was resumed and completed the day after Lafleur left and delivered the day following.

I believe Lafleur was somewhat ashamed of having been imposed upon by scandal mongers, and it was remarked that the chiefs, captains, and warriors rarely ever spoke of the affair.

Mushalatubba's resignation and re-election was never alluded to in my

Mushulatubbee, "He Who Puts Out and Kills," ca. 1770-1838, by George
Catlin in 1834. Choctaw chief of the Northern District (Courtesy of National
Museum of American Art, Smithsonian Institution, Gift of Mrs. Joseph Harri-
son, Jr.)

presence. He and Netuckijah continued their annual visits to Mr. Glover
and myself to give their joint order for their annuity goods. Nothing further was heard of opposition to schools and churches.[63]

In the latter part of the summer of 1829 we were informed by Col.
Ward that the government had ordered a treaty with the Choctaws for the
purchase of all their lands on this side of the Mississippi river; and for
their comfortable removal to their large and valuable country, between
the Canadian Fork of the Arkansas and the Red rivers, west of Arkansas

Territory. The treaty was to take place in September on Dancing Rabbit Creek.[64]

To make our Indian establishment profitable we granted credit to many traders, and their indebtedness at this time amounted to more than ten thousand dollars which required my presence at the treaty ground. I went taking my servant Dick with me. Also a tent, blankets, etc. on the pack horse. Soon after my arrival Maj. Eaton, Secretary of War, Col. John McKee, Gen. John Coffee, the commissioners arrived. After putting up my tent and making arrangements for comfort I paid my respects to the Commissioners, who occupied a large rough cabin erected lately. Maj. Eaton invited me to partake of the conveniences of the cabin and make myself at home. I thanked him at the same time informing him that I had brought a tent, servant, etc., but notwithstanding would be much in their company.[65]

The Chiefs and many of the Captains called on me that evening. A day or two passed in friendly meetings of friends and acquaintances and commonplace conversation before there was any formal commencement of business. I think on the third day there was a formal council—our commissioners made known the object of their mission. There was a meeting of the commissioners, chiefs, and captains every day afterward.[66]

On the night of the third day of these proceedings several of the old Captains came to my tent. They told me the tribe could not meet the wishes of the President to move to their new country west of the Mississippi. I replied, "I have been told it is a very fine country, well stocked with game; that one was hardly ever out of sight of deer in the prairies; and at certain seasons of the year herds of buffalo are seen, beside there were plenty bears in the canebrakes, wild horses, etc." Several spoke at once saying, "We cannot move our old people. Many of them would die on the path were we to attempt it." I said, "You could obtain a stipulation in the treaty to have them removed comfortably in covered wagons, and in steamboats." The Indians remarked, "We have been told that the President gave orders to have the Indians comfortably removed in wagons and steamboats but agents—strangers to them—, appointed to superintend, would curse and abuse and would sometimes drive them through the mud like hogs." "But," said I, "you could have it in the treaty stipulation that the Superintendent must be a humane, careful man—one who is your friend."[67]

The State of Mississippi had already given unmistakable evidence of her intentions to have her laws executed in every part of her territory. I thought it would be best for the tribe to emigrate to their new country as soon as it could be done comfortably and satisfactorily to the Indians;

therefore I advised the Captains to recommend their people to reflect cooly upon the subject. If they would do so, I believed they would be convinced that it was best they should make the most favorable treaty possible with the Commissioners and be removed as soon as it could be done with comfort to themselves. They left my tent about midnight promising not to forget my words. In the morning I met the Secretary of War walking near my tent. He said, "Mr. Gaines, I am just thinking whether I should not give an order to the contractors of beef and corn to cease bringing it in to the Camp as the Indians do not appear willing to treat for their removal west. What is your opinion?" "It is in my opinion, Maj. Eaton, that you had better move slow in this business. Encourage your contractors to keep up the supplies, and see that full rations are issued to the Indians every day." I informed him that I was visited the night before by the old captains who had conversed freely with me. I repeated the conversation to Maj. Eaton.[68]

At the council that day I witnessed a better feeling on the part of the Indians and more liberality on the part of the commissioners. The day following a rough draft of the treaty was interpreted to them and a good deal of friendly discussion took place on both sides resulting in some amendments. On the day following a treaty was agreed upon and signed by the chiefs and Commissioners.[69]

This treaty was bitterly opposed by some of the leading men of each district, who went off in a passion to where there was some whiskey in the neighborhood. Major Pitchlyn heard through a confidential friend, who was present at whiskey drinking, of the discontented men, that threats were made against the signers of the treaty; and that they intended to break it at all hazards. This was immediately communicated by Maj. Pitchlyn to the Commissioners, who were preparing to set out for Columbus. He suggested to them that the Secretary of War had better see me and prevail upon me to lead the exploring party, provided for in the treaty, to examine their new country, giving it as his opinion that if I would consent to go and would call upon the chiefs that evening to request them to select a delegation at once and let me know next day at what time they would be ready to set out to examine their new country, and report to me tomorrow. This Maj. Pitchlyn believed would quiet the discontented Indians and would probably save bloodshed.[70]

The Secretary came to my tent and gave me the information he had received from Maj. Pitchlyn. He said, "If you consent to go you shall have the pay of exploring agent, and also a commission for treating with the Indians." I replied, "I have been working for the government for nearly twenty years of my life not making anything to support a family in the future. I am now a merchant in profitable business, which I cannot in justice to my family give up. My partner desires to withdraw from business and would not consent for me to leave suddenly for so long a journey." The Secretary said, "There is a necessity for you to go. I promise if you consent that after your return you shall also be appointed superintendent for the removal and subsistence of Indians."[71]

I consented to go. He then told me that it was desired by the Government to remove and settle the Chickasaw Indians upon a part of the Choctaw country, as it was believed they would be satisfied with the country lying north of the Canadian fork of the Arkansas river, which the Chickasaws are to examine by a delegation of chiefs and captains led by Col. Reynolds, who would be instructed to cross over the Canadian fork and visit my delegation, when Col. Reynolds and myself would take such measures as we might deem best to effect the object of the government by suggesting to the two delegations that they had better remain together and examine the Choctaw Country thoroughly and if found large enough for both tribes, the Chickasaws could purchase a portion of it from the Choctaws and live neighbors as they had always before. The Secretary added, "Your drafts for what money you will need for fitting out your exploring party comfortably, and also for carrying out your mission, will be promptly paid." This was said while shaking hands with me when about to depart from the treaty ground.[72]

I called at once upon the three great chiefs of the nation, requesting each of them to select six or seven of their captains for the exploring party and report to me their names, places of residence, and at what time and place they would congregate to set out with me. Each man, I informed the chiefs, must furnish his own horse to ride, but I would furnish tents, pack horses, a new rifle for each man, and everything else to make the journey comfortable. The arms were to be supplied after reaching Fort Smith. The chiefs promised to comply in relation to selecting men etc. and report at my tent after breakfast next morning. This interview appeared to give great satisfaction. The grave faces of the signers of the treaty relaxed in smiles, and the pleasing intelligence was soon spread through the camp. Nothing more was heard of the discontented parties.

Next morning the three Chiefs made their reports to me jointly. Afterward we departed for our homes—the Indians apparently well satisfied.[73]

Mr. Glover, as I expected would be the case, expressed some dissatisfaction that I should have consented to set out so suddenly. But he acknowledged that there seemed to be a necessity for it; and that it would prevent serious trouble. "We will buy no more goods," he continued, "I will help our clerks to sell those we have on hand so that upon your return we can wind up our business, and you can continue in the public service."

At the time appointed I joined Netuckijah and his six Captains near the Shuquanochie. We proceeded to Lafleur's in the Yazoo valley where I was joined by the Captains of Mushalatubba and Lafleur—the latter chieftain having declined to go with me. Our party now consisted of twenty all pretty well mounted on hardy Indian ponies.[74]

The days journey in the swamps was rainy. We rafted over the Yallobusha, Yazoo and dead rivers swimming our horses. After camping that evening the delegation made me a formal visit at my tent, after supper.

Netuckijah addressed me as follows:—"Mr. Gaines, we have called upon you to express our appreciation of your kindness and condescention in consenting to accompany us on so long a journey to examine our new country and provide for our wants. The weather has been fine until to day causing our travel to be pleasant. But today we had a foretaste of the exposure, peril and fatigue of the journey before us. We promise here to make the journey as safe and as pleasant to you as may be in our power. Each of us will obey an order from you with the same promptness as your good servant Dick, there."

In the morning we continued our journey following a "blind path" which we were told led to the Mississippi River opposite Montgomery's, an old trading point a short distance above the mouth of the Arkansas. Two days travel took us to the river where we found a large, old Kentucky flat boat which we used to ferry us over. The crossing occupied a day. That night we camped on the low grounds of the Arkansas river. I think it was a delegation from the Quapaw tribe that camped so near to us that fires of each camp could be seen from the other.[75]

We were visited by the delegation after supper. They were received in a formal but friendly manner. One of Netuckijah's Captains held the office of Speaker, and he was told to speak to our visitors. He began by asking, "What is the name of your tribe? What river do you live near?" He was answered, "On the other side of Red river"—"How many sleeps from here? Where are you going?" "Ten sleeps. We are going to visit our father, the President," was the reply. "How many hundreds or old hundreds does your tribe number," inquired the Speaker. "Two or three hundreds." The speaker at this reply turned his back upon the visitors, with a contemptious expression on his face. But Netuckijah took up the thread of conversation which soon turned to questions on their part of who [we] were, the number of our tribe, where we were going, &c.[76]

The next day we proceeded up the valley of the river. After travelling three or four days we were informed that we had passed Little Rock. This town was situated on the south side of the river, and was the seat of government. I deemed it my duty to halt the party, pass over the river for the purpose of paying my respects to the Governor, and inform him of the object of my mission. I spent a day with him partaking of his hospitality then returned to my party. Continuing our journey several days up the northern side of the Arkansas we crossed near Fort Smith where we camped for a few days rest and to make our outfit more comfortable and abundant for the exploration. Here a new rifle, with an abundance of powder and lead, was issued to each of the party.[77]

The plan agreed upon with the delegation was to travel in the direction of the dividing ridge a day or two then back again toward the Arkansas river, zig-zag, as to obtain a knowledge of the lands in that portion of country. Col. Arbuckle, stationed at Fort Gibson, was instructed to furnish me with whatever I might order to carry out the object of my mission. We therefore crossed the Canadian fork a few miles above its mouth, then the main river a few miles higher up to a salt works, in the new Cherokee country, for the double purpose of obtaining supplies from the fort and a supply of salt. I forwarded an order on Col. Arbuckle for a sergeant and twelve men, with sixty days rations of flour, &c.[78]

My messenger took with [him] three or four careful [men] and all of the pack horses for as much flour as they could carry—also two or three hundred pounds of pork or bacon—for the exploring delegation. The Colonel immediately wrote me that as soon as the horses could be shod the sergeant and men would be sent—that the sacks for transporting the flour were being made; and that he would see that my pack horses were well loaded as soon as practicable. One of his lieutenants and a surgeon who desired to see our party volunteered to bring the note. They expressed a wish to accompany me through the new Choctaw country.[79] I said, "If you wish to do so, gentlemen, you can go with me." They seemed surprised and were hardly convinced I was not jesting when I read them a note I had written to Col. Arbuckle stating that upon reflection that if I deemed it necessary to have a surgeon and lieutenant in addition to the sergeant and mounted men, and if he could [spare] those officers he would please send them to me. The surgeon and lieutenant returned to the fort when they received orders to join me. Accordingly my party was increased to forty-five men.[80]

We travelled in a south western direction the first day and the next in a northwestern. In this way we made thorough examination of the country between the dividing ridge and the Canadian as far west as the Cross Timbers. We then passed over the ridge until we reached the waters of the false Washita and then travelled southward.[81]

After crossing the Canadian we were soon joined by Col. Reynolds and the Chickasaw delegation. The Choctaws were delighted to meet them inviting them to accompany us which they consented to do, one of the inducements being that they might enjoy a buffalo hunt with us. The two parties now united numbered about sixty men. We began exploring the country between the Canadian and Red river. We had rain after crossing the dividing ridge. The weather began to get very cold. The two delegations expressed a desire to travel toward home which was agreed to accordingly. The morning after my delegation commenced its march eastward, expecting to find the Chickasaw delegation ready also, but the weather threatening snow or sleet, they supposed we would all remain in camp that day. As it was late in the forenoon I suggested that our delegation should move on, encamping at the first cane we found for the benefit of our horses, & the Chickasaws might overtake us next day—This was agreed to.[82]

We moved on until the afternoon when we camped near the head of a canebreak. After breakfast the next morning we continued our journey until we reached a small river—the L'eau Bleu. We crossed it just below a bluff on the east side, camping on the bluff so that our horses might have the benefit of a canebreak below. We had put up our tents, stored our baggage, turned our horses in the cane and were making fires when two young men of the Chickasaw party rode up in a gallop. They informed us that the Chickasaws, after passing the place we camped the night before, discovered the trail of a large party of Indians which had struck our trail, & turned upon it, following as if intending to overtake and attack.[83]

The Chickasaws hastening their march overtook the strangers in a thick grove of timber when they suddenly turned aside hiding themselves behind trees. It was supposed they numbered over a hundred warriors. The Chickasaws expected to be attacked and dispatched the messengers to us for immediate assistance. No gun had been fired on either side when they left but a battle was momentarily expected to begin. We were soon on a rapid march to the relief of our friends. At a short distance from our camp we met the Chickasaw Delegation. They stated that they moved on slowly through the forest without having been fired upon but they had no doubt that the strangers would pursue and attack us that night, therefore they deemed it best for them to camp with us.

Returning to the camp we had a meeting when I proposed Col. Reynolds should be appointed commander; and that he should give such orders as he deemed best to strengthen our encampment for defence. The bluff was perpendicular and probably more than fifty feet high. Col. Reynolds thought it perfectly safe for one side. He directed the tents to be pitched in a half circle; and that before dark our horses should all be brought up and tied to the post oak saplings within the half circle—that each tent should have a good log fire in front—sentinels be placed on the river bank above and below and at several points in the rear of the semi-circle so that those in the tents could take position near the horses if we were attacked; and that the sentinels after firing should retreat to the same position when the enemy would hasten to the tents and the fires would afford us light to shoot them down.[84]

All of this work preparing for our attack had to be done before dark although the sun was not more than half an hour high. We performed it, however, under the skillful directions of Col. Reynolds. The arrangements of the tents and fires had quite a military appearance. The men were seen busily engaged cleaning and loading their rifles, moulding bullets while the cooks were preparing supper. The fires were kept burning all night. The sentinels were relieved from time to time. The night passed away without an attack having been made on us. The young men of both delegations had such confidence in the programme of Col. Reynolds that they seemed to feel an injury in their disappointment of a victory they had promised themselves.

It was thought advisable before we marched to send scouts in front to lookout for the enemy. While passing over a ridge that evening the scouts reported smoke in the valley before us. We approached the place prepared for any emergency. We soon discovered the smoke was from a camp in the canebreak. Our scouts cautiously penetrated the brake and found nothing but a pot, skillet, a parcel of beaver skins and traps. Just as we were listening to this report two men rode up apparently well pleased by meeting us. They heard the tramp of our horses as we were crossing the ridge, and believing we were hostile Indians retreated from their camp making a circuit to fall on our trail. Looking at the tracks of the horses, they knew that they were shod. Therefore, they concluded that we were not wild Indians and hastened to overtake us. When we informed these trappers of the Indians we passed the day before, they said they would go with us as it would not be safe to remain.

We went on leaving the trappers to follow after getting their skins and other articles at the camp. Before night they overtook us. When we camped for the night the trappers gave us a brief account of themselves. They were in relationship uncle and nephew; they lived in the new settlements below in Arkansas Territory. I invited them to supper at my tent. The old man remarked he always preferred cooking his own meals, at the same time looking earnestly upon some quarters of venison near by, then added he would be thankful for one of the ribbed quarters. Receiving it he prepared a stick, forced one end of it in the ground, near a fire, then hung the venison on it, taking great pleasure in watching the roasting process. After the meat was thoroughly roasted he moved it to where he had left his baggage and invited his nephew to partake. The nephew seemed to be a moderate [eater] but the uncle never ceased eating until naught save the bones remained.[85]

We found the land on the Red river side of the dividing ridge generally very rich—much more so than on the Arkansas side. I think it was a week after leaving L'eau Bleu we camped in the valley of Red river. About dark we heard chopping and sent a couple of young men to find out about it. Returning they reported several small log huts occupied by Indians. The trappers informed us that these Indians were refugees from the Shawnee tribe; that they had been living here ever since the British war (1815). We received an invitation from the chief to come to their council house and have a talk. After supper the chiefs and the oldest Captains of our delegations walked to the council house which was lighted by a fire in the center of the floor.

A half breed woman, looking at me, said, "You are a white man. I hoped never to see the face of another white man." I inquired her reason for such a hope. She answered her husband and several members of her family had been killed by the whites. "The remnant of my relations," said she, "were compelled to leave their homes, and we travelled to this country where we hoped to live in peace." I replied, "You should not entertain hatred for white Americans. It was not their fault your tribe joined the English who came over in their ships to fight us. In fighting them, with your people among them, we could not helping killing the Shawnees."

The council commenced—Netuckijah, through his speaker, told the Shawnees that the land they were living on belonged to the Choctaws— they had exchanged their old country east of the Mississippi for this—but if the Shawnees conducted themselves properly they would not be disturbed and would be adopted by his tribe. They would then have all the rights and privileges of Choctaw families. This liberal offer was accepted by the Shawnee chief with promises that they would not lie or steal; and he would see that they conducted themselves properly conforming themselves to the laws and customs of the Choctaws. The Council after thus settling public affairs, entered into commonplace conversation. Soon after we retired to our camp.[86]

Our journey was resumed next morning. Our flour was exhausted, and our Fort Gibson friends became tired of substituting lean venison for bread, and fat venison and bear meat, signified their intention to seperate from us next morning, returning to Fort Gibson, which they did.[87] The Chickasaw delegation continued to remain with us—in fact they seemed to have made up their minds to do so until we reached our houses. The Red river slope was so generally fertile both delegations were highly pleased with it. At Fort Towson we expected to find a supply of flour but on our arrival there were disappointed. I proposed we should travel several days up the Kiametia river to examine the fine land in that region.[88] The delegations expressed themselves already satisfied; and proposed that we should proceed to a settlement in Arkansas Territory for the purpose of obtaining flour or corn. We went down the Arkansas river in an eastern course.[89]

Col. Reynolds and I were informed by a man at Towson that there was a family residing above the western line, who owned a small mill where he thought we might obtain meal. We determined one morning to make a forced march to this mill, leaving our delegations to follow. We promised to purchase corn and have meal prepared by the time they arrived next day.

Reaching the cabin of the miller about sundown we found an active industrious woman at home, her husband being absent. We told her we had not eaten bread for more than ten days, begging her to prepare supper for us as soon as possible while we were seeing to the welfare of our horses. She said, "Gentlemen, I will set about it at once if you will promise you will be satisfied with what bread I give you. A man came here, sometime ago, who had not eaten bread for two or three weeks and he eat so much it killed him." We of course promised. After attending to our horses we returned to the cabin, found "a hoe cake" baking, a small table neatly set and a plate of yellow butter and pitcher of milk upon it. Our hostess gave us small pieces of bread at intervals until the cake, etc. were consumed. I thought that I had never met with any luxury so delicious as these pieces of corn bread, the butter and milk. We wished another small hoe cake but she told us we could have no more until supper.[90]

Next morning, telling the good woman we felt no inconvenience from the bread, she said, "Then I'll get you a good breakfast which you may eat in your own way." The miller having returned home busied himself with preparing meal. The delegations enjoyed both bread and "tom fuller,"* the night of their arrival, to their content.[91] From this place it was deemed advisable to move on to Washington Arkansas where we expected to obtain necessary supplies; also to recruit our horses on some of the neighboring plantations for the journey home. The delegation was halted at a pla[nta]tion in the neighborhood of the village where we purchased provisions for men and horses. Col. Reynolds and I went to the village engaging board at a tavern for a week. The Colonel went out next day among the store keepers to raise money by the sale of a draft on the war department. When he returned he told me no one wanted to buy a draft. "What shall we do?" he said. "We cant leave here without money—both of us have not enough to pay our bill at this house for one week; and there is the bill for the corn and provisions for the delegations—it will amount to several hundred dollars."[92]

"We will no doubt find some one who wants a draft," I replied, "I will go out and try my luck." Accordingly I stepped into a store and inquired of an elderly man if he did not wish to buy a draft on the War Department. He said he did not. "It is very strange," said I, "my friend, Col. Reynolds, has been around the merchants of this place and they all tell him they don't want to purchase a draft. How do you make your remittances?" He answered, "We make our purchases in New Orleans, and have opportunities of remitting as often as we have money to send. To tell you the truth, sir, there has been a good deal of trouble to make the drafts of Indian agent on the war department answer our purposes in New Orleans. Some drafts have been returned and money lost by them." I told him that I could convince him that my drafts would not be returned. Without replying to this, he said, "I suppose you are Mr. Gaines. I knew a gentleman of that name in Alabama who resided in Demopolis. I was at that time living in Greene County." "Did the Gaines you know favor me?" I inquired. "Well, I had'nt much acquaintance with him," he replied, "but I knew his partner Mr. Glover, very well." When I informed the merchant who I was, he said, "Give yourself no further trouble, Mr. Gaines. You shall have as much money as you wish to draw for. Your draft, I know, will answer my purpose in New Orleans."

We spent the week pleasantly in Washington—paid off all our bills, then set out for home rejoicing. When we reached Little Rock, I arranged with Col. Reynolds to take care of the delegations for the balance of the journey as I intended to return by steamboat. My horses were taken charge of by

*Big hominy prepared by beating the corn in a mortar.

Netuckijah who promised to send them to me when he reached home. The morning after the delegations departed.[93]

As there was no steamboat expected for several days, I sent my servant Dick to the river to look out for a suitable skiff or canoe in which we could go down to the Mississippi. Before leaving I spent a pleasant day with the Governor who the day before called upon me and invited me to dine with him. Dick found a small skiff at the river, hunted up the owner, purchased it, and after breakfast next day we departed. Dick handled the oars very well, and my task as steersman was easy and pleasant.[94]

We had a fine run until late in the evening it began to rain. We landed at a plantation and went to the house which was near the landing. We asked permission to remain the night which was promptly refused; and my attempt to persuade was cut short by the man telling me that he did not entertain travellers,—had promised himself never to permit another "Indian country man" to stay in his house—he had been treated badly by them. I told him that though I wore a blanket overcoat I was not a savage. He said it was no use talking—his mind was made up. Of course I left him, returned to the boat, and went down the river in the rain and rapidly increasing darkness.[95]

After travelling about an hour we saw a light on what we supposed was a bluff. Dick's shouting was soon answered. He requested the person to come to the landing with a torch. With the assistance of the man we landed and carried our baggage up to the house where we were informed, travellers were sometimes entertained. At the door I was met by a lady who refused to receive us, saying that her husband was very sick. I then asked if there was a cabin in the yard we might stay in for the night. She replied there was no cabin except the kitchen. I said as it was raining very hard if she would permit I would go into the kitchen. A servant girl led the way. We found it a clean, neat cabin. I presented the man, who helped us up from the river, a half dollar and he aided Dick in making a good fire. Dick insisted upon me to put on dry clothes. I did so and in a few minutes after I was comfortably situated.

While Dick was preparing supper, the servant girl came in to inform me that her mistress wished me to take supper in the dwelling house. I followed the girl to partake of her mistress' hospitality. A sick man was lying on a mattress before the fire and as I entered looked at [me] intently then broke into immoderate laughter. His wife, who evidently supposed he had gone out of his senses (as I must say I did also) exclaimed, "What on earth is the matter with you?" He replied, "I was laughing because you sent my old friend Gaines in the kitchen!" After welcoming me warmly he spoke of meeting me frequently in Huntsville while I was examining the land office there. We spent the time pleasantly until rather late in the night when I accepted the invitation to enjoy the comfort of a bed room.

After a good breakfast we departed on our voyage to the mouth of the Arkansas. When we reached that place we crossed over to the east bank of the Mississippi. While I was speaking to the proprietor of a cabin for entertainment until the arrival of a steamer descending we heard one approaching. Our baggage was put in the skiff; and I offered to give it to the man if he would assist us in getting aboard. We had a comfortable passage to New Orleans. Remaining a day & night in the city, I took passage in the mail boat to Mobile and thence to Demopolis—reaching home about the last of February—having been absent nearly five months.[96]

It will be seen by the conversation which occurred between the Secretary of War and myself, on the evening of the day the treaty of Dancing Rabbit Creek was signed, that I engaged to leave with the exploring party very reluctantly; and that I consented from a sense of duty to my country and to the Indian tribes I had been so long associated with as the United States Agent of the Choctaw trading house. I could not doubt that on my return I would receive the promised instructions of the Secretary, jointly with Col. Reynolds, to carry out the wishes of the Government by the treaty between the Choctaws and between the government and the Chickasaws; and that in addition to my appointment of Exploring Agent I would receive that of Commissioner for holding treaties with both tribes, and Superintendent of their removal and subsistance. And although Col. Reynolds and I made a joint report of the Exploration and the feelings of the two delegations in regard to the extent of the country examined, and its sufficiency for both tribes, and expected to receive special instructions soon after our return home, yet we heard nothing from Washington City. There was a rumor Gen. Jackson had some trouble with his cabinet and Maj. Eaton had been sent as Minister to Spain.[97]

Mr. Glover and I went actively to work closing our mercantile business. I was still in expectation of receiving instructions from the War Department until June when I concluded Secretary Eaton had left no record of the verbal contract with me. I determined to commence business on my own account in Demopolis. I went to Mobile to make some purchases of goods when Mr. Jonathan Emanuel, who was carrying on a wholesale dry goods business, proposed a partnership with me. I was so well satisfied that we should agree upon the terms of the partnership that I declined to purchase goods and returned home to consult with my family. Mr. Emanuel was about setting out for New York to purchase goods. Before leaving Mobile I agreed to write to him at New York should my family willingly consent to move to Mobile. Also giving him my views about the terms of the partnership.[98]

In July Capt. Frank Armstrong, a worthy friend of mine, called upon me to state that he came to take the census of the Choctaw tribe and wished me to introduce him to the chiefs. I rode with him to Netuckijah's residence introducing the Captain as my friend whose word the Indians might rely upon. When parting with Capt. Armstrong I gave him letters of introduction to the other chiefs.[99]

I do not remember that I told the Captain of my engagement with Secretary Eaton, but learned from him, after he had been several weeks taking the census, that his instructions required him to know from the Chiefs and Captains of each town when they would be ready to move, and they uniformly answered, "Whenever Mr. Gaines is ready."[100] This, Captain Armstrong repeated to the War Office, which (I supposed) produced a long letter from Gen. Gibson to me. Gen. Gibson was the Commissary General and managed the removal and subsistance of Indians. He enclosed me the appointment of Superintendent of removal and subsistance of Indians, which he urged me to accept "if only to break the ice and pave the way for future removals." Such sums of money as I would require would be placed in the branch of the Bank of the U.S. at Mobile and at Vicksburg— that I might appoint as many assistants as I deemed necessary with such compensation as I might deem reasonable and proper, that no bond would be required of me, and that I should take the treaty for my instructions.[101]

I could not refuse to accept though it was not in my interest to do so. But there appeared to be a necessity under the circumstances that I should. Accordingly I wrote to Gen. Gibson I felt it my duty to accept the appointment tendered me by the Secretary of War if it was "only to break the ice and pave the way for future removals." I requested him to have thirty thousand dollars placed to my credit in the branch Bank of the United States at Mobile and the same amount in the Branch Bank at Vicksburg— in the meantime I would appoint assistants and begin the work.[102]

I appointed Thomas McGee my assistant to operate in Mushalatubba's district, Dr. J. B. Earle and Gen. Sam Dale in Netuckijah's and ——— in Lafleur's. Mr. McGee employed teams, wagons and teamsters, soon got in motion several hundred families to cross the Mississippi at Vicksburg. Sam Dale was sent to Netuckijah's residence, with wagons and teams to get the Sucarnochie and other towns of Indians in the neighborhood. Dr. Earle was sent to the Chickasawha and Six Towns to get them in motion also for Vicksburg. Mr. ——— was dispatched to Lafleur's.[103]

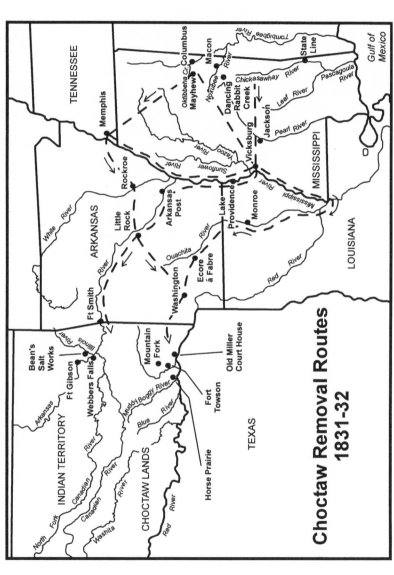

Choctaw Removal Routes, 1831–1832

The plan I adopted of having active preparations going on in all the districts at the same time was successful, as I believed it would be, for the Indians in each district hearing these operations were proceeding in all the other districts went actively to work to be in readiness. Had I been active in one, the other districts would have been slow in preparing to move. I lost no time in riding to supply my assistants with money to pay for corn, etc. for the teams and provisions for the Indians, and to see that my orders were strictly carried out.

After these emigrants were fairly on the way to Vicksburg, I went forward to that place to engage steamboats and purchase necessary supplies. It was now October. I chartered two boats for the emigrants bound for the Red river slope, and one to transport such of them who wished to settle on the Arkansas slope of their new country.[104] Mr. McGee moved off a number of families from Mushalatubba's district crossing the river at Memphis.[105]

It was about the last of October before I could dispatch the two boats up Red river. About the same time the Indians desiring to settle on the Arkansas slope were ready to embark. Dr. Earle and I were going with them.[106] Before leaving, I called at the bank and checked out two thousand dollars to carry with me. I had paid all the bills except my bill at the hotel. I went to the office where I had a desk given to me by the proprietor to transact business. It was enclosed by a green curtain or screen to cut off intruders when I wished to be alone. I took the money out of my pocket, took from the package two hundred dollars, and wrapped the balance— $1,800—in a piece of paper and inserted it in the waistband of my drawers. After paying the hotel bill I went to the landing and found the boat waiting for me. A man stepped on board at the same time and applied to the Captain for passage to some point on the river. He said, "I cannot take you, sir. The boat is chartered by Col. Gaines, an agent of the Government." The stranger said he was sorry he could not be accommodated— that he belonged to the Commissary's department and wished to reach Fort Towson as early as possible to have provisions in readiness for the Indian emigrants. I remarked, "If that is the case you have as good right to a passage as I have." The Captain said, "Every berth is engaged in both cabins." "He can have the upper berth in my stateroom," I said. This matter settled we were soon steaming up the Mississippi. I walked around both cabins to relieve the fears of the women and old people telling them that it was an easy and pleasant way to travel; and that there was no danger. Then I went below to quiet the families on deck. By the time I got through with this, supper was announced. After supper I was so much fatigued by the labors of the day I determined to go to bed. I was soon asleep, and have no recollection of waking before sunrise next morning. While I was dressing I found the roll of bank notes was not in the lining of my drawers. I examined the floor, the bed clothes and mattresses thoroughly but could not find the money. Sending for Dr. Earle I told him I was apprehensive the money had been stolen. He brought the Captain. During the consultation which followed I remarked that the cabin boy assisted me in undressing. The Captain, remarking that if he had committed the theft he would soon find it out, left the stateroom and in a few minutes returned saying the boy knew nothing about it. I then asked, "Where is the gentleman who occupied the upper berth?" Dr. Earle and the Captain said that they had not noticed him that morning. The Captain searched for him in vain. One of the deck hands stated that while "wooding" about midnight he saw a well-dressed man walk off the boat but did not recollect seeing him return.[107]

I consulted with Dr. Earle what was best to do. It was agreed he should proceed with the boat and I should return, on the first boat we met, to the woodyard where the man got off and take such measures to capture the thief as circumstances permitted. It was evening before we met a boat. I was placed on board; the Captain promised to land at the woodyard until I conversed with the proprietor.

I was sitting quietly in the cabin when a gentleman came to me and said, "I am informed your name is Gaines, Sir, and that you have lost all your money." I assented. He continued, "My name is Gaines. Don't look so melancholy. I am told you reside in Alabama therefore you are a considerable distance from home. If you wish, it I will lend you money enough to bear your expenses." I thanked him for his kind offer—I had some money at Vicksburg. "It will afford me pleasure to lend the money," he said, "Don't decline because I am a rough looking fellow. I am a mechanic, and have on board a large amount in wagons, carts and plows, manufactured in my shops. I hope you will go on to New Orleans with us. The boat will get to Vicksburg tonight, but you need not stop there unless your business is of importance." I was compelled to stop I told him but hoped to meet him in New Orleans.

The proprietor of the woodyard could give no information beyond what the deck hand told us. He expressed the opinion the thief would be hard to find—that it was more probable he crossed the river and was in the swamp on the east side—that whether on one side or the other it would be like hunting a needle in a hay stack to look for him. He promised to write to me if he could gain any information. I determined to give up the search and return home as the terms of my partnership with Mr. Emanuel had been agreed upon in our correspondence. I went on to New Orleans, with my kinsman, and from there took the first mail steamer to Mobile. Remain[ed] there for a week, then went up to Demopolis.[108]

Mr. Glover had made good progress in bringing our business to a close. Being satisfied with his arrangements, I returned to Mobile with my family taking rooms at Cullom's hotel. The new firm of Emanuel & Gaines was doing a good business. Our two clerks Mr. Saml. W. Allen and Henry Lazrus, and our bookkeeper Mr. Schuyler, were active business men. Mr. Emanuel left little for me to do the balance of the winter and spring which was a holiday I enjoyed after my late laborious public service.[109]

I returned to Demopolis with my family the last of June intending to recommence the removal of the Indians when I learned that my old friend Armstrong was in the western part of the nation at work as my successor. Before leaving Mobile, all assistants had rendered their accounts for money disbursed by them in the removal and subsistence of Indians, and I had transmitted my accounts, including theirs, to the War Department for settlement. I was rather pleased than otherwise to be relieved from my public duties, as my time could be more profitably employed in my new business. My letter to Commissary General Gibson in reply to this letter persuading me to accept the office "if only to break the ice and pave the way for future removals" might be fairly considered as intending nothing more.[110]

Returning to Mobile with my family in October I took rooms at White's hotel. Early in the succeeding spring I rented Mr. Swift's place opposite the Nursury, on Spring Hill road, intending to spend the summer.

Soon after the meeting of the Legislature in November of this year a law was passed for the establishment of the Branch of the Bank of Alabama at Mobile, the President and directors to be elected by the Legislature. I was not a little surprised when I learned I was elected President as I had never solicited or thought of the office. The capital was fixed at a million and a half dollars; and State bonds were authorized to be issued, and sold for capital for this branch and those at Decatur and Montgomery.[111] No time was lost in organizing my board of directors. I was appointed an agent of the Bank to sell its fifteen hundred thousand dollars of bonds. I started at once for New York via Tuskaloosa to get the bonds. On my arrival at Tuskaloosa, Gov. Gayle told me the bonds had not been executed but that they would be as early as practicable, which would detain me a week in Tuskaloosa.[112]

Before the end of the week the Legislature passed a law authorizing me to sell the bonds issued by the State to furnish capital for the three branches, above named, amounting to three millions five hundred thousand dollars. Also authorizing me to appoint an assistant if I deemed it necessary. I was furnished with a manuscript copy of the law with the signature of the Governor and the great seal of the State affixed. With this and the bonds I proceeded on my journey. When I reached Washington I deemed it advisable to spend a few days there as much as excitement prevailed throughout the country about affairs in South Carolina. Gen. Jackson was then President of the United States. I lost no time, after obtaining comfortable quarters at a hotel, in calling on the President who received me with the warmth of an old friend. When I told him my business North he advised me to spend several days in Washington and become acquainted with the members of Congress from Philadelphia, New York, and Boston.[113]

As I was taking leave of him he said, "You must dine with me day after tomorrow. Come an hour before dinner so that we can talk of old times." Accordingly I attended the dinner party which was composed chiefly of members of the cabinet, foreign ministers and members of Congress. When we went in to dinner Gen. Jackson asked me to take the seat next to him, on the right. Towards the close of the dinner a gentleman at the other end of the table asked the President to take wine with him. He replied, "My physician has advised me not to take wine. My friend, Mr. Gaines, on my right who has supported me on a more serious occasion will, I am sure, be my substitute now." Filling my glass as he ceased speaking. I received a bow from the gentleman, a foreign minister, returning it, we took wine together.

I was invited next day by the Hon. Wm. R. King to take wine with the Hon. James Buchanan and himself. Theirs was good wine—excellent. My mission became the subject of conversation. Mr. Buchanan seemed highly pleased with the account I gave him of the resources of Alabama, and the advantages of Mobile for a great commercial city—regretted he was not able to invest in our bonds but said he would recommend them to his friends in Philadelphia. I called upon the President the day before I left Washington. I stated to him that it was probable that I might deem it the interest of my state to proceed to Europe and offer the bonds for sale. In the event I would like letters to our minister in London introducing me as the agent of the young and promising state of Alabama. He said I should have the letters. I spoke about the existing political excitement in South Carolina. He remarked, "You are endeavoring to obtain an expression of my opinion as to the result of the excitement you speak of. Go to Philadelphia and New York, offer your bonds to the capitalists—I think you will find purchasers. If not write me and I will have you supplied with documents which will make you favorably known in England."[114]

I went to Philadelphia where I spent a week. Arriving in New York I delivered my letters of introduction, called upon Bankers and Capitalists, offered the bonds for sale but as I expected I was everywhere met with the remark "that Southern State bonds were not in demand at that time."[115]

After spending several weeks here I went to Boston finding the capitalists there even less inclined to purchase. After a week's absence I returned to New York where I imagined I had "a nibble" before going to Boston, from a worthy gentleman to whom I had brought letters of introduction from Mobile. He usually called upon me after supper, spending an hour or two in friendly conversation. On the second night after my return he visited me, and I thought looked unusually grave. I inquired if he had any late news from Mobile? He said that he received a letter the day before from our mutual friend Mr. Leavins (one of the directors of the new State Branch Bank). "It is a private letter," he said, "but I think I ought to show it to you. Here it is." Mr. Leavins wrote:—"The Board is becoming very impatient at what they consider the tardiness of our President. It was suggested at our last meeting to send on some person to aid him, or as his successor but I opposed the measure." I handed the letter back to the gentleman, opened my portfolio and taking out the manuscript copy of the act appointing me sole agent for the sale of bonds issued by the state of Alabama, said, "Our friend Leavins does not seem to know that the Legislature, when I called on the governor for the bonds and was waiting for their execution, passed this law." Handing him the copy I continued, "Dont you think the gentleman sent here to aid or succeed me would make an awkward figure?" He read the law then answered "I think so. It is very unusual, I believe, for states to appoint agents in this way. This is highly complimentary to you." A long conversation followed, on the resources of Alabama and commercial prospects of Mobile.[116]

On leaving he said, "I will see you tomorrow," I imagined I felt his visit to be a second "nibble" at the bonds. His visits continued almost every night our conversations generally being on the subject of my mission. He told me what he thought could be obtained for the bonds, terms of payments—interest and principal payable in Liverpool. I offered the bonds at par, interest and principal in New York or Mobile. Becoming tired of the negotiation I concluded I would call upon Mr. Gallitin, the President of one of the banks in the city, and have a conversation about the sale of the bonds in Europe. I carried with me the copy of the law appointing me agent. He was of the opinion that the bonds could be sold in Europe quite as advantageously as if sold, at my offer, in New York. I asked him if he could be induced to go with me? He replied that he should like it very much if Mrs. Gallitin would consent to go with him. He stated that while the Secretary of the Treasury he had correspondents in Europe which he had kept alive ever since for the benefit of his bank.[117] I remarked if I did not succeed in making a sale in the course of a week or two I would go there, in that event I would remunerate him handsomely if he would go with me. He replied, "There will be a party at my house tonight. Come to it and make a speech to Mrs. Gallitin on the subject." I consented. Fortunately my tailor that day brought home a new suit of clothes made in the latest fashion. I found a large party at Mr. Gallitin's. Leading me to the back part of the parlor where Mrs. Gallitin was sitting with some ladies he introduced me as the brother of Gen. Gaines. Mrs. Gallitin received me very cordially remarking that my brother was a favorite of hers, their acquaintance having begun when he was a lieutenant. I thought this a good opportunity to make the "speech" and said, "I am permitted by Mr. Gallitin to make a speech to you, madame. I have been here more than a month as a financial agent of Alabama to sell some bonds but so far have been unsuccessful; and if I cannot sell them in the next two weeks I must go to Europe to sell them. Mr. Gallitin in that event consents to go with me provided you will accompany him. Now, madame, if you will consent I promise that you shall choose the ship and have everything your own until we return, except the business which Mr. Gallitin and I must manage." She answered that she would like to go very well and would think of my proposition.[118]

Next day several of my acquaintances said to me, "So you are going to Europe." My answer was that I would go if I did not succeed soon in selling the bonds in New York. At night the gentleman, before mentioned, called upon me after supper as usual. "I hear you are going to Europe, Mr. Gaines." "Yes," I said, "unless some of the New York capitalists purchase the bonds." We were sitting beside a table on which were writing materials. He remarked the bonds were not in form for the market. I said I could return them to Tuskaloosa and have others executed in a more desirable form. "If you have made up your mind that the interest and principal should be paid only in the United States then make both payable at the Pheonix Bank here; and the purchasers of the bonds might possibly contract with the bank to pay both as some banking house in England. Such a contract might be printed on the back of the bonds which would make them marketable in England. Think of it, and we will talk the matter over tomorrow night."[119]

Accordingly next evening he came. Taking our seats at my little business table I said, "We have talked a good deal upon this subject now, write down what you think can be done in New York if the bonds are replaced by others in the form you suggested, then I will write what I think my State will be satisfied to do." He commenced by writing:—"It is my opinion that if Alabama will replace the bonds, neatly executed on better paper, with interest and principal payable at Pheonix Bank, New York, semi-annually, with the interest coupons on the margin of each bond, they might be sold in New York provided the bank will contract with a banking house in England to furnish funds in payment of the coupons and the bonds as they fall due, in that country. This contract between the Pheonix Bank and the banking house in England might be printed on the bonds here." I wrote:—"Alabama will execute new bonds in the form you suggest—coupons and bonds payable at the Pheonix Bank." He was of the opinion the bonds might be sold at par Alabama paying the rate of exchange between New York and Liverpool at the date of each payment. I wrote that Alabama would have nothing to do with the rate of exchange. He expected par for the bonds, and would pay the coupons and bonds promptly at the Pheonix Bank. He replied it was no use in prosecuting the matter any further—the bonds could not be sold at that time on the terms I demanded. He departed somewhat out of humor.[120]

On his return [next] night I proposed to resume the subject. He remarked we could do nothing, that he had had a conversation with the president of the Pheonix Bank, who told him the bank would willingly collect and pay the interest and principal; and would readily contract with a first class banking house in England to pay the coupons and bonds promptly, such contract being executed on the back of the bonds would render them salable in England and give them a preference over bonds, principal and interest made directly payable by the state in England. After more conversation and a continuation of our suppositions writing he said he believed his friends would take half of the bonds with the privelege of taking the other half after paying for the first in satisfactory instalments. He proposed that at our next meeting we should engage a confidential lawyer to draw up a contract, in conformity to what we had both written, which he would submit to his friends. If satisfactory to them it would be executed on their part, but this like our discussions must be confidential until after the payment of the first instalment the better to enable his friends to negotiate their drafts on England. The contract was drawn up, approved by us, submitted to his friends and the day after was executed.[121]

It will be seen by the foregoing paragraph that I was placed in a [dilemma] as I would have to leave New York without even informing Mr. Gallitin that I had sold the bonds.

I lost no time in returning home via Tuskaloosa where I returned the first bonds issued to the State Department and placing in the hands of the Governor a copy of the contract with form of bonds to be issued which he promised to have executed as early as practicable and in time to be sent to the Pheonix Bank for payment of the first installment. In the meantime notes for our Branch Bank at Mobile had been prepared. The Bank was soon put in operation. The new banking house on the corner of Royal and St. Francis streets was built, with superior vaults, &c. The operations of the institution the first year was very satisfactory. I was re-elected President without opposition, and there was but little change in the Directory. The second years operations were also satisfactory to the Legislature and I was again re-elected without opposition but there were several new directors elected from different parts of the state. The Bank began to show some of the evils of the state banking system, exclusively state property. Speeches were made at our discount table advocating the discount of notes supposed to be weak and unsafe.[122]

State politics more and more every year weakened the bank; and, although our branch became a national depository enjoying every favor the Government could safely grant it was unable to continue specie payments during the financial crisis produced by the refusal of Congress to recharter the Bank of the United States after its suspension. In 1837, I had for the first time, powerful opposition to my re-election. I was, however, elected and served out the year 1838 with the determination to serve no longer. I required rest as my health was a good deal impaired.[123]

Our State Bank with all its branches became so deranged and embarrassed by the financial crisis, just passed through, that the Legislature, having lost confidence in State banking, took measures to wind them up. It must, however, be admitted that they had been instrumental in developing the resources of the new State, and facilitating commerce. Mobile from an ordinary town grew to an important commercial city.

In the early part of the summer 1843 my health was so much impaired my physician ordered me to the mountains of Virginia for the benefit of the air and mineral waters. Mrs. Gaines and I proceed via of New Orleans and the Mississippi and Ohio to Guyandotte—thence by stage to the White Sulphur Springs. The water of that and several other mineral springs during the summer benefitted me. The pleasant weather of September, which had contributed much to the restoration of my health, enabled me to take a retrospective view of the state of my affairs for the past two or three years.[124] I again went to work with them by addressing a letter to the Secretary of War stating that before I left home a writ had been served upon me for an alleged balance of about four hundred dollars due the government when in fact the government was indebted to me several thousand dollars; and I requested the favor of him to direct the re-examination of my accounts, by the proper accounting officer, and to instruct him to correspond with me here in relation to any items requiring explanation, as I would remain here some weeks longer for the benefit of my health. I waited several weeks without receiving an answer, therefore determined to go on to Washington and urge a final settlement of my accounts.[125]

Upon arriving in that city I took lodging at Willard's Hotel, and early next morning called upon the Secretary of War, Judge Porter. I thought he received me coldly. I told him that I had addressed a letter to him from White Sulphur Springs several weeks ago and hoped to have received an answer but none had come to hand.[126] He inquired, "What was the subject of the letter?" I informed him. He then inquired, "What were the services?" Upon telling him, he said, "I must have referred your letter to Mr. Crawford of the Indian Bureau," directing me to his office. Mr. Crawford informed me such a letter had been referred to him. He said that on inquiring at the third Auditor's office he found my accounts closed and that they would not be reopened for further examination. I informed him that the service had been urged upon me by Major Eaton, then Secretary of War, and Commissary General Gibson; that it had been performed by me at no little sacrifice of my interests, because it seemed to be a necessity, under the then existing circumstances,—to save bloodshed and preserve peace among the Choctaws in one case and to remove them willingly in the other. Mr. Crawford was cold and "crusty." Leaving him I returned to my hotel to reflect upon what I should do next. I had left at home all the papers relating to the service. I made up my mind to call the following morning on Gen. Gibson for copies of his letters to me on the subject of removal and subsistence of Indians; and through him to obtain from the War Department evidence of the promises of Secretary Eaton made to me on the Treaty ground at Dancing Rabbit Creek.[127]

Accordingly I went to Gen. Gibson's office. He promised to do as I requested. I called next day for the copies, etc. He furnished me with copies of his own letters, but could find neither record or any paper in the War

Office of Maj. Eaton's verbal promises to me. He said that about the time Maj. Eaton returned from the southwest there was some trouble in General Jacksons cabinet, and Maj. Eaton was appointed Minister to Spain. In consequence of the change an[d] excitement it was probable he may have omitted to have made any memorandum of his verbal agreement with me. I read the copies while in General Gibson's office—one, enclosing me the appointment of Supt. of removal and subsistence of Indians, urged me to accept "if it was only to break the ice and pave the way for future removals"—saying that my requisitions for money should be promptly complied with and no bond would be asked of me; and no instructions given me but the treaty for removal, &c. My answer to this was that I accepted the appointment though at much personal sacrifice. Gen. Gibson's second letter, after I had made the first removal in the fall of the year before, stated that "it was determined to continue the removal of the Indians under the superintendance of officers of the Army." He was standing by me when I read this. I looked up saying, "General, how did you happen to write this lie!" He replied in evident anger, "What do you mean, sir?" "When this sentence was written," I said, "my successor, a citizen like myself, was actually among the Indians, as my successor making preparations to recommence their removal." "That letter," said the General, "was dictated by the Secretary of War, who stood by me while I was writing it." "I thought so," I said, "for you know, General, I accepted the appointment reluctantly upon your urging me to accept, 'if only to break the ice and pave the way for future removals.'"—[128]

I returned to Secretary Porter's. Not finding him in I set out for my hotel. It was raining as I stepped out on the portico. Upon opening my umbrella the Secretary passed by me when one of the ribs, I think, gave him a little scratch on the face. I apologized, saying, that I had called at his office to hand him some copies of correspondence, furnished by Gen. Gibson, which he would oblige me by putting in his pocket and reading them when he returned to his office—I would call on him next day for his decision on my petition for the re-examination of my public accounts. His reply to this was, "I am on my way to attend a cabinet meeting." By this time we had reached the White House—we were walking during the foregoing conversation—so, when he made this remark we separated. When I called at his office next morning I was informed he had gone to Philadelphia. No message was left for me.

Returning to my hotel, I addressed a letter to President Tyler giving him the substance of the details of Secretary Eaton's promises to me; and of the necessity of accepting the verbal appointment. Also of my acceptance of the appointment of Superintendent of removal and subsistance of Indians, my letter from White Sulphur Springs to the Secretary, and the incidents relating to the case since my arrival in Washington, concluding by requesting the President to order my accounts reopened, examined and settled.[129]

Two or three days after dispatching this letter, I called upon the President. He told me he had read my interesting letter and was of the opinion I had been badly treated—that Secretary Porter was called to Philadelphia by sickness in his family there. When he returned he would act upon my petition and would do what was right in the matter. It was not customary to issue such an order as I requested but he would have a conversation with Porter about my affairs as soon as he returned.

I was now pretty certain I should be detained in Washington for several weeks, therefore the state of my purse rendered it necessary our expenses should be moderated by going to a boarding house. Mrs. Gaines expressing herself willing I determined to look out next day for a boarding house, and accordingly ordered my bill. Mr. Willard called upon me to inquire whether I was dissatisfied with my room or treatment. I told [him] I was not but found I would be detained in the city for several weeks [so] the state of my purse rendered it necessary I should have cheaper board than I could expect in a hotel. Asking him to recommend a comfortable establishment, he said, "I wish you to remain with us. I will make your bill as moderate as could be afforded at any good boarding house, and you can pay it after you return home. I have a handsome suite of rooms vacated to day which you can have if you consent to stay. If you prefer it your meals shall be served in your own dining room." I could not refuse such an offer so that evening we were in possession of the best suite of rooms in the hotel.

A week or two of leisure was now before us which was rendered very pleasant by the attentions at my brother's friends and seeing the sights the Capitol offered at that period. I lost no time in calling on Secretary Porter after his return. I was received with an apology for his sudden departure without leaving a message for me. He said he was ready for the re-examination of my accounts—a comfortable room was being prepared for the accomodation of the gentlemen who were to examine them; and for myself, as it was desirable that I should be present to make such explanations as justice might require. He asked me to come to his office at ten o'clock next morning when he would introduce me to the accountant and the meeting should be commenced. I accordingly called at the Secretary's office at the time mentioned, was introduced to the clerk, then shown into a comfortable room. The clerk was a lawyer by profession. He was an interesting, intelligent gentleman which rendered my attendance there as agreeable as it was necessary.

The re-examination was completed in about a week. When it was reported to the Secretary of War, he issued an order discharging the suit against me, and allowing me about two thousand four hundred dollars. He expressed the opinion I was entitled to more by the verbal promises of Secretary Eaton. I petitioned Congress at once for a further allowance for leading the exploring party, in conformance to my verbal engagements at the Treaty of Dancing Rabbit Creek, at great personal sacrifice to myself to quiet the discontented Indians and prevent bloodshed. Congress did not seem to understand the personal and pecuniary sacrifice I encountered by suddenly leaving my mercantile business for so long an absence required for exploring the new and wild country of the Choctaws acquired at the Treaty of Doaks Stand, their removal, and aiding in bringing about a sale of a portion of their territory to the Chickasaw tribe thereby "paving the way" for the sale of the lands belonging to both tribes on this side of the Mississippi river.[130]

of a Good Man

FROM THE *HAYNEVILLE EXAMINER*

Hon. George Strother Gaines died at State Line, Mississippi, in Feb. 1873, at the age of 89 years. He came to Alabama in 1805 — sixty-eight years ago — and it was over him that Colonel Aaron Burr, ex–vice president of the union, watched as he lay afflicted of a fever at St. Stephens, in 1806. He sent news of the massacre at Fort Mimms to General Jackson in 1813, and explored the west for a home for the Choctaws in 1829. He was a Senator from Marengo and Clarke in 1825 — forty-eight years ago — and owned the first "store" at the town of Demopolis. For many years he was president of the branch bank at Mobile. When General Jackson was about to retire from the presidency, he stood on the porch of the White House, and, in the presence of Mr. Gaines, told the president elect, Mr. Van Buren, that if Mr. G. should ever apply for an office, he hoped that he would not refuse him; "for," said General J. "Mr. Gaines will ask for no position he cannot fill." The town of Gainesville, in Sumter County, was named for Mr. Gaines in consequence of the incident, so flattering to him, to be found in "Brewer's Alabama," page 526. He was truly a noble man, with but one side to his honorable nature. And he deserved to live out the full measure of a useful life, if life be a blissful existence. Born in 1784, he was a young man when the century began. He was the brother of Major General E. P. Gaines, and uncle of Hon. F. S. Lyon, of Marengo. His eye had glanced over the most memorable period of the world's history; and he had lived from the simplicity of the old time to the grossness of the present without being corrupted by its vices and follies. There are but few men like George S. Gaines was, and the fact is a grievous one.[1]

The Southern Argus, Selma, Ala., Feb. 21, 1873.

$\mathcal{A}$ppendix A

Gaines to Dillard, Peachwood,
8 August 1857[1]

Dear Sir:

In the hasty sketch I gave you of the Dancing Rabbit Creek treaty, I stated that the *stroke of policy* recommended by Majr. Pitchlynn to the Secretary of War prevented the discontented Indians from carrying out their threat to mob the Chiefs & Captains who signed it, and thereby prevent its ratification by the President and Senate.[2]

The exploring party was named on the treaty ground. Netuckeijah headed it. The other members were selected for their popularity & superior intelligence, numbering in all about eighteen.[3]

I returned home and hastily arranged with my partner, Mr. Allen Glover, for closing our mercantile business; and set out with the party before the end of October.

My instructions were verbal, and as before stated, given hurriedly, with the promise of written instructions in relation to the arrangement which Col. Reynolds the Chickasaw Agent, & myself were expected to make, after the examination of the new Chaktaw Country, by which the Chickasaws should also settle on the Chaktaw tract. So far as related to the expenses of the exploration my instructions were to draw for money I might want, having a due regard to the interest of Govt.[4]

The objects sought by the exploration, & by inducing me to abandon my lucrative business to accompany it, were so important to Alabama & Mississippi as well as to two favorite tribes of Indians, that I deemed it my duty to fit out the deligation in comfort for the journey. We travelled westwardly intending to cross the Mississippi near the mouth of Arkansas river; & had fine weather until we entered the swamp, near the residence of the Cheif Lafleur.[5] The first days journey in the swamp was rainy. We rafted over Yellobusha, Yazoo and a dead river, this day, soaked with the falling rain. After encamping and supper, the deligation made me a formal visit at my tent. Netuckeijah addressed me thus.

"Mr. Gaines we have called upon you to express our appreciation of your kindness & condescention in consenting to accompany us in so long a journey & provide for our wants in the examination of our new country. The weather has been fine until today, and our travel pleasant: but today we have had a foretaste of the exposure peril & fatigues of the journey before us. We promise *here* to make the journey as safe and as pleasant to you as may be in our power and to that end we invite you to give to any one of us such instructions as you may deem proper in promoting your comfort & safety; and we pledge ourselves to obey you as promptly as your good servant Dick obeys you."

The third day after entering the swamp we reached Mississippi river. We crossed in a large flat boat, which I found in possession of a hunter, and purchased for the purpose. Keeping up the north side of the Arkansas river to Fort Smith, where we crossed; & fited out with packhorses loaded with Ham Sugar & Coffee. Each member was here furnished with new rifles & ammunition for two or three months use in an almost unexplored country.[6]

We asscended, examining the new Chaktaw Country carefully from Fort Smith between the Ridge (dividing the waters of Red & Arkansas rivers) and the Arkansas & Canadian fork of Arkansas. Halting to receive a fresh supply of Flour sent me on my requisition upon Col. Arbuckle then stationed at Fort [Gibson]. Col. Arbuckle wrote me, with the flour, that a Leiut. Surgeon & 12 mounted men would overtake us in a few days & accompany us in the examination of the country.[7]

We packed & secured our Flour Sugar Coffee & Salt with coverings of Bear Skins & proceded on our examination, backwards & forwards between the river & Ridge, as we asscended northwestwardly. The country was very beautiful, gently undulating, principally prairie,—relieved by strips of woodland on the water courses. These strips were generally narrow or wide, as the streams were small or large, small branches shaded with narrow & larger creeks with wider strips of woods. Every morning when I mounted my Horse I was soon surrounded by the party all mounted, to know the programe for the day. Then the hunters would spread out to the right and left—always bringing into camp, in the evening, plenty of game for the whole party, venison turkeys Prairie hens & occasionally Bear meat.

Before reaching the mouth of the Canadian Fork the Leiuts. command overtook us. The examination was intensely interesting every day,—novelties in country, an abundance of game, & fine weather to enjoy the chase, rendered each day & night joyous & happy. The Leiut. & Surgeon were both jolly soldiers & good hunters and entered into our hunts in the day & feasts & jollifications at night with great spirit & zest. The Buffalow now became plentiful, and were daily killed for their humps & tongues. The rest of the carcass we found coarse & inferior to our beef.[8]

Above the mouth of the Canadian fork we were joined by Col. Reynolds & the Chickasaw deligation. Netuckeijah invited them to join us & travel with us to enjoy our sports,—Wild Horses were now plentiful, and his invitation was accepted.[9]

The weather, now December, became quite Cold: but our sports & our enjoyments were encreased. Large log fires at neight, & longer nights, lengthened our Social enjoyments. Our Chaktaw hunting, War love stories, & wit, were now seasoned by Army stories & wit.

About the last of Decr. we crossed the dividing Ridge, & fell upon the Waters of *L'Eau bleu* and False Washita: two small rivers that head in the dividing Ridge & empty into Red River.[10] The slope from the Ridge to Red River is two or three times as wide as that on the Arkansas side of the Ridge. Our Flour Sugar Coffee & Salt growing alarmingly small after we reached the Cross Timbers the Cheif Netuckeijah proposed that we turn our course downwards being homewards pursuing the same plan of examination as we persued up, between the Ridge & Arkansas River,— inviting the Cheif Levi Colbert & his party to continue with us. This proposition was agreed to, and his invitation to the Chickasaw deligation was also accepted.[11]

This slope is so wide that it affords besides the False Washita, & the beautiful River *L'Eau bleu,* the Boggy river, & the still larger Kiametia, & also several smaller water courses, all emptying into Red river, below the Cross Timbers & above the Western boundary of Arkansas Territory (now State). It is much more fertile than the slope north of the Ridge. The greater part being underlaid with Limestone.

Our Military friends left us on the Boggy river, for their Fort [Gibson]. Our Flour had given out & they did not like to do without that part of their rations.[12]

We had many interesting adventures during our examination of this slope, but I need not detain you any longer so far from the field of your labors. Suffice it to say that the country was highly satisfactory to the Chaktaws; and was found to be large enough to settle the Chickasaw tribe upon it also.

After reaching the white settlements we found it necessary to rest some days, & recruit our horses, at Washington Hempstead County. Here Col. Reynolds & myself made a joint report to the Secy. of War of the Exploration of the Chaktaw Country: of its capacity & ample room for the comfortable settlement of both tribes; and asking to be favored with new instructions, found to be necessary in effecting the desired arrangement between the two tribes, which we had ascertained could be done on good terms. The instructions hastily made out by Maj. Eaton when returning from Dancing Rabbit Creek, & handed Col. Reynolds, were so defective & wanting in liberality that the terms were never mentioned to the Cheifs. They differed materially from what he told me they would be.[13]

After recruiting our horses we hastened home, I think, about the last of February 1831.[14]

I lost no time after my arrival at Demopolis, in closing my mercantile business, to be ready to commence the removal of the Indians early in the summer.

About that time some misunderstanding took place in President Jackson's Cabinet resulting in changes. Maj. Eaton Secy. of War became our minister to Madrid, and Genl. Cass took his place in the War Office.[15]

It is charitable to suppose that Genl. Cass knew nothing of his predecessors engagements with the Indians, that I should remove them; and with me, promising me the appointment of "Supdt. of the Subsistence & removal of Indians," and of Commissioner for treating with Indians. Yet it would be uncharitable to believe that Majr. Eaton should have persuaded me to abandon my lucrative business to undertake a public service so important as saving a most advantageous treaty, which could not have been made but for [his] promise that I should remove them, and which would have been broken (there being a very large majority opposed to it) & possibly a good deal of Bloodshed: but for the stroke of policy recommended by Majr. Pitchlynn, & which no other man, in his opinion, but myself could carry it out, and which Majr. Eaton told me he believed also. I say that it would be uncharitable to suppose that he left no record in the War Office of his engagements, so important to the Govt. & Indians.[16]

The truth is Genl. Cass having his eye, even at that early day, upon the Presidency, looked more sharply to his own interest than to that of the Govt. in dispensing the patronage of the War Office—My Brother & him were not very friendly; and he could not expect much from me. No man in the Govt. has been so careful, in my humble opinion, as Genl. Cass, to make capital out of everything within his reach, both of popularity & property; and none has been more successful, although he did not quite reach the Presidential chair.[17]

Majr. F. W. Armstrong was a clever man & was brother to Genl. Armstrong a pet of the President had served with credit in the army—had after the war entered into business in Mobile *supported by my friends*—had been unsuccessful, & had turned politician. He had talked loudly in the Presidential canvass in Alabama (where by the bye there was no need for it) for General Jackson had by his services, on our soil, intrenched himself firmly in the hearts of the people: But Majr. Armstrong wanted office; and Genl. Cass wanted Tennessee; & was looking out to secure that State & for an office for the Major. It is not strange then, the treaty being ratified, the discontented Indians quieted; and the new Chaktaw Country examined & found to be large enough for the Chaktaws, & to spare ample territory for the settlement of their Chickasaw neighbors; and being informed that the two tribes were inclined to meet the wishes of the Govt. in this respect—With a knowledge of all this I say that it was not strange that *Genl. Cass* overlooked the engagements of his predecessor; and determined to do something for Tennessee & at the same time for himself.[18]

When poor simple me was making ready and in daily expectation of receiving instructions to commence the subsistence & removal of the Indians in May 1831, I learned with surprise that an Agent Capt. Colquehoun was already in the Western division of the nation preparing for their removal.[19] Very soon after this Majr. Armstrong paid me a visit, and invited & urged me to ride with him & introduce him, as my friend, to some of the most influential cheifs; having been sent by the Secy. of War to prepare them for removal. He appeared to be entirely ignorant of the actual state of things; & I am satisfied had no knowledge of my expectations. I made no allusion to them; and rode with him several days, introducing him as my friend, & desiring the Cheifs to confide in him as they had always confided in me, and aid him in preparing for their removal.[20]

I was not sorry to be relieved from a service of great labor & privation, and heavy responsibility:—So I made no complaint and cheerfully set about building up a new business.

Mr. J. Emanuel of Mobile offered me a copartnership in his business in June: But the terms had not been agreed upon. He went to New York, & we were in correspondence about the terms. The Indians had afforded to Majr. Armstrong, in taking their Census, all needful assistance. But when he enquired when they would be ready to move to their new country the answer was always "When Mr. Gaines is ready we will be ready," which was reported to the War Office by the Major; and caused Genl. Cass to tender me the appointment of "Superintendant of the Subsistence and Removal of Indians" which was sent me by the Commissary General of Subsistence Gibson, an old friend of mine, through whose bureau the Removal was to be managed. The General accompanied the Commission with a long letter urging me to accept *"if only temporarily to break the ice & pave the way for future removals."*[21]

I reluctantly accepted at the additional solicitation of distinguished friends in Alabama & Mississippi. I think some time in Aug. 1831 quoting in my letter of acceptance Genl. Gibson's words *"if only temporarily to break the ice & pave the way for future removal"*: adding that seeing that the Govt. had lost sight of Majr. Eatons engagements with me, which had caused me to abandon a lucrative business, I was then intreaty for a partnership in a Mercantile House in Mobile; & if my offer was accepted, I could remain but a short time in the Service of the Govt.[22]

Genl. Gibsons letter imploring my services, authorized me, if I would accept, to employ as many Assistants & at such compensation as I might think proper; and to remove the Indians according to the treaty; without any particular instructions from him; and he requested me to forward my requisition for money, which would be promptly sent to any points I might name. The sum of $60,000 was promptly remitted me on my requisitions & no security required of me.

I selected several active influential assistants and commenced the work at once—Stationing them at different points in the nation; so that the work would go on in every part of it at once. The fall months was the season for comfortable immigration; and the arrangements for it, were all to make,—Waggons to hire, contracts for Subsistence to be made, roads to be opened, Steam Boats to be engaged. It was a task without preparation, when I began the work about the 1st of Sept. that promised but little success before the winter set in.[23]

Having stationed my assts. at desirable points in this wide field of labor,—more than 150 by 200 miles of area, & set each to work, by written instructions, I travelled taking no rest, but at night, from one to another around a circuit of several hundred miles: furnishing each with such sums of money as were required, from time to time, cheering them on; in their labors, and hastening the Indians in their preparations by every means in my power.

Before the end of November I had crossed over the Mississippi and landed at the highest point accesable by Steam Boats, (at that season of the year) on the Arkansas & Washita rivers six thousand Indians.[24] At these points they were recd. by other agents, and conducted to their new homes. At that period of our Govt. there were created many useless public Agencies: but those in aid of Chaktaw immigration were worse than useless. My assistants with their experience, and knowledge of the Indians, collected by them from their old homes, and removed from their old homes with great labor, opening roads as they went. Some of them, from the Tombigbe river to the Mississippi, then embarking with them in Steam Boats and landing them at the highest accesable points on the Arkansas, and Washita rivers, were the proper persons to conduct them to their new homes; and would have done so with perfect satisfaction to the Indians, and far less expense to the Govt.[25]

I am satisfied that the same amount of work was never done in the way of subsisting & removing Indians by the Govt. & never will be done hereafter at so little expense, as was incurred by me. I claim no credit for it. It was not owing to any financial skill or superior management but to my perfect knowledge of the Indians and the country they inhabited; & that they were going to; and also the intervening (Arkansas territory now State) country. When I look back taking a birds eye view of the wide field of my labors, without roads, in its then wild state:—the Indians confused by Genl. Cass two Agents Capt. Colquehoun & Majr. Armstrong's summer's operations, I am myself astonished at my success. Although these Gentn. named were highly respectable & judicious & faithful in their labors, (according to their instructions) confusion & dissatisfaction alone were the fruits. So that there was in fact no preparation, when I entered upon the work, about the 1st September, under General Gibsons *carte blanche* instructions. With money in hand, & my perfect knowledge of the resources of the country, my contracts were made on the very best terms to the Govt.:—add to this, the understanding between the Indians and Commissioners, when making the Treaty, that they were all to be removed by me, and you have the secret of my success.

Mr. Emanuel having agreed with me upon the terms of our partnership it was announced in the newspapers, of the day, and having closed the emmigration: for that season on my part, I returned home in December; and went to Mobile—spending the winter there, making settlments with my assistants; & making up & transmiting my accts. to Washington City for settlement.

My services were not necessary in my new business at Mobile only in the winter & spring months; and my partner advised me to continue in public service until the Indians were all removed—The summer and fall months only being proper for that work.

In the early part of the next summer 1832 when preparing for removal, I received from Genl. Gibson a letter thanking me for my efficient services, and requesting me to render my final a/cs. up to a day named ahead, for settlement. *The President having decided to remove all the Indians under the Superintendence of officers of the Army in future.*[26]

I rendered my a/cs. accordingly, without complaint, up to the day named. Majr. F. W. Armstrong a citizen like myself, appeared among the Chaktaws again as my successor, so soon after I received Genl. Gibsons letter of thanks, that I think it probable that the appointment was in his pocket before the Commissary General's letter was written to me.[27]

The settlement of my a/cs. went on slowly, items were suspended by Auditors under the most frivilous pretences. My charges for compensation for my services, as an Exploring agent, and as a Commissioner for holding treaties with Indians, agreeably to Secretary Eatons engagement with me, were rejected under a rule established in the War Office by Secy. Cass subsequently to Secy. Eatons engagement with me, and a trifling, per diem offered me. This I of course rejected: it was hardly sufficient to cover my own outfit and personal expenses. My accts. for subsisting and removing Indians fared the same fate: numerous items were suspended & rejected.

In the mean time, my attention to the Branch Bank:—my private affairs, & to my new business at Mobile, fully occupied my head & hands.

Having been elected President of the Branch of the Bank of Alabama at Mobile, by the Legislature at their session in 1832–3 and appointed by an Act of the same, sole agent of the State, for negotiating the sale of State Bonds, created for the use of the Banks; I was compelled to visit New York early in the year 1833. I stopped a few days at Washington City, and called upon Secy. Cass & explained to him the nature of my engagements with his predecessor, my own personal sacrifices in abandoning my own business to perform a public service, which no other man could successfully perform. I complained to him of the Auditors not settling my subsistence & removal accounts and of their holding me to the forms prescribed to regular disbursing officers, in the face of Genl. Gibson's letter releiving me from those forms. Having a pretty good knowledge of Genl. Cass' character for accumulating all sort of capital, I requested the Alabama delegation to be present at this interview, and I believe every member was present. My late friend Col. Wm. R. King spoke of me to the Secretary, and of my public services in the warmest terms of praise. The Secy. promised that my accts. should be settled to my satisfaction before I returned from New York: where he was told by Col. King that I was going as the honored & trusted agent of my State on important public business. The negotiation at that time of $3,500,000 of State Bonds in New York detained me there nearly three months; and when I called at Washington returning home, nothing had been done for me. I could not wait for the settlement. But

Genl. Cass assured me that every thing should be settled as I wished, as soon as the press of business by calls of Congress upon his Dept. was gotten through with.[28]

On calling to take leave of the President Mr. Van Buren was with him & I have no doubt remembers our conversation to this day. On remarking to the President that I had merely called to take leave of him he asked me if I would accept office, & before I could answer addressing himself to Mr. Van Buren remarked that Mr. Gaines services whilst U.S. Agent to the Chaktaw trading house, in restraining the Indians during the war, and engaging them as allies against the Creeks, were of the greatest importance to the Govt.—that he knew me from a boy and that I was entitled to any office in his gift that I wanted.[29]

Expressing my gratitude for his good opinion I told him that I desired no office, and had no favor to ask from the Govt. on my own account. But in behalf of my Chaktaw friends I begged that the provisions of their late treaty might all be carried out by the Govt. in the spirit of kindness & liberality;—which he assured me should be done.

I have mentioned this interview with the President before: but I repeat now what occured in detail, to relieve your mind from the erroneous impression that he was aware of the shuffle & cut game his Secretary of War was playing to get clear of me & place a friend where he could make him useful to himself at some future day. The President was from my boyhood to his death a warm friend of mine.

I was reelected by the Legislature to the Presidency of the Bank until the session of 1838–9 when I declined to run for the office. My health gave way about that time. In 1843 my physicians ordered me to the White Sulphur Springs in the mountains of Virginia as a dernier resort for the restoration of my health.[30]

My public accts. remained unsettled. A few months residence at various mineral springs restored my health; and I determined to visit Washington, & if necessary appeal to President Tyler for justice. Mrs. G. was with me. Judge Porter of Pennsylvania was then Secy. of War. I had written to him from the Springs urging the settlement of my accts., hoping that I might not be compelled to incur the expense of going to Washington: but I got no reply. When I called upon Judge Porter & complained that he had not replied to my letter, he seemed not to have recd. it; & turned me over to the Commissioner of Indian affairs, saying that if my letter was received it had been sent to him for his action. This functionary acknowledged that my letter had been sent to him: but he had not examined it. After three weeks attention at the War Office, Judge Porter decided that my accounts could not be opened, my having acquiesed in their settlement, as reported for suit. This I disproved by shewing my correspondence with Genl. Gibson & the Auditors: having demanded & obtained copies of the same.[31]

Judge Porter however left the city for a visit to his family without giving me any satisfaction. I then appealed to the President, with a full statement of the whole matter, demanding the settlement of my accounts. He advised me to await Judge Porters return quietly, without complaint; promising me that he would speak to him, & advise the opening and reexamination of my accts. Three weeks more passed by before Judge Porter returned from Pennsylvania. He then took up my case issued an order for the settlement under the rules prescribed. Majr. Eaton had returned to the U.S. and was then in Washington and had made out & filed in the War Office a certificate confirming my statement of his engagements with me, on the treaty ground. In the order of Judge Porter, he admits the justice of my entire claim but says that the whole cannot be paid without an act of Congress ordering it. Armed with this order, and supplied, now kindly, with an intelligent clerk & a fine room, I went to work & reexamined with him the account & great mass of accompanying vouchers: The fruits of which (being about three weeks more detention) were the dismissal of the suit pending against me & the payment to me of about $2,500, acknowledged to have been kept from me more than ten years: no interest was allowed.

I then petitioned Congress for the balance, being composed of rejected items, Judge Porter admited justly due me under Majr. Eatons verbal contracts, with me: yet could not be paid without an act of Congress for my releif. My petition was denied by that Congress, and again laid before another Congress, and fared the same fate. I intend to appeal to the next Congress, & hope to be more successful, not so much for the amount justly due me, although it would be very acceptable, as for the example of maintain[in]g my rights, which I wish to leave to my children.

In looking over this batch of hasty sketches I find that I have been a little hard upon Genl. Cass & might be considered as having judged him wrongfully—This I would be sorry to be guilty of. No one will deny Genl. Cass tallents or patriotizm: but still as a politician he has proved that selfishness predominates over his patriotizm, a little too much.

When I called at Genl. Gibsons office to receive the copies of my correspondence with him made out for me to use in the settlement of my accts. I was carefully looking over his letter to me, & coming to the last thanking me for my efficient services, and informing me, that *The President had decided to cause all the Indians in the future to be removed under the Superintendence of officers of the Army.* I addressed the Genl. rather familiarly asking him *how he came to write me this lye.* He straightened up his tall figure as he turned around to me from a desk he was standing by, and asked me angrily what I meant. I pointed to the paragraph handing him the copy of his letter; and before he had time to remark upon it; I said Genl. you know that there was no use for any excuse in superceding me for I accepted of the appointment, reluctantly; & *only temporarily to break the ice & pave the way for future removals* after the Govt. lost sight of their engagements with me made by their Secy. of War Maj. Eaton. He read the copy all over carefully, and I went on to tell him that F. W. Armstrong, a citizen like myself, appeared among the Chaktaws, as my successor, so soon after I received that letter that I believed very probable that he had his appointment in his pocket before it was written. He appeared embarrassed & said that Genl. Cass dictated every word of that letter, (he now remembered very well) standing at his elbow whilst he wrote it. I replied that I had thought so from the first; for I knew him incapable of falsehood, or any sort of deception knowingly. The honest old General was never after, so cordial in his intercourse with me as previously.

I feel no enmity to Genl. Cass. He only acted the part of *his* class of politicians. No mans rights are regarded, in carrying out their plans of self aggrandizement. He was a bold old fox to make a Catspaw of Genl. Gibsons hand,—few men would have had the nerve to attempt such an act. In all that makes up the character of a perfect gentleman and a soldier no man stands higher than Genl. Gibson.

It may be that we have found the secret of the failure of Genl. Cass's efforts to reach the Presidential chair. It may be this defect in his character—want of candor which the people believe cannot be dispensed with in their Cheif Magistrate: candor being an essential ingredient in the composition which makes up a great man.[32]

Genl. Cass, I dare to say, whilst acting as Territorial Govr., Superintendent of Indian Affairs, Commissioner for treating with Indians &c. &c., and receiving the greatest pay ever allowed by the Govt. for each service performed all at the same time, saw no impropriety in the allowance to himself. But I was told that whilst he was Secy. of War he established the rule that the Govt. pay an officer or agent in his Dept., rendering the duty of several officers or Agents at the same time, for only one service. This rule exists, I believe, in the War Office, only as a ghost to be brought forward at the pleasure of the Secretary. Yet Judge Porter, acknowledging the justice of my whole claim, turned me over to Congress to beg for a large portion of it. That body has twice refused me justice: but I do not dispair; for, although the hot party agitations which has for years past stirred up

& floated into Congress some of the very dregs of society, too light & too filthy to comprehend any duty, save that of obedience to party leaders. There is too much good sense in the people to suffer this state of things to exist much longer.[33]

Is it not to the demoralizing influence of party spirit, which the good people of the United States have permitted to controul the elections, that we are indebted for the existing controversy between the Northern and Southern States, threatening the dissolution of the Federal Govt.? There is nothing else that could have blinded & besotted our keen sighted Northern Bretherin; than this mischeivous demon, seducing from their holy calling ministers of the Gospel to aid in the work. Blind & besotted they must be to beleive it their duty to meddle in our domestic affairs, to keep up a cowardly agitation for years to the injury of the very class they pretend to favor; And more mischeivous, it must be in its results, if permited to continue much longer; than if they were to poison the water we all drink, as well as the whiskey they send us. I am a firm believer in the ability of the people to govern themselves,—in the stability of this good Govt. of ours—& in the waking up of the people, although stupefied for a time by a party Press, party stump orators; and cheated out of their votes by party machinary.

But I am running out into muddy water; and will hasten back. In a very few words then I will give you my opinion of the requisite antidotes for the cure of the poison infused into the body politic by the demon party spirit. It is not to muzzle the Press but to encourage education and the spread of useful knowledge—to honor truth and virtue—to frown upon vice and all sort of deception—to select our rulers for their good sense and moral lives; and not for their party predilections. These antidotes rigidly observed North & South in electing one Congress, would consign the agitators to oblivion, if not contempt; and the operations of the Govt. would no longer be clogged, but go on dispensing justice to all; and carefully fostering our commerce with the nations of the world, and continue to grow in strength, as our fathers designed that it should: and become in time a blessing to the whole human family.[34]

Respectfully
Geo. S. Gaines

$\mathscr{A}$ppendix B

Conversation with George S. Gaines[1]

BY ALBERT JAMES PICKETT

Mr. Geo. S. Gaines was born in North Carolina & raised in Tennessee. In 1805 he was appointed by Mr. Jefferson a Chactaw factor & that year he settled on the Tombigbee in discharge of his duties. Here he resided & was living about the time Tecumpse visited the Creek Nation for the purpose of influencing the Indians to take up arms against the Americans.[2]

Some time about 1795 the Creeks had established a town at the Tuscaloosa falls.[3] A chief of that town named Oseoche-emauhla used to visit Mr. Gaines trading establishment & would purchase goods to the amount of $100 on a credit, a credit which the factor had been allowed to give to all the chiefs, should it at any time appear to him necessary to allot them to our [government] & people. This chief used to bring down canoes full of peltry twice a year & honestly & faithfully discharged his debt. Mr. Gaines having at length such confidence in the man's punctuality & honesty, on several occasions pressed him to purchase goods to the amount of $500. But the chief refused to go in debt beyond $100. Upon Mr. Gaines first arrival at St. Stephens, he became acquainted with Tandy Walker who had once been one of the government blacksmiths for the Creeks & who once lived with Col. Hawkins.[4] He spoke the Creek language in its purity. Mr. Gaines noticed this man & treated him kindly for the reason that good & honest men were rare, about that period about St. Stephens & Walker in return became very much attached to Mr. Gaines.

Just before the breaking out of the War of 1813 & about the time Tecumseh was prosecuting his schemes, the Tuscaloosa Chief with a good many warriors came down the River in canoes & brought with them Walker for interpreter who then lived a few miles above the factorage.[5] The chief stated to Mr. Gaines that he had often rejected the offer to purchase goods to the amount of $500, but upon reflection & had come down then with the view of embracing the offer, & that Mr. Walker would go his security. Mr. Gaines remarked that since he had made him the offer times had changed. A war was about to be waged between the U.S. & Great Brittian that the latter government were using at that time all means to array the indians against the White American & that in the uncertain condition of things he did not feel himself authorized to let him have so large an amount & that he could not do it.

While this conversation was going on, Walker paced the floor with sad countenance & appeared very much distressed. The chief became warm & angry in his expostulations for the large credit and the warriors became excited & talked very loud. While Walker continued to manifest more un-happiness. Mr. Gaines told the chief as it was now near dark to go to his [camping] ground & to dream about it & that he would in turn dream for [himself] & that possibly by morning they might come to a better un-derstanding. The indians then took their leave with Walker who had upon going out left his knife on the counter. Walker soon observed to the indi-ans that he had left his knife on the counter & he must go back for it. Returning in the store he whispered to Mr. Gaines to meet after dark at the rock a place well known down at the river. This knife was left on the counter with the design to give him an opportunity of speaking to Mr. Gaines.

Mr. Gaines went to the place designated & there Walker approached him in a cautious & circuitous manner & whispered in his ear to follow & cautioned him to be still lest they both should be killed. Mr. Gaines unconscious of intended mischief followed him into a thicket 1/4 mile off & when getting in the thickest place Walker with great trepadation & alarm informed him that the chief had acquainted him with the determi-nation of the Creeks upon war & the distruction of the Factorage & all the Tombigbee settlers, that they had disclosed all their plans to him tell-ing him that, when the $500 worth of goods were purchased he & Walker could carry them up to Tuscaloosa moving Walkers family up there out of danger & there divide them—that no risk would be run in standing his security for the factorage would be destroyed & all persons murdered very soon. Walker appealed to Mr. Gaines to say nothing about it & said be on your guard—let us separate for if we are found together we will both be shot.

The next morning the chief & his party came to the store—he reported that dreamed that Mr. Gaines had let him have the $500 worth of goods—that he had carried them to his town & had a fine store & that his people thought him considerable man. Mr. Gaines in reply said I also have dreamed, but my dream is altogether different from yours. I have dreamed that war existed, that the hostiles had killed many people & had endeavored to burn up my store, & I cannot let you have the goods. Why said the chief in an angry tone, you make me a small man. I told my people to expect me soon with the goods & built me a new store. You must let me have the goods. Walker has negroes near you & he will be good for the debt. But Mr. Gaines positively refused, told him however he would so soon as the anticipated war was settled amicably which he expected would be done soon, he would then trust him for $1000 without credit. Finally the matter was compromised by the chief taking up goods to the amount of $100 & neither the goods nor the indians were seen afterwards by Mr. Gaines.

Soon after the Burnt Corn fight, the people about St. Stephens became much alarmed & commenced erecting some temporary forts—and It was uncertain which sides the Chactaws would take. While all was doubt & terror & alarm, and a few days after the fall of Fort Mims,[6] one day Pushmatahaw rode to St. Stephens & sought an interview with Mr. Gaines & commenced making proposals to join the Whites with his warriors. Mr. Gaines told him he was not a war chief. Genl. Flournoy was at Mobile & that if he would go there with him—Mr. Gaines [was] delighted [at the] idea of receiving the assistance of the Choctaws, rode rapidly to Mobile with Pushmatahaw. They had an interview with Flournoy in the old Spanish Fort & Pushmatahaw introduced the subject of his mission in a speech, & requested to be mustered himself and warriors into service of the U.S. To this generous & manly proposition, Flournoy replyed with great indifference & said he was not authorized to receive any indians & would not. Pushmatahaw being much astonished again besought him in a very eloquent appeal saying that he desired to join his standard for many reasons, but principally to restrain his warriors, some of whom had already joined the Creeks & he was fearful if not engaged soon by the Genl. that they would go over *en mas* to the ranks of the Hostiles. But Flournoy treated his offers with coolness & rudely rejected them.[7]

Mr. Gaines being much mortified at the want of foresight in this officer, now addressed him & advised him by all means to receive Pushmatahaw & his warriors—that altho he was not authorized, yet the President would approve such a course for he was put here to protect the Frontier & to adopt any measure which would be necessary to effect the purpose, but Genl. Flournoy returned him the same answer which he had made to the brave Pushmatahaw, & further, intimated to Mr. Gaines that when he needed his advice he would send for him & avail himself of it. The Chief

& Mr. Gaines with heavy hearts left the Fort & the unfeeling commander, mounted their horses & entered the trail to St. Stephens the latter deeply mortified but endeavoring to conciel his shagrin from the Pushmatahaw who enquired if that was one of our great warriors remarked that the great warrior at the Fort was in his opinion of very small calabre. He informed that Genl. Jackson, a much greater warrior would soon be down with a force & that he would receive Pushmatahaw & his warriors with great pleasure, which appeared to relieve the old warrior considerably.

When they [were] in sight of St. Stephens the anxious citizens, men women & children who had forted at the place were now seen to rush out & surround the two riders. What news what news cried a hundred voices at the same time. They were informed of the unsuccessful application to Flournoy & dispair was seen in every face & feelings of indignation pervaded the assembly at the foolish & ill timed rejection of the proposition—but before Mr. Gaines had ceased answering their questions a man at a distance was riding up with his horse lathered with sweat & panting—the rider delivered letters from Flournoy requesting Mr. Gaines to raise all the Chactaws he could muster them into service—a shout of exultation rose up from the crowd & all was joy & among the number, Pushmatahaw felt exceeding rejoiced. Mr. Gaines was now urged to proceed with him to the nation & after hastily preparing some jerked beeff & bread they left St. Stephens in company with Mr. Flood McGrew.

But before the trip to Mobile, the fall of Fort Mims had produced alarm throughout the weak & feeble settlements upon the bigbee & Mr. Gaines with great sagacity turned his operations towards the country he had been raised believing that among these [brave] citizens was Andrew Jackson & Gov. Blunt, who could be appealed to with success.[8] At his own expense he dispatched Edmunson on a fleet horse and gave him authority to press horses on the route & give drafts upon him—the man rode day & night & soon reached Coberts ferry on the Tennessee River, & was in a short time afterwards in the executive council room at Nashville where he fortunately found both Gen. Jackson & Gov. Blunt.[9] Handing a letter to each at the same time—Jackson rose up from the perusal & walked rapidly across the floor saying By the eternal these people must be saved. I know the young man who wrote these letters & I rely upon his statements. Gov. Blunt was equally enthusiastic & they resolved to send troops to Alabama. Jackson at that time had his arm in a sling from an encounter with Benton, but nevertheless volunteered to command. Gov. Blunt requested him to issue his orders and he would sanction his acts.[10]

Col. McKee happened to be in Nashville and ordered to repair to the

Chactaw nation & to enlist an army of indians. He reached the [residence] of John Peachland U.S. interpreter about the time Mssrs. Gaines McGrew & Pushmatahaw did. Pushmatahaw resolved to return & assemble his indians.[11] Mushalatuba did the same, confering with Col. McKee a few day. Mssrs. Gaines & McGrew started back to St. Stephens travelling the lonely trail by themselves & camping out at night.[12] In a few days they reached the great assembly ground where they saw over 5000 indians encamped. The young men at Ball play—They rode to where Mrs. Nail a half breed was and took a seat with her on a log who welcomed them warmly expressing her joy at their success & loudly denouncing those who had massacred her friends at Fort Mims. This was near Marion in the present state of Mississippi.[13]

After while Pushmatahaw & his wife were discovered riding up. They alighted near Mr. Gaines. Pushmatahaw took no notice of Mssrs. Gaines & McGrew—he had previously always been sociable & was accustomed to receive Mr. Gaines with great cordiality. But he now observed a distant bearing & Mr. Gaines was at a loss to account for his conduct & McGrew became alarmed & advised Mr. Gaines to acost him, but Mrs. Nail requested that Mr. Gaines should be left to manage him his own way. Presently Pushmatahaw lay down under a tree, apparently slept for half hour with his hand over his face. By this time it was announced that the chief was to address the vast assembly—then [their] noise rent the very air, now all was hushed in silence [simultaneously] the vast [congregation], formed around the chief squatting on the ground in silence one circle within another. He arose and addressed them to the following effect. "Warriors. Many years ago Genl. Washington send for a deputation of our nation to visit him. We resolved to go. We passed through Virginia & the Virginians treated us with great kindness. Every where we went the Virginians shewed us much attention & were kind & made us presents. We went on to Philadelphia and were received with open arms by the Virginians there Genl. Washington took us in his house. Every time he opened his mouth good talks came out of it & he gave us good advice—told us not war upon each other or other nations—that war was a bad thing at best. And that we ought to quit it & even if the Americans had to go to war, the Chactaws must not. Genl. Washington dismissed us with many presents. He told us to go home & not rely so much upon hunting, but to cultivate the earth more & raise corn & other produce. That we would soon be a much more happy & prosperous people. Genl. Washington sent us that beloved man there, to sell us goods & he has let us have what we want on good terms."[14]

This speech was continued in this strain to great length & Mr. Gaines still remain[ed] in doubt as to the gist of it, or the real disposition of Push-matahaw who had acted so strangely throughout the meeting. He could not tell from the speech the object of it & nor could he read any thing upon the faces of the numerous audience. But Pushmatahaw continued "You know Tecumpseh—he is a bad man, he had come among the Creeks. He has got many of them to join him & even some of our own warriors have gone over to his side. You know the Tensaw people—they were our friends. We have played ball with them & whenever we journeyed to Pensacola we stoped at their houses and they fed us. What has become of these good people. Most all of them killed in one day in that [large] slaughter pen. Their Bones ly there now. The people of St. Stephens are good friends. They are defenseless. They want soldiers to fight for them & if they don't get there soon they will all be killed like the Tensaw settlers. They have been kind to us"—Pushmatahaw, here drew out his sword & flourishing it said "I am resolved to join the settlers & fight for them—you can all do as you please & take which side you please. I do not intend to advise you but if you have a mind to follow me I will lead you to glory & to victory"—Here a warrior slaped his hands upon his breast & said "I am a man, I am a man & I will follow you"—a general slaping of breasts took place, a shout went up, Pushmatahaw was surrounded with a large army immediately. Mr. Gaines much rejoiced & relieved, Mr. McGrew delighted and Mrs. Nail the [patriotic] half breed danced with extacy.

About the same time Col. McKee had raised 500 warriors commanded by Mushulatuba & some Chickasaws through the influence of John Peachland U.S. interpreter & had marched upon the Tuscaloosa town—the indians of that place hearing of his approach abandoned it & McKee burned the town. Returned to Peachlands who lived on the Tombigbee river immediately at the mouth of Ochtibbaha meaning fighting water. Mushulatubba lived near there [where] Col. Bluit has a plantation.[15] About this time Dinsmoor faithful & indispensable Agent of the Chactaws was removed & Col. McKee was put his place.[16] The agency was at Jackson Mississippi Capital Miss. established there 1809. It had been formally held on the Chickasaha river near the present town of Quitman Clarke County Miss. The army raised by McKee after spending a little time at home joined Col. Claiborne at St. Stephens.[17] In the western a Puckshenubbee district that Warrior led several hundred warriors to St. Stephens. When all together then there were upwards of 1500. The Chactaw Nation at that period consisted of three districts, the eastern under Pushmatahaw, the North Western under Mushulatubba & the Western under Puksinubba.

These chiefs had their own district councels and in general councel the eldest chief presided.[18]

In 1805, Col. Dinsmoor & Genl. Robinson of Nashville were appointed commissioners to hold treaty with these indians for the purchase of a strip to connect the Tombigbee settlements with the Miss. settlements. Before this, the Tombigbee settlements were between Ellicotts line on the West side Tombigbee and Creek named [Cintabogue] running 9 miles above it into the Tombigbee including also a small settlement lying east of the Ala. called the Tensaw settlement. The Indians were invited to St. Stephens to negotiate with the commissioners and they met in great numbers some 10,000 souls fed by the Gov. & not-withstanding of the talents of Col. Dinsmoor & high standing of Genl. Robinson with the Indians they failed to effect a treaty. But they agreed to meet the commissioners again in the latter part of the same year, at Mount Dexter on the Noxubee river[19] — which they did & agreed to cede all their lands within the following lines commencing at the cut half way between the two rivers & running North-wardly on the dividing ridge between the Tombigbee waters & those of the Ala. up to a point now known as Chactaw corner in the south east corner of the present county of Marengo. Running then westwardly to the Fullucktobanna, old field on the Tombigbee River a few miles below Tuskahooma.[20] Thence to the settlements of the Mississippi, then South down to Ellicotts line, then along Ellicotts line to the place of beginning. Shortly afterward Dinsmoor run the line & at the Chactaw corner erected a mound & inserted in it a red cedar post made corners at Fullucktobanna & other places. After the survey was completed settlers in 1808 from all parts marched in and the county of Clarke was organized, about the same time Wayne county in Miss. was settled & then Greene county and sub-sequently several counties on Pearl river were settled.[21]

The population of Washington county as these settlements were then called, consisted of about 2000 souls principally from So[uth] Ca[rolina] & Georgia & a few from North Carolina. Among the settlers were Maj. Boykin who had distinguished himself in the Revolutionary War under Marion, the two Col. Callers from North Carolina, the Bates from Geor-gia, the Johnsons, Hollengers Mims & Gaines & Linders.[22] The Linders, the Mims & Hollengers were the wealthiest citizens some of them own-ing over 100 slaves. They cultivated corn principally & potatoes—lived mostly on what they raised had large stocks. The Mims, Hollengers & Gaines the heads of these families were originally indian traders & accu-mulated their property in that way. Some of them had 5000 head & put up beeff & Gaines (Young) put up beeff in tierces to supply the West India

House of Forbes & Co. On one occasion he got out a great cargo load of hickory [hard] spikes for the same House to be sent to England by that House.[23] There was not a solitary town in the whole settlement about 1805, & the traveler was much troubled to get out of the neighborhood every one was wanting him to go to his home to stop—they were the most hospitable [persons] upon the face of the earth. They were destitute of enterprise but lived easy & comfortable. Besides these principal families, there were many others no one knew where they came from & they were adventurers & men of very bad character many of whom after the gospel & education was introduced returned westward. About that time they were fond of dancing parties and Samuel Mims one of the wealthiest men then lived where Fort Mims was destroyed—had a large house there. People would collect from all parts of the settlements & and dance there several days then go to the Duns Thompsons and other houses. They were fine dancers having been associated much with the Creoles of Mobile. Taffia & wine were principal drinks.

The U.S. Chactaw factory was established at St. Stephens shortly after the withdrawal of the Spanish authorities below Ellicotts line in the year 1802. At that period the U.S. had trading houses which they called factory among all the larger tribes. The object of the establishment was to aid in the civilization of the Indians & to protect them against the cupidity of private traders. Joseph Chambers Esq., of Salisbery North Carolina was the first factor 1802 of the Chactaws.[24] About this period commissioners were appointed to adjust the claims to lands in the Tombigbee settlement. Their first meeting was at Fort Stoddart in 1803—one of the commissioners having died there, the Board held its sessions afterwards at St. Stephens.[25] Joseph Chambers was also one of the Commissioners & Robert C. Nickolas of Virginia afterwards an officer in the army was appointed to fill the place of the dead one.[26] The settlers claimed land from grants under Great B[ritain], France & Spain. Those living on public lands about the time of Elicotts survey were afterwards presented by Congress with a donation 640 A each family. Others who settled in the country & resided in it at the time the board of Commissioners was established were entitled to a preemtion from 160 to 64 a.[27] The Commissioners had high authority & set like a court with a secretary testimony was received & recorded— they decided subject to the approval of the president & he always sanctioned their decrees. The secretary of the Board was a lawyer of some eminence named Parmalee from New England. The Board scrutinized the claims most rigidly which gave dissatisfaction to persons presenting weak & incomplete claims but it was soon made apparent to the people that the board had an object in view in the investigations they made, which was to do justice to the parties. No further complaint was heard of them. Mr. Chambers was a man of fine mind highly cultivated of industrious business habbits. He brought with him [in] 1802 as an assistant Factor Thos. H. Williams from N.C. who being a man of ability was required soon after to discharge the duties of Secretary of State at Washington Adams Co., then became collector of the Port of New Orleans then U.S. senator from Miss.[28] About this time Mr. Geo. S. Gaines then living in Gallatin Tennessee 20 years of age was appointed to fill Williams place with the understanding that so soon as he became familiar with the duties, he should be allowed to succeed Mr. Chambers the principal factor. In those days when men were appointed Gen. Agents, they looked upon themselves as strictly servants of the government & did not enter into pollitics. The Commissioners terminated their labors in about two years & in the spring of 1807 Mr. Gaines became principal factor having discharged the whole duties from his first arrival.

Thomas W. Murry, from [Albermarle], Virginia, was appointed Receiver of the land office in 1806. Being dissatisfied with his station he resigned in 1807[29] & Lemuel Henry from Tennessee was appointed in his place.[30] Nickolas Perkins of Tennessee also having previously being appointed Register upon Chambers retirement who for several years held various offices connected with the lands.[31] The first public sale of land at St. Stephens was in 1811 at which time all the public lands in Washington County was offered for sale—only the river lands were sold generally brought from $1.25 to $3 per acre. The government would not sell any lands for less than $1.25 & as the almost entire portion of Washington County with the exception of the river lands were miserably poor, these lands continue vacant to this day. The pollicy of the government has been injurious to the treasury & of the inhabitants of Ala. They should have sold the lands at their actual value this pollicy has been to make squatters & to prevent a good population & to encourage the plundering that public [?].

It should have been mentioned that surveyors were appointed shortly after the organization of the Board of Commissioners to locate private claims & run the public lands off into townships & sections. Appointments were made by Mr. Briggs Survey[or] Genl. [of] Washington Miss., and after the treaty of Mount Dexter the ceded lands were also laid off and prepared for sale.[32]

2nd second public sale took place in 1816 when the lands of Clarke Wayne & Greene counties were offered. There were few French grants—

mostly English & Spanish in Washington county. The grants generally called for 400 or 800 Arpents & an arpent not quite an acre—the English called for (see Magoffin about this & about the sealing wax seal).

Fort Stoddert named after Secty. of War was established shortly after (see 1 vol. public lands p. 618) the running of Ellicotts line—dont recollect the first man who built in 1805. It was a stocading with block houses & Bastions was of wood. The Barracks were comfortable frame houses. The Fort was established immediately on the river bank just above the present Arsenal landing—in 1805 two companies were there he thinks under command of Capt Skyler.[33] The discipline was rigid & the young officers not having the advantage of a military education were almost daily mustering & practicing artillery, sword exercise, or in reading military books. The place proved unhealthy & the troops in 1805 and '6 were sent to St. Stephens to spend the sickly months—leaving a small garrison to take care of the Fort under the command of Lieut. Gaines who was also a Collector of the Port. After this the summer encampment was established on a hill called [Mount Vernon] 3 miles west of Fort Stoddert, the site for the present arsenal. This place proving more healthy & sufficiently near the river & the Spanish line it became the permanent location of the troops intended for the defense of this section. With the exception of a detachment always kept at the Fort. Fort Stoddert was a port of entry.

It will be perceived in consequence of the isolated situation of the Tombigbee settlements, their commerce being subjected to taxation by two ports of entry languished & owing to this may be attributed the want of enterprise & industry of the settlers. It was impossible for this state of things to exist always. The supplys for the army & the U.S. factory as well as the commerce of the whole settlement were interupted & taxed by the Spanish authorities in passing through Mobile. Mr. Gaines U.S. Factor in respectful remonstrance personally made to the Spanish government at Mobile against the detention of some goods for his establishment & the execution of duties upon the [government] came well nigh being imprisoned. He took the ground that the goods were the property of the U.S. intended to promote civilization of the indians a matter in which the Spaniards ought to be in favor of & that further the detention of the goods & the duties imposed were in violation of the treaty between the two governments. Being informed that he must reduce his remonstrance to writing was delivered in person to the Commandant. After reading which his Lieut. returned it to Mr. Gaines in an insulting manner with the reply that the Commandant was not accustomed to receive a communications in english. He then applied to the Spanish interpreter to translate it—he informed Mr. Gaines that he had translated the document for the Gov. & he was instructed to hold no interview with Mr. Gaines. Mr. Gaines reported the affair to the Gov[ernment of the] U[nited] States who ordered him to pay the duties & take charge of the goods—remonstrance was made in 1806 or 7. Every craft that passed with goods through Mobile Bay was anoyed by the exactions & detentions—The duties were high & not regular—& imposed at exorbitant rates frequently upon [timid] persons.[34]

The Government [site] continued to receive goods & to pay duties until 1810—When [they] ordered the goods to be sent to Mr. Gaines of the Ohio from Pitsburg to the mouth of Tennessee thence up the Tennessee to Colberts Ferry just below the Mussel Shoals. In 1810. Gaines was instructed by the secretary of war to proceed up to Cotton Gin Port, (the government having several years before built a gin there to encourage the Chickasaws to raise cotton) & to examine that country from Gin Port to Colberts Ferry toward opening a good waggon road—and to obtain the consent of the Chickasaws to open it. Mr. Gaines examined the route but the indians refused the privilege of opening a waggon road & he was compelled to transport large quanties of goods on pack horses to the residence of Peachland where he built boats & took the goods down to his factory. [He] got the Colberts together at George Colberts—first stock was 25 thousand dollars worth.[35] At the same time Mr. Gaines received instructions to buy lead on his way to the lead mines above the mouth of the Ohio, found a sunken barge near fort Massack laden with lead & he contracted with the owner for the quantity he wanted which was raised by penetrating the bars of 56 lbs by means of screws cut in the sockets of boat poles.[36] It [the lead] was conveyed to Colberts ferry with the [trade] goods there. 50 pack horses transported with the goods to Peachland. The goods designed for the factory were received this way until after the change of government in Mobile.

The factor had interpreters, and an assistant and when occasion required another clerk—also a skins man who received the skins beat them during the summer months every week to keep the worms out of them— had laborers besides this to aid in beating the skins & packing them for market. The factor received a salary of $1000, $365 in lieu of rations & furnished with furniture & and anual allowance to keep up the furniture. Assistant factor received $500 salary & $150 in lieu of rations. The skins man was Joseph Gillaspie who is now about 70 and lives in Sumter County. The interpreter & clerk one man received $400 per year. As the design of the factory was solely to civilize the indians & attach them to the government, the factor was instructed to sell goods at a profit sufficient to cover expenses & produce a fund to counter ballance losses.

The factory in 1802 was first kept in a block house of the old Spanish fort at St. Stephens, the Barracks of the fort affording accommodation for the offices of the factory & warehouse goods—the old Spanish church had then recently fallen down, but the parsonage was a large frame building & was in a state of good repair, & was used as a skin house. In 1812 the block house & buildings become so decayed & the Gov. refusing to repair. The factor moved the effects into his own private building of brick, which after the Burnt Corn fight was enclosed by bastions & pickets as a fort.[37] The citizens built a fort on Mount Republic Hill close by. In the fall of the year & during winter months the shipment of furs took place in the factory. The skins having been carefully kept free from worms during the summer, were neatly packed, the deer skins in bales weighing 250 lbs having been previously assorted the reds to themselves, the grays to themselves & blues to themselves. The beaver otter and small fur skins in hogsheads carefully placed pelt to pelt. The beeswax was melted & run into kegs. These shipments alone amounted to between $15 & $20 per annum besides moneys transmited annual amount in skins in money about $25 to $30. The great House of John Forbes & Co of Mobile was the competitor of the factory and the trade was at length almost entirely diverted from them. The resident proprieter [of] this house lived in princely style. The principal articles sold at the factory were blankets and strouds a kind of coarse broadcloth half yard of this made flaps 1/2 yard made leggings. 3/4 yd made a petticoat for a woman—1 1/2 yards made a covering to answer as a shawl or blanket for a women. The more wealthy indians & bows & bells of that class wore in lieu of strouds fine scarlet cloth with highly ornamented mockascins and head dressed—the skins, etc. were put on scooners, duties paid in Mobile to the Spaniards & shipped to Orleans then shipped to Philadelphia to the indian agent. Besides the articles above mentioned purchased at the factory & shipped, Bears oil honey in kegs, bacon, ground nuts & tobacco in [cartons]—then articles were sold at the factory to settlers and not shipped.[38]

In consequence of the enormous duties imposed by the Spanish authorities of Mobile upon our citizens & the many insults added to the injuries our citizens became provoked beyond endurance & many of them became willing aids of Col. Kemper in his efforts to revolutionise West Florida. He thinks in 1810 that a company was organized in the settlements, to take Mobile.[39] Maj. Hargrave, a worthy old Revolutionary officer became a prominent actor & marched with the company to Saw Mill Creek. Hargrave among others being taken was sent to Havannah, remained in the calaboose a long time & through the interference of the Gov. was released.[40]

Aaron Burr—Mr. Gaines states that whilst on a visit to his Brother at Fort Stoddart, Maj. Nicholas Perkins arrived at his Brothers quarters about sun up & he was awoke by their conversation.[41] Maj. Perkins said he had not slept the past night that a little after dark yesterday evening, he was engaged at a game of whist with his friend Thomas Malone clerk & Theodore Brighwell[42] Sheriff of the county and another gentleman in a cabbin at Wakefield[43] the C.H. when a gentleman rode up to the door of the cabbin & asked the direction to Maj. Hinsons—the person addressed answered that it was 7 miles to Col. Hinsons & it would be difficult for a stranger to find the path in the dark it forked & there was a creek with a bad crossing place.[44] Nothing daunted the stranger [and he] carefully enquired the distance to the creek & the way. Whether he should go directly across or bear up or down the channel—how far to the forks &c. This attracted the attention of Perkins he turned his head towards the door at which the stranger was siting upon his horse. The light of the candle shined in his face which was highly interesting with large black penetrating eyes. He then glanced at his form & horse. His dress was a coarse grey round about & pantaloons of the same, fashionable hat & boots. His horse a noble animal with elegant saddle & bridle.

After receiving directions the stranger departed & Perkins remarked to his friends that that was Aaron Burr, who had been denounced by his government as a traitor & rewards had been offered for him by the Gov. of Miss. & the President of the U.S. & that he considered it his duty to endeavor to apprehend him.[45] He proposed to the Sheriff that they too should follow him to Hinson's & accordingly ordered their horses for that purpose. When near Maj. Hinsons Perkins recollected that he & the Maj. were on bad terms & that he could not go to his house. Brightwell agreed to proceed to the house & ascertain if it was Burr & then to return & devise means if necessary to take him. Being near the house Perkins waited several hours for Brightwell in vain. He then concluded that was really Burr & that the sheriff who was much under Hinson's influence, had advised him Brighwell, to abandon the attempt to take Burr, supposing that he Perkins would return to Wakefield. He then determined to proceed to Fort Stoddart as speedily as possible to apprise Lieut. Gaines of the whole affair. It being midnight & the road from there to Fort Stoddart being nothing but a path with several bad creeks on the way, he travelled on horse back to old Mr. Joe Bates, residing on Nannahubba Bluff (Fish

Bluff) arrived after riding 15 miles before day light. Bates let him have a canoe & negro man. They proceeded 8 or nine miles down the Bigbee river & [the] Mobile & arrived at Fort Stoddart, between daylight and sun up. Having stated to Gaines the particulars.

Lieut. Gaines having heard these particulars at once called his orderly & directed him to mount himself & 4 or 5 men, be ready immediately for service also ordered horses for himself & Perkins took a harty breakfast. In the afternoon the party returned with Aaron Burr. & Perkins related to me the following particulars of his arrest. The party took the road for Wakefield in a brisk trot crossing some bad creeks on the way & met Col. Burr in company with Maj. Hinson & the sheriff Brightwell, a short distance below Hinson's residence. Lieut. Gaines on meeting Col. Burr, accosted him politely said I presume I have the honor of addressing Col. Burr. Burr said I am a traveller & stranger in the land & do not recognize your right to ask such a question. Lieut. Gaines said I arrest you at the instance of the U.S. Burr said by what authority do you arrest me a traveller on the highway on my private business—Gaines, I am an officer of the U.S.A. I hold in my hand the prochlamation of the Gov. & President directing your arrest. Burr, you are a young man & may not be aware of the responsibility of arresting a traveller. Gaines, I am aware of my responsibility. I know my duty. Burr then entered upon an argument to show him that such prochlamation ought not to have been issued & that in carrying them out he was wrong. After speaking sometime in a forcible & animated manner Lieut. Gaines informed that his mind was made up that he should accompany him to Fort Stoddart & that he should remain there untill he Gaines could send him to Washington City comfortably—that so long as he showed no disposition to make his escape he should be treated with all the respect due to the Vice President of the U.S, that any attempt to escape would forfeit the respect he was bound to entertain for him & would very materially change his treatment of him. While the conversation was going on Burr's manner was lofty and commanding, but so soon as he saw no chance of making an impression upon young Gaines, his interesting face suddenly relaxed in its sternness & was lighted up with smiles. Gently noding his willingness, they passed on.[46]

Without further remonstration, he accompanied the party to the Fort. Hinson and Britwell not accompanying them. He rode on silent & dignified to the fort. He was shown to his room where he remained declining dinner or supper with the family, but taking his meals in his room. His room was adjoining that of Mr. Geo. S. Gaines who suffering from sickness. Burr about midnight hearing him [groan] got up, opened the door

and in a kind manner asked Mr. Gaines what was the matter with him—
& offered his services to give him relief if in his power. Said that he had
traveled much & knew something of diseases. He then felt of Mr. Gaines
pulse & took a seat by him & talked for some time with [Gaines] conven-
ing up very agreeable subjects. His manner was facinating and seductive.
He dined with Lieut. Gaines the next day—he was introduced to Mrs.
Gaines the daughter of the late Judge Toulmin & to Mr. Geo. S. Gaines.[47]
At the kind invitation of Mrs. Gaines he agreed to take his meals in the
family when they had no company but otherwise he must be excused. His
conversation at the table was sprightly and very interesting. He played
chess with great skill Mrs. G. being a frequent competitor with him. He
made the evenings he spent with the family most delightful—by his
sprightly conversation & interesting accounts of his travels & incidents.
Mr. Gaines staid with him a week & he frequently set up of nights late
his (G) room talking with him about the indians &c. Gaines returned [to]
the factory.

About three weeks after his arrest, Lieut. Gaines had made arrangements for his departure to Washington City. In mean time his Secretary
who had charge his bagges & papers attemted to follow him from Natchez
but struck the Tombigbee above the sight of Gainesville employed John
Jones an indian countryman to bring him in a perogue to St. Stephens.[48]
He was invited by Mr. G. S. Gaines to his house where he remained until
a conveyance was arranged by [Lieut.] Gaines who sent him after Col.
Burr who had preceded him about three weeks. He was a German, but
highly intelligent.

Maj. Nicholas Perkins was a lawyer of some distinction that emigrated
from Franklin, Tennessee to Washington County in 1802 or 3. He purchased land in the Sun flower bend on Tombigbee. He was a man of high
standing & much firmness. In consequence of these qualities Lieut. Gaines
selected him as the leader of a party of gentlemen Thomas Malone, a
planter by the name of Slade, and one or two others all respectable gentlemen, and they left for the North.[49]

Appendix C

2nd Conversation with Geo. S. Gaines, Spring of 1848[1]

BY ALBERT JAMES PICKETT

The Spanish Government established a Fort at hobuckintopa & called it St. Stephens. This Fort & Fort Confederation at Jones' Bluff was abandoned some years before Mr. Gaines came to the country. It is probable they were dismantled before Ellicott surveyed the line of the 31st degree in 1799.[2]

On a path, being the route from St. Stephens to the present city of Jackson, lay a large indian mound embracing at the base about two acres & rising in a conic form some thirty or forty feet—apparently a large ditch had been once cut around it enclosing in a square form some twenty acres. This mound was called by the Chactaws Nanna (hill), wyah (mother) & according to their tradition was the Mother of the whole tribe, out of whose hole in the top, their ancestors sprung up suddenly one day. This hole was quite large & deep immediately in the top & was about 10 feet in circumference. The indians had great regard for this mound & when hunting in its vicinity, would always throw down a portion of the killed game into the hole—thus *feeding their mother* as they believed.[3]

One day Mr. Gaines on his way to the agency at Jackson rode upon this mound & while surveying the hole, observed Pushmatahaw & a number of indians pass on their way to the agency. Presently he overtook them & Pushmatahaw with a smile full of meaning & mischief observed, "Well I suppose you have been visiting our Mother & what did she say to you." It was the constant custom of all the government agents to take every favorable occasion to impress upon the indians the propriety of selling their lands & emigrating West. Mr. Gaines in reply to the interogatory of Pushmentaha, said "Your mother told me (when I felt it my duty to pay my respects to her just now) that you, her children were getting in a bad condition—that the game of your county was disappearing & that it greaved her very much for fear her dear children would starve & she hoped they would cede their lands & emigrate west where every thing was more plenty." Many of the common indians gave a grunt believing that their Mother had really so discoursed to Mr. Gaines, but Pushmentaha did not believe in the tradition about the mound & when Mr. Gaines had finished relating these words of the Mother, the old chief laughed immoderately saying Holauba, houlholauba, feenah!!! its a lie, its a lie, its a real lie—our good Mother never could have made such a remark. On their journey Pushmatahaw discoursed much upon the subject of indian traditions & said that the true account was that the Chactaws originally came from the West. This was in 1810.

THE COLBERTS AND BROWN

The Colberts were the sons of an intelligent & wealthy Scotch Trader in the English influence & enjoyed the patronage of that government. He probably emigrated to So. Carolina, before Oglethrope settled Georgia & from there came into the Chickasaw nation—his wife was a full blood Chickasaw. By her he had three sons, George the elder, Levi & James & several daughters.[4] At an early day George Colbert established a ferry at the foot of the Mussel Shoals which was long known as "Colberts Ferry" being the crossing place on the main route from Natchez to Nashville & from the Big bee settlements to that place also. In 1800 Mr. Gaines was at this ferry & George Colbert then lived a little ways south of it.[5] George Colbert was middle size, with features strongly indicative of intelligence & shrewdness & cunning in trade. He was chief of the Chickasaws in *fact,* but not by office. About 1800 Levi settled 10 miles south of the ferry on the Nashville trace & kept a house of entertainment.[6] James lived still farther south on the same route & kept entertainment. He was educated & was a polished gentleman but possessed less influence than his uneducated Brothers, both of whom were men of strong native minds.[7]

James Brown lived 40 miles south from Colberts ferry on the "Nashville trace" and also kept entertainment. He was a large fine looking half breed whoes father was an Englishman—he married a sister of the Colberts.[8]

In N. W. Alabama & No[rth] E[as]t Miss. there were few Chickasaw towns. The bulk of the tribe lived below Colberts Ferry on & west of the Natchez trace. The Chickasaws in numbers were greatly inferior to those of the Chactaws. They sprung originally from the same people & spoke the same language but with a different pronunciation. Altho there was less general intelligence among them than the Chactaws, yet in consequence of the sagacity of their head men & rulers they came off better with their treaties with the whites & are now a much richer tribe.[9]

The Cotton gin, at Cotton Gin Port was established in 1800, by our government to encourage the Indians to raise cotton.[10]

In going from St. Stephens to Colberts Ferry in 1806 the trail led by the North West corner of Washington County, thence by the house of a Frenchman named Charles Juzan near the Lauderdale Springs. He had an Indian family having married a niece of Pushmatahaw—lived well in a neat cabin entertained travellers & sold goods to the Indians, was respected by the whites & indians, was of a respectable Mobile (French) family. The indian town of Coonsha was where he lived. This was the residence of Pushmatahaw. The route continued through the old Yazoo towns to Noxobee River & crossed near where the town of Macon now is—where resided an Indian countryman, named Starnes, a sensible Yankee Blacksmith, who had been living here many years with an indian family & entertained travellers—(half way between Starnes & Pytchlyn's lived Mushilletubba who was the son of Mingo Hooma Stubbee the [senior] chief of the nation—Hooma Stubbee died indebted to the factory $1000 in 1809 & his son assumed & paid the debt—)[11]

Thence to Pitchlynn's U.S. interpreter who lived near the mouth of Oaktibbeehaw river—this was in part the dividing line between the Chactaws & Chickasaws & took its name from a great battle fought upon it at the Ford near the mouth & hence it was called fighting water.[12]

Pitchlynn was the son of a Brittish officer in the commissary's department. During the revolutionary war his father was passing from Natchez to Georgia & was necessarily detained in this nation. Pitchlynn then a lad born in So. Ca[rolina] accompanied his father—who died while in the Nation, when the Boy became very much attached to the Indians—was so perfect in their language, he was thought to be more perfect in it than the indians themselves. He was 40 years old when Mr. Gaines first saw him in 1805. Got hold of some books & made himself something of a schollar. In course of time married a half breed Chactaw & had a numerous family of children. Maj. Peter Pitchlynn of Arkansas is his son. To him & his influence may in a great degree be attributed the friendly state of feeling exhisting between the whites and Chactaws. He prevented the tribe of Chactaws from becoming hostile in 1813. Had the confidence of both tribes and the U.S. Had about 500 horses in the range. The Colberts also had many horses.[13]

Horses of various Colours looked splendid in the Prairies—settlers sold ponies at $10 to $20—better kind of horses $50 to $100—drove them to N[ew] O[rleans], Pensacola, and Mobile.

	Miles
From St. Stephens to No. Wt. Corner Washington	30
Charles Juzans	30
Starnes—near Macon	40
Mushilitubba	20
Pitchlynn	12
George James (Cotton Gin Port)	35
Jim Brown on the Natchez trace	10
Levi Colberts	30
George Colberts	6

CONTINUATION OF THE NOTES OF HON. GEO. S. GAINES

The remaining part of the Chactaw country was sold at the treaty of Doak's Stand in 1822 & at Dancing Rabbit Creek in 1830. By this treaty it was provided that they should be removed comfortably in waggons & steam boats under the superintendence of discreet men, but the chiefs refused to sign to the treaty until the Secretary of War assured them that Mr. Gaines was to move them & the Secretary of War prevailed upon Mr. Gaines to undertake it. There was perhaps not a majority of the nation in favor of this treaty. The least intelligent among them was violently opposed to it & commenced drinking on the treaty ground with the view of breaking it up by a mob. Soon as it was perceived the chiefs were inclined to make it. The Commissioners Genl. Coffee & John H. Eaton, then being secretary of war, at the moment of signing the treaty being apprised of the discontents, urged Gaines to accept of the appointment of an exploring agent to lead off at once a delegation of indians to explore their new country W[es]t of the Arkansas—which Gaines refused but the secty of war continued to urge him as he had consented to remove them—but his principal object was to draw the attention of the discontents from the Treaty to the exploring expedition led by Mr. Gaines. Their new country lay west of the then territory of Arkansas bounded on the South by Red River & on the North by the Arkansas River & the Canadian Fork of the Arkansas & extending W[es]t to the American line which they acquired at the Treaty of Doak's Stand (above Jackson) in exchange for the country they then ceded including Jackson but they could not be induced to occupy it.[14]

Mr. Gaines was a merchant very lucratively engaged in that occupation, but seeing that a great point was to be obtained by leading off the exploring party & examining their new country, agreed upon the secretary of war's proposing to appoint him also an agent for treating with the Indians with the pay of both offices—to wit: the reconcilement of the discontented indians to the treaty & effecting an arrangement between the Chactaw & Chickasaw tribes by which both might settle upon the Chactaw lands—a few weeks previous to this, the Chickasaw had treated for the sale of their country provided the govt. could give them a suitable new home in the W[es]t.[15] Mr. Gaines acceptance being made known, the chiefs were requested to select 12 or 15 leading men to proceed forth with to the new country and the commissioners hastened as speedily as possible from the treaty ground. Dancing Rabbit is in Noxubbe county. Mr. Gaines made arrangements with his partner by dissolving his business & set out immediately with the exploring expedition. Col. Reynolds with a delegation of Chickasaws the agent of the Chickasaws was sent over to greet Gaines upon the Canadian Fork of the Arkansas. Gaines proceeded from Coonsha towns[16] across the country by Col. La Fleurs on the Yazoo thence through the Missi Swamp (fall of 1830) to Montgomery's point on the Mississippi thence to Arkansas Post Little Rock & Fort Smith to the new country—Col. Arbuckle at Fort [Gibson] was instructed to furnish him with necessaries for the expedition.[17]

The party ascended the country between the Arkansas River & the dividing ridge between these waters & red river—And met with Reynolds & his Party on the Canadian Fork which they ascended to the Cross timbers & then crossed over to the waters of the Red River. Then descended the false Washita Branch of Red River thence to within a short distance of Red River then struck easterly to & crossed Blue River. Here a very interesting scene occurred. Before leaving the false Washita at the camp it was agreed [then] overnight to strike across the country eastwardly the next morning. The Chactaw party saddled up early & came to the Chickasaw camp who supposed that the Chactaws would not travel as it was raining that day. In the evening the Chactaws encamped in wooded Ravine in the Prairies—next morning marched to the Blue water about 12 o'clock & encamped to await for the Chickasaws. About one o'clock Pitman Colbert & another Chickasaw indian came up with a message from Levi Colbert, that they had set out early in the morning to overtake us and hapend over last nights encampment, where they found that a trail of 100 indians had struck on our trail with the appearance of being in rapid pursuit—fearing that we would be overtaken they had hastened on & overtook the party 10 miles from the encampment & In a peace of woodland. They expected every moment would be fired upon. When Gaines party got ready to go back to their assistance, the whole Chickasaw party [drove] up & reported that they had endeavoured to speak to them but got no answer, had kept behind the trees but did not fire upon them. Col. Reynolds assumed the command of the party & they run bullets till midnight & sentinels passed & lay all night without being attacked, continued down the valley of Red River crossing the boggy River to Arkansas line stoped a few days at Washington Arkansas. Here reported to the Secy. of War the result of the exploration. The country was found extensive enough for the two tribes rich & well watered—stating that their was no inclination on the part of the Chactaws to defeat the wishes of the Chickasaw but our instructions were so limited we could proceed no further.[18]

A dissolution of the cabinnet took place. Genl. Eaton went out & Cass came in. In the spring of 1831 commenced preparing to emigrate. In April or May was informed another agent had been appointed to emigrate them. F. W. Armstrong was appointed for that purpose & solicited G[aines] to go with in the nation. He did so & introduced him to number of the chiefs. But the Indians said Mr. Gaines was the one to go with them & asked him if he did not promise it. Armstrong not being able to do any with them, reported to the govt. About 1st Sep. Cass sent him an appointment to remove them. He accepted temporarily—appointed agents collected waggons & in the month of Nov. Mr. Gaines crossed 6000 indians over the Mississippi. Remained in Mobile in the winter & spring Mr. Gaines was relieved by the determination of the President to emigrate the indians in future by officers of the army.[19] About 6000 more were removed during the year 1832 3 & '34. Their progress in Christianity & civilization has been astonishing since their removal. They have adopted a civil form of gov. Republican in its character. They have schools and accademies—have their lawyers, doctors &c and are an orderly Christian people. Their still remained upwards of 7000 indians in 1834. By a clause in the treaty those who thought proper to remain, were to have a section of land to each head of a family a half section to each child over 10—& 160 for each child under 10. They were to signify their intention to take lands within 6 months after the ratification of the treaty & the agent had to received such applications. In '32 the lands were surveyed and an agent was sent out to locate their claimants, but finding only about 70 out of 1500 families on the record, the lands for these 70 families only was designated on the maps and revenue from sale and all the lands occupied by the remaining families upwards of 1300 that were [with] the minimum

price were sold & many of the families violently turned out of their pos-
sessions—& have been ranging about ever since until a few year ago until
Congress appointed Commissions to investigate their claims which Commission expired in '46 confirming nearly all their claims. These families
after the Gov. from time to time turned a deaf ear to their rights, fell into
the hands of agents & speculators—who used up all they obtained from
them so that they are poor & more miserable than they ever were &
within the last few years the Govt. after making great efforts have succeeded in removing about 3/4 of the 7000—the remainder reside principally on the head waters of the Pascacola.[20]

Companions & Associates

of George Strother Gaines

Matthew Arbuckle (1776–1851), a career army officer and native of present-day Greenbrier County, West Virginia, served as commander and founder of Fort Gibson (1824–41), Indian Territory, on the Grand River near its confluence with the Verdigris and Arkansas Rivers. He served as an aide to Andrew Jackson at the Battle of New Orleans, was commissioned colonel of the 17th infantry in 1820, and was brevetted brigadier general ten years later for faithful service. Arbuckle provided supplies and a military escort to Gaines and Benjamin Reynolds and the Choctaw and Chickasaw exploring parties in December 1830–January 1831.

Francis W. Armstrong (1783–1835), a native of Virginia, served in the 24th Infantry Regiment in Andrew Jackson's Tennessee army during the War of 1812 and reached the rank of major before his discharge in 1815. He represented Mobile County in the Alabama legislature, serving in both houses (1820–21, 1823–25). He was appointed in April 1831 to conduct a census of the Choctaw before their removal from Mississippi and was appointed Choctaw agent west of the Mississippi in September 1831. His brother, Captain William Armstrong, replaced Gaines in 1832 as superintendent of Choctaw removal east of the Mississippi.

Willie Blount (1768–1835), a native of North Carolina, served as governor of Tennessee (1809–15). In September 1813 Samuel A. Edmondson delivered to him Gaines' letter reporting the Creek assault on Fort Mims and asking for his aid in defending the lower Tombigbee and Tensaw settlements. Blount authorized Andrew Jackson to raise and march Tennessee volunteer forces to the defense of the Mississippi Territory.

Aaron Burr (1756–1836), a native of Newark, New Jersey, and Revolutionary War veteran, served in the U.S. senate (1791–97) from New York and as vice president (1801–05) under Thomas Jefferson. On 11 July 1804 Burr killed his chief antagonist and political rival Alexander Hamilton in a duel, setting in motion events that led to treason charges as part of the "Burr Conspiracy." He apparently planned to establish a colony on the Washita River in present-day Oklahoma and perhaps to seize control of Mexico, but wilder stories circulated about the possible seizure of the U.S. government or the western territories. After warrants were issued for his arrest, Lieutenant Edmund Pendleton Gaines intercepted him a short distance from Wakefield, Washington County, Mississippi Territory, on 19 February 1807 and held him briefly as a prisoner at Fort Stoddert. While there Burr engaged George Strother Gaines in conversations about the Southern Indians and their commerce and upon occasion took his meals with and spent evenings with the Gaines family.

James Caller (1758–1819), a native of Virginia, emigrated to Washington County, Mississippi Territory, in May 1802 and later removed to Clarke County. He served as a senior militia officer, member of the legislative council for the territory, and territorial commissioner in 1807. Caller led a militia force of 180 whites, mixed-bloods, and friendly Indians that attacked a Creek Red Stick party led by Peter McQueen, High-Head Jim (or Jim Boy), and the Creek prophet Josiah Francis (or Hillis Hadjo) on the morning of 27 July 1813 at Burnt Corn Creek in present-day. Escambia County, Alabama. He and his brother John Caller (1758–1819) were also associated with Reuben Kemper, Joseph P. Kennedy, and others in Mississippi Territory who plotted (1810–11) to drive the Spanish out of Mobile.

Joseph Chambers, a native of Salisbury, North Carolina, was appointed by President Thomas Jefferson in 1802 as factor of the Choctaw factory, known as the Choctaw Trading House, at old Fort St. Stephens, Mississippi Territory. He was also appointed register of the U.S. land office for Washington County, Mississippi Territory, in 1803 and postmaster at St. Stephens in 1804. Chambers resigned as factor in 1806 to return to North Carolina, and he recommended that his young assistant, George Strother Gaines, be appointed to replace him. Gaines was confirmed as factor in 1807.

Lewis Cass (1782–1866), a native of Exeter, New Hampshire, served as Andrew Jackson's secretary of war after John H. Eaton's resignation over the "Peggy Eaton affair." Although trained as a lawyer, he spent much of his life in the political arena, serving as governor of Michigan Territory (1813–31), secretary of war (1831–36), minister to France (1836), U.S. senator (1845–48, 1851–57), and secretary of state under James Buchanan (1857–60). An old-line Jacksonian Democrat, Cass was defeated by Gaines' cousin, Zachary Taylor, in the presidential election of 1848.

Ferdinand L. Claiborne (c.1772–1815), a native of Sussex County, Virginia, emigrated to Natchez, Mississippi Territory, in 1805. He was appointed brigadier general in command of volunteer forces in Mississippi Territory east of the Pearl River and ordered by Major General James Wilkinson to defend Mobile in the War of 1812. He arrived at Fort Stoddert on 30 July 1813 with seven hundred soldiers in time to defend the Tombigbee and Tensaw settlements in the Creek War of 1813–14. He established Fort Claiborne in present-day Monroe County, Alabama, as a defensive position on the Alabama River in November 1813 and destroyed the Creek town of Ecunchate, or the "Holy Ground," on 23 December 1813.

John Coffee (1772–1833), a native of Prince Edward County, Virginia, emigrated to Davidson County, Tennessee, and became a close personal friend of Andrew Jackson. He marched two thousand cavalry from West Tennessee to relieve the Mississippi Territory after the Creek assault on Fort Mims in 1813. Coffee removed to present-day Huntsville, Alabama, in March 1817 and later to Florence to serve as surveyor of the northern district of Mississippi Territory, and he was reappointed surveyor and served until his death in 1833. Jackson appointed him as a commissioner along with John H. Eaton to negotiate for the removal of the Choctaw, and the negotiations resulted in the Treaty of Dancing Rabbit Creek in September 1830; Coffee also negotiated the removal of the Chickasaw by the Treaty of Pontotoc in 1832.

George Colbert (c.1744–1839), the second oldest of five mixed-blood sons of James Logan Colbert (c.1720–1784), owned a plantation and slaves and operated Colbert's Ferry (c.1802–18) on the Tennessee River on the Natchez Trace. He exercised great influence over the economy and in the councils of the Chickasaw Nation and blocked Gaines' effort in 1810 to develop a wagon road from the Muscle Shoals on the Tennessee River to John Pitchlynn's at the mouth of Oktibbeha Creek on the Tombigbee. Although he opposed land sales to the U.S. government and removal, he emigrated west with his slaves and established a sizable farming operation near Fort Towson, Indian Territory, where he died on 7 November 1839.

Levi Colbert (c.1759–1834), another mixed-blood son of James Logan Colbert, operated a stand (c.1812–15) on the north bank of Buzzard's Roost Creek on the Natchez Trace and owned a plantation, slaves, grist mill, and salt springs. He led the Chickasaw delegation that explored the country west of Arkansas Territory with Colonel Benjamin Reynolds, Chickasaw agent, and Gaines' Choctaw delegation in 1830–31. He emerged as the principal leader of the Chickasaw and led the opposition to removal until his death in Colbert County, Alabama, on 2 June 1834.

Albert C. Coles (b. 1852), a native of New Jersey, emigrated to Mississippi where he became Gaines' partner in the nursery business at State Line, Wayne County, Mississippi, before the 1870 federal census. He is listed as a "farmer" in the 1870 census and was skilled at grafting trees and plants. Coles became Gaines' amanuensis in the summer of 1871 and recorded Gaines' reminiscences as published in the *Mobile Register* in 1872 and in the *Alabama Historical Quarterly* in 1964. He continued to operate the Peachwood nurseries as Gaines, Coles and Company and issued an 1887–88 catalog celebrating thirty-two years of business in the Gulf states.

William Scott Colquhoun, a native of Dumfries, Virginia, was appointed as an assistant agent for Choctaw removal on 29 June 1831 by George Gibson, commissary general of assistance. Colquhoun arrived in Mississippi on 28 August and served as a special agent under Gaines. He worked in LeFlore's district and conducted a party of 253 Pearl River Choctaw from Vicksburg, Mississippi, aboard the steamboat *Walter Scott* in December 1831. In 1832 Colquhoun organized a party of over 1,700 emigrants in Nitakechi's district, but he was dismissed by William Armstrong after landing them on the White River in Arkansas Territory.

Sam Dale (1772–1841), a native of Rockbridge County, Virginia, emigrated to Georgia and later to Mississippi Territory where he became a noted frontier guide and Indian fighter. He settled in Clarke County around 1810 and served with Colonel James Caller's militia force in July 1813 at the Battle of Burnt Corn Creek where he was wounded. His fame as an Indian fighter was further enhanced by the famous "Canoe Fight" on the Alabama River on 12 November 1813 when Lieutenant Jeremiah Austill, Lieutenant James Smith, and Captain Dale killed nine Creek Indians. In 1814 he removed to present-day Monroe County, Alabama, where he served as tax collector and in 1817 as delegate to divide Mississippi Territory. He served in the first general assembly for Alabama Territory in 1817 and represented Monroe County in the state legislature for eight years (1819–21, 1823–24, 1826–29). He served as an assistant to Gaines in the Choctaw removal of 1831, and he spent his final years on a farm near Daleville, Lauderdale County, Mississippi.

Charles Lefebre Desnouettes (1773–1823) was the acknowledged leader of the French emigrants (1817–23) who settled on four townships in present-day Marengo County, Alabama, in 1817. He used his contacts and personal wealth to aid his countrymen in their efforts at building a vine and olive colony first at Demopolis on the east bank of the Tombigbee River and later at Aigleville on the south bank of the Black Warrior River. General Desnouettes served as an aide-de-camp to Napoleon at Marengo, shared his carriage in the retreat from Moscow, supported his return from Elba, and served at Waterloo. He and Gaines became close friends, and he left Gaines in charge of his estate and business affairs when he left Alabama in 1823. He sailed from Mobile to seek refuge in Belgium in hope of returning to France but lost his life in a shipwreck off the coast of Ireland.

Anthony Winston Dillard (b. 22 April 1827), a native of Tuscumbia, Alabama, emigrated to Gainesville, Sumter County, Alabama, in 1848. He was a lawyer and educated at Centre College (Kentucky) and Jackson College (Tennessee). He served as probate judge of Sumter County (1856-62) and as chancellor of the western chancery division (1868-80). Dillard, an avid historian and writer, contributed several articles to newspapers and magazines (1857-85) and published several chapters of his "History of Sumter County" in the *Livingston Messenger* and the *Gainesville Independent* in 1857-58. He corresponded with Gaines and other early settlers in writing his "History" and an article on the Treaty of Dancing Rabbit Creek.

Silas Dinsmoor (d. 1847), a native of New Hampshire and graduate of Dartmouth College, was appointed U.S. agent to the Choctaw on 12 March 1802. He and James Robertson negotiated and signed the Treaty of Mount Dexter with the Choctaw on 16 November 1805. In 1807 Dinsmoor moved the Choctaw agency from the Chickasawhay River valley near present-day Quitman, Mississippi, to the Pearl River valley "on the main wilderness road from Natchez to Nashville" near present-day Clinton, Mississippi. He was dismissed as Choctaw agent and replaced on 28 June 1814 by John McKee. He moved to St. Stephens where he became a valued member of the community and an active member of the Masonic Lodge #9, but he struggled as a businessman.

Lorenzo Dow (1777-1834), a native of Coventry, Tolland County, Connecticut, emigrated to Georgia and made his first trip to Mississippi Territory in May 1803. A rather colorful and eccentric itinerant Methodist preacher, he visited the Tensaw and Tombigbee settlements on several occasions while making his way between Georgia and Natchez (1803-12). Dow was the first protestant minister to preach in present-day Alabama, and he preached in several of the scattered settlements of early Alabama in 1803 and 1804 and perhaps on at least seven other times not recorded in his writings.

John H. Eaton (1790-1856), a native of North Carolina, served in the U.S. senate (1818-29) and became a political ally and personal friend of Andrew Jackson. He served as Jackson's secretary of war (1829-31) until his resignation on 7 April 1831 when Jackson's cabinet broke up over the "Peggy Eaton affair." He was appointed governor of Florida Territory in 1834 and later served as minister to Spain in 1836-40. Eaton and John Coffee served as U.S. commissioners and in September 1830 negotiated the Treaty of Dancing Rabbit Creek that led to the Choctaw removal from Mississippi.

Samuel A. Edmondson (c.1794–1869), a native of South Carolina, delivered Gaines' letters to Governor Willie Blount and General Andrew Jackson at Nashville in September 1813 reporting the massacre at Fort Mims and requesting protection for the lower Tombigbee settlements. He was appointed militia captain by William Wyatt Bibb, governor of Alabama Territory, on 29 March 1818. He later settled in Lowndes County, Mississippi.

Andrew Ellicott (1754–1820), a native of Solebury township, Bucks County, Pennsylvania, became nationally prominent as a surveyor and ended his career as a professor of mathematics at West Point. He served as a member of the Virginia surveying party for the Mason and Dixon Line, surveyed the southwestern boundary of New York, and surveyed and published the first map of the new "Federal City" in 1793. He surveyed "Ellicott's Line" in 1797–1800 for the southern boundary of the United States with Spanish Florida as provided for in the Treaty of San Lorenzo in 1795. Ellicott's line formed the southern boundary of Mississippi Territory with West Florida and followed the thirty-first degree line of north latitude from the Mississippi River east to the Apalachicola River.

Jonathan Emanuel (1798–1875), an English-born merchant and entrepreneur, emigrated to Mobile in the 1820s and became a prominent cotton broker and business and civic leader. He offered Gaines a partnership in his dry goods business in 1831, and they remained business associates for several years and lifelong friends. Emanuel served as president of the Mobile Insurance Company and was on the boards of several other businesses including the Alabama Life Insurance and Trust Company, the Bank of Mobile, and the Mobile and Ohio Railroad Company.

Thomas Flournoy (d. 24 July 1857), a native of North Carolina, succeeded James Wilkinson as a brigadier general and commander of the Seventh Military District with headquarters at New Orleans. He coordinated the defense of the lower Tombigbee and Tensaw settlements from Mobile during the Creek War of 1813–14, and he initially rejected Pushmataha's offer to raise forces in defense of Mississippi Territory. Although criticized for inaction and indecision, he operated with scarce sources and limited communications from the War Department.

Edmund Pendleton Gaines (1777–1849), a native of Culpepper County, Virginia, and older brother of George Strother Gaines, was a career soldier who entered the U.S. army in 1797 and reached the rank of major general before his death. He served as post commandant at Fort Stoddert (1804–07) and served in the War of 1812, the first Seminole War (1818), the Black Hawk War (1832), the Second Seminole War (1835–36), and the Mexican War (1846–48). His first wife was Frances Toulmin, daughter of Judge Harry Toulmin.

Young Gaines (1760–1829), a native of South Carolina, emigrated to the lower Tombigbee with his wife, Esther Lawrence Gaines, and children around 1790. He became wealthy in the Indian trade and a prominent landowner who acquired some 2,400 acres of land on the Tombigbee River and approximately 1,200 acres in present-day Perry County, Mississippi. He served as U.S. interpreter at the Treaty of Hoe Buckintoopa in 1803 when the Choctaw surrendered the land between the Tombigbee and Mobile Rivers and the Pascagoula River. His daughter, Ann Gaines (1795–1868), married George Strother Gaines in 1812.

Albert Gallatin (1761–1849), a native of Geneva, Switzerland, emigrated to the United States in 1780 and settled in Pennsylvania after the Revolutionary War. He served three consecutive terms in Congress (1795–1801) before his appointment as secretary of the treasury by Thomas Jefferson in 1801; he remained through James Madison's first term as president (1801–13)—the longest service in that office. Gaines visited Gallatin in New York City in 1831 and solicited his advice and assistance in marketing $3,500,000 in Alabama bonds to raise capital for three new state branch banks. Gallatin, president of the National Bank of New York (1831–39), introduced Gaines to business and social contacts that led to Alabama's first multimillion-dollar bond sale.

George Gibson (d. 29 September 1861), a native of Pennsylvania and career army officer, served as brigadier general and commissary general of subsistence in the War Department under several secretaries of war, including John H. Eaton and Lewis Cass. He was given responsibility for coordinating the removal of the Indians east of the Mississippi River and confirmed Gaines' appointment as superintendent of Choctaw removal in 1831. When the Jackson administration placed Indian removal under the U.S. army in 1832, Gibson notified Gaines of the decision to use military personnel. He was promoted to major general on 30 May 1848 for meritorious conduct for his service in the Mexican War.

Allen Glover (1770–1840), a successful planter and native of Edgefield District, South Carolina, emigrated to Demopolis, Marengo County, Alabama Territory, in 1819 with his family, slaves, and livestock. He purchased land from the French colonists and Gaines, and he and Gaines became close friends and business partners (1822–32). He became a wealthy and influential merchant and planter with more than 100 slaves before his death in 1840.

Homastubbee, a great medal chief of the Choctaw Nation, served as chief of the Northern District or Okla Tannap. He signed the treaties of Fort Adams (1801), Fort Confederation (1802), Hoe Buckintoopa (1803), and Mount Dexter (1805) that opened up lands in Mississippi Territory. At his death in 1809, his son, Mushulatubbee, succeeded him as district chief.

Hopia-skitteena or **Little Leader** (c.1752–1852), an important Choctaw subchief (captain), served in the War of 1812 and lived on the east bank of the Sucarnochee River near Narkeeta, Kemper County, Mississippi, in 1830. Described as a small man with a fiery temper and great courage, he was an outspoken opponent to removal to the west. Although he opposed removal, he signed the Treaty of Dancing Rabbit Creek on 27 September 1830, received a section of land on the Sucarnochee, and refused to emigrate to the west.

John Jones (c.1740–1843), a native of Virginia, was an Indian countryman and trader. He and his brother, Samuel Jones, settled near present-day Epes, Sumter County, Alabama, around 1780. Their log cabins were built near the site of the old French Fort Tombecbe on Jones' Bluff on the Tombigbee River. The brothers remained at Jones' Bluff through the Spanish occupation at Fort Confederation (1794–97), the operation of the Choctaw Trading House (1816–22) built by Gaines, and the private trading house operated by Glover and Gaines (c.1822–31).

Charles Juzan (1784–1846), a noted French Indian countryman, married a niece of Pushmataha and lived at Coonsha near present-day Lauderdale Springs, Lauderdale County, Mississippi. His home was located on the "Tennessee Road" between St. Stephens and the Natchez Trace and was a stopping place for travelers including Gaines on several occasions. He was a nephew of Pierre Juzan and operated several trading houses in the Choctaw country at Coonsha, Chunky, and Tuscahoma. One of his sons, also named Pierre Juzan, emerged as a Choctaw leader in Indian Territory.

William Rufus King (1786–1853), a native of Sampson County, North Carolina, served as U.S. congressman (1810–16) from North Carolina and emigrated to Alabama Territory in 1818. King served as U.S. senator from Alabama (1819–44, 1848–52), president pro tem of the U.S. senate (1836–41), and minister to France (1844–48). He supported Gaines' petitions for reimbursement in Congress and the development of the Mobile and Ohio Railroad. Elected as Franklin Pierce's vice president in 1852, he died of tuberculosis at King's Bend, Alabama, in 1853.

Cyrus Kingsbury (1786-1870), a Presbyterian missionary and native of Alstead, New Hampshire, entered the mission field for the American Board of Commissioners for Foreign Missions with the Cherokee in 1817. He moved to the Choctaw Nation the next year establishing the Elliot school on the Yalobusha River in the Western District in 1818 and the Mayhew school on Oktibbeha Creek in the Northern District in 1822. He emigrated to the Indian Territory in 1836 and continued his work among the Choctaw until his death in 1870.

Greenwood LeFlore (1800-1865), a mixed-blood, became the district chief of the Western District in 1826. He supported the missionary efforts of the Methodists and Presbyterians and became an advocate of Choctaw removal. He attempted to eliminate the system of district chiefs and consolidate the Choctaw under one chief, but his efforts brought about a power struggle with Mushulatubbee and Nitakechi (1826-30). Although he became an advocate of removal and signed the Treaty of Dancing Rabbit Creek in 1830, he remained in Mississippi, became a successful planter and slave owner, and served in the Mississippi senate (1841-44).

Francis Strother Lyon (1800-1882), a native of Stokes County, North Carolina, was Gaines' nephew and the son of James G. and Behethland (Gaines) Lyon. He emigrated to St. Stephens in 1817 where he lived with his uncle and studied law with William Crawford. Lyon served as secretary of the Alabama senate (1822-30), as state senator (1833-35, 1876-78) and representative (1861), as U.S. congressman (1836-40), and as a representative in the Confederate Congress (1862-65).

John Flood McGrew, a frontier leader and prominent landowner in the Tombigbee settlements, worked with Gaines and John McKee to promote an alliance with the Choctaw and Chickasaw against the Creeks in the Creek War of 1813-14. He was appointed to the five-member legislative council for Mississippi Territory in 1808.

John McKee (1771-1832), a native of Virginia, was appointed in 1792 by Governor William Blount (1749-1800) of the Southwest Territory to negotiate a boundary settlement with the Cherokee. He served as temporary agent to the Cherokee in 1794 and as Choctaw agent from 1799 until Silas Dinsmoor's appointment in 1802. McKee and Gaines negotiated a cession agreement with the Choctaw in December 1815 to locate a new federal trading house near the site of the old Spanish Fort Confederation. He replaced Dinsmoor in 1814 as Choctaw agent and resigned in 1821 to enter politics, serving three consecutive terms (1823-29) as U.S. congressman from the Tuscaloosa District. McKee's plantation, Hill of Hoath, was in present-day Boligee, Greene County, Alabama.

Thomas L. McKenney (1785–1859), a native of Maryland, was the last superintendent of Indian trade (1816–22) and became the first head of the Bureau of Indian Affairs (1824–30) when the bureau was established by Secretary of War John C. Calhoun in 1824. McKenney urged Gaines to remain as Choctaw factor when Gaines resigned in 1818, and he supervised the closing of the factory system after it was abolished by an act of Congress in May 1822. Although the factory system was eliminated, McKenney succeeded in establishing fifty-two Indian schools with an enrollment of 1,512 students before Andrew Jackson dismissed him from office in 1830.

Thomas Malone served as assistant factor at the Choctaw Trading House at St. Stephens and at Fort Confederation (1807–17). He was an early settler in Mississippi Territory and developed sizable land holdings in the lower Tombigbee River valley. He was also a member of the party that escorted Aaron Burr to Washington, D.C., in 1807 to stand trial for treason. Malone surveyed the lands ceded by the Choctaws for the trading house built by Gaines in 1816 near the site of Fort Confederation.

John Mason, a former president of the Bank of Columbia, served as superintendent of Indian trade under the secretary of war (1807–16) and expanded the influence of the factory system. He supported Gaines' relocation of the Choctaw Trading House from St. Stephens to a site near Fort Confederation in 1815–16. He resigned as superintendent to return to private business and was replaced by Thomas L. McKenney on 12 April 1816.

Samuel Mims, a wealthy Indian countryman, settled on Tensaw Lake and operated a ferry about a mile east on the Alabama River. His large frame house became a palisaded stockade, Fort Mims, following the Battle at Burnt Corn Creek when people feared the outbreak of an Indian war. It was the sight of a bloody carnage when destroyed by Creek Red Sticks on 30 August 1813. The destruction of Fort Mims led to an invasion of the Mississippi Territory by several thousand volunteer soldiers from neighboring states to fight the Creek War of 1813–14, and Gaines emerged as an important wartime leader of the lower Tombigbee and Tensaw settlements.

Mushulatubbee (c.1770–1838), a great medal chief and district chief of the Northern District (1809–30), lived on the "Tennessee Road" or "Big Trading Path" about four miles northwest of old Brooksville Station, Noxubee County, Mississippi. He signed the treaties of Fort Confederation (1816), Doak's Stand (1820), Washington (1825), and Dancing Rabbit Creek (1830). He supported the educational efforts of the missionaries, but he opposed their religious activities. He emigrated to the west and died of smallpox on 30 August 1838 near the Choctaw agency on the Arkansas River.

Molly Nail, a mixed-blood Choctaw, was married to Henry Nail, an Indian countryman and trader, who resided in Pushmataha's district. She served as an interpreter and was present at the Choctaw council in 1813 where Pushmataha urged his followers to ally with the white settlers in the Tombigbee and Tensaw settlements against the Creeks. She was also present at the treaty conference on Dancing Rabbit Creek near present-day Macon, Mississippi, in September 1830. One of her sons, Joel Nail (c.1794-1846), became a prominent chief in the Southern District, led a removal party to the west in 1831-32, and died near Fort Towson on 24 August 1846.

Nitakechi (c.1780-1845), a nephew of Pushmataha and a member of the 1824 Choctaw delegation to Washington, D.C., replaced John Garland in 1829 as chief of the Southern District. He signed the Treaty of Dancing Rabbit Creek in 1830 and led the Choctaw delegation that explored the new Choctaw lands west of the Mississippi River with Gaines in 1830-31. He emigrated west in 1832, and made his home at Horse Prairie southeast of present-day Hugo, Oklahoma. Nitakechi was reelected chief of Pushmataha District, Indian Territory, until his death in 1845.

Nicholas Perkins, a native of Virginia, emigrated to Tennessee and later to Washington County, Mississippi Territory. He served as register of the U.S. land office in Washington County (1806-08) and attorney general for the county and district of Washington (1808-09). He assisted with the capture of Aaron Burr in 1807 and escorted him to Richmond, Virginia, for his trial. Perkins later returned to Franklin, Tennessee, where Gaines visited him in 1815.

John Pitchlynn (c.1764-1835), an Indian countryman and trader, married into an important Choctaw family and served Gaines and the U.S. government as adviser, subagent, and interpreter. He lived near old Plymouth, Lowndes County, Mississippi, near the mouth of Oktibbeha Creek on the Tombigbee River. His first wife was Rhoda Folsom, daughter of Nathaniel Folsom, and on her death he married her cousin Sophia Folsom, daughter of Ebenezer Folsom. Their son, Peter Pitchlynn, led the rebirth of the Choctaw Nation in Indian Territory.

James Madison Porter (1793-1862), a Pennsylvania jurist and politician, was appointed secretary of war on 8 March 1843 by President John Tyler, but his nomination was rejected by the senate on 30 January 1844. Gaines met with Porter in 1843 to request reimbursement of his expenses for serving as Choctaw exploring agent and commissioner (1830-31) and as superintendent for Choctaw removal in 1831.

Puckshenubbee (c. 1739-1824), a great medal chief of the Choctaw Nation, served as chief of the Western District or Okla Falaya. He was involved in several treaty conferences and signed the treaties of Fort Adams (1801), Fort Confederation (1816), and Doak's Stand (1820). He joined Pushmataha and Mushulatubbee as a member of the 1824 Choctaw delegation to Washington, but died from injuries sustained in a fall at Maysville, Kentucky, on 13 October 1824, at the age of eighty-five.

Pushmataha (c. 1764–1824), a great medal chief of the Choctaw Nation, served as chief of the Southern District or Okla Hannali (c.1805–24). Noted for his oratory, he spoke at the "great council" in 1811 addressed by Tecumseh near old Brooksville Station, Mississippi, and rejected Tecumseh's war message. He journeyed to St. Stephens in September 1813 after learning of the destruction of Fort Mims and offered his services to Gaines and the people of the Tombigbee and Tensaw settlements. He led the first body of 135 Choctaw volunteers to St. Stephens, where he was commissioned a lieutenant colonel. Pushmataha died of pneumonia at Tennison's Hotel, Washington, D.C., on 24 December 1824 and was buried in the Congressional Cemetery.

Benjamin Reynolds (1788–1843), a native of Fayette County, Kentucky, served in both houses of the Tennessee legislature. He served as a captain of the 39th Tennessee regiment and was wounded at the Battle of Horseshoe Bend in 1814. Jackson appointed him as agent to the Chickasaw in 1830, and he led a sixteen-member exploring party that included Levi Colbert, Pitman Colbert, Henry Love, William D. King, and Elaptinkbahtubbe to the West in 1830–31.

James Robertson (1742–1814), a native of Virginia, was a co-founder of Nashville, Tennessee, and served as agent to the Chickasaw (1792–97, 1812–14) and as a treaty commissioner to the Chickasaw and Choctaw (1802–05). He and Silas Dinsmoor negotiated and signed the Treaty of Mount Dexter with the Choctaw in November 1805.

Harry Toulmin (1766–1823), a native of Taunton, Somersetshire, England, emigrated to Virginia in 1793, served as president of Transylvania University and later as Kentucky secretary of state. He was appointed Mississippi territorial judge by Thomas Jefferson in 1804 and became the first federal judge for the Tombigbee district. He led the Alabama opposition to the Mississippi request to establish the "natural boundary" of the Tombigbee and Mobile Rivers as the eastern boundary of the new state of Mississippi. Toulmin also played a major role in the constitutional convention of 1819 that framed the first constitution for the new state of Alabama.

Tandy Walker, an Indian countryman and trader, served as a government blacksmith in the Creek Nation and removed to the lower Tombigbee around 1800. He advised Gaines on Indian relations and resided in the West Bend area of the Tombigbee between Coffeeville and Fort Easley in present-day Clarke County, Alabama, prior to the War of 1812. He was seriously wounded in November 1813 while scouting near Burnt Corn Creek.

William Ward, a native of Kentucky, replaced John McKee as Choctaw agent in March 1821. The Choctaw accused him of misappropriating their annuities, exchanging whiskey for Choctaw property, and turning away land claimants or failing to register their land claims as provided for by the Treaty of Dancing Rabbit Creek. Despite his incompetence and intemperance, Ward's abuses of the Choctaw went uncorrected by the federal government.

Nathan Bryan Whitfield (1799–1868), a native of Lenoir County, North Carolina, served in both houses of the North Carolina legislature and reached the rank of major general in the state militia by 1835. He emigrated to Jefferson, Marengo County, Alabama, where he developed a plantation of over 4,000 acres by 1837 and purchased Gaines' property near Demopolis in 1842. He incorporated one of Gaines' log cabins into his classical Greek Revival home of Gaineswood, which he constructed between 1842 and 1861 and named in honor of Gaines by 1856.

Notes

INTRODUCTION (JAMES P. PATE)

1. George Strother Gaines, "Gaines' Reminiscences," *Alabama Historical Quarterly* 26 (Fall–Winter 1964): 140; Gaines to J. T. Gaines, Natchez, 12 April 1805, "Letters from George Strother Gaines Relating to Events in South Alabama, 1805–1814," *Transactions of the Alabama Historical Society, 1898–1899* 3 (1899): 185–86; Toulmin to Jefferson, Fort Stoddert, 25 February 1809, Clarence E. Carter and John Porter Bloom, eds., *The Territorial Papers of the United States, Territory of Mississippi, 1798–1817,* 27 vols. to date (Washington, D.C.: Government Printing Office, 1934–), 5:705 (hereafter cited as *Territorial Papers*).

2. *Territorial Papers,* 5:133–229; George Strother Gaines, "Notes on the Early Days of South Alabama," *Mobile Register,* 19 June–17 July 1872; "Reminiscences of Early Times in the Mississippi Territory [Second Series]," George S. Gaines Collection, 1784–1873, Alabama Department of Archives and History, Montgomery, Alabama; "Conversation with Geo. S. Gaines" and "2nd Conversation with Geo. S. Gaines Spring of 1848," Albert James Pickett Papers, 1799–1922, Alabama Department of Archives and History, Montgomery, Alabama.

3. Anthony Winston Dillard, "The Treaty of Dancing Rabbit Creek between the United States and the Choctaw Indians in 1830," *Transactions of the Alabama Historical Society, 1898–1899* 3 (1899): 99–106; Gaines to Dillard, Peachwood, 8 August 1857, Gaines Collection; "George S. Gaines to A. W. Dillard [in reference to the Dancing Rabbit Creek Indian Treaty], Peachwood, 8th Aug 1857," *Arrow Points* 11 (September 1925): 25–39; George S. Gaines, "Removal of the Choctaws," in *Dancing Rabbit Creek Treaty,* Historical and Patriotic Series No. 10, State Department of Archives and History (Birmingham: Birmingham Printing Company, 1928), 9–24. An important section of the original letter, more than three paragraphs, is printed out of sequence in the 1928 publication (see pp. 10–11).

4. Zella Armstrong, *Notable Southern Families,* 6 vols. in 3 (1918–33; reprint, Baltimore: Genealogical Publishing Co., 1974), 1 & 2:88–97; James W. Silver, *Edmund Pendleton Gaines: Frontier General* (Baton Rouge: Louisiana State Uni-

versity Press, 1949), 4–6; George J. Leftwich, "Colonel George Strother Gaines and Other Pioneers in Mississippi Territory," *Publications of the Mississippi Historical Society*, centenary ser., 1 (1904): 442–43.

5. "Gaines' Reminiscences," 139; Silver, *Edmund Pendleton Gaines*, 5–6; Leftwich, "Colonel George Strother Gaines," 443.

6. "Gaines' Reminiscences," 139–40, 147–48, 150; Records of the Choctaw Trading House, Office of Indian Trade, 1803–24, National Archives, Washington, D.C. (microfilm, 6 rolls), 1:37, 39–43, 47, 51, 101, 142, 166 (hereafter cited as CTH: Indian Trade); Secretary of Treasury to Turner and Chambers, Treasury Department, 27 July 1803, *Territorial Papers*, 5:227–35; Secretary of Treasury to Chambers, Treasury Department, 10 and 28 December 1804, ibid., 359, 369–70; Postmaster General to Seaman, [Washington, D.C.], 23 October 1804, ibid., 342.

7. [List of Goods Requested for 1816], in Gaines to Mason, 25 January 1816, Records of the Superintendent of Indian Trade, Choctaw Trading House, Indent Book, 1805–20, National Archives, Washington, D.C., p. 21 (hereafter cited as CTH: Indent Book); "Recd in George S. Gaines letter of April 1817 [List]," in Gaines to Mason, 14 April 1817, Chaktaw Trading House near Fort Confederation, ibid., 23–24; "A List of Articles wanted at the Chaktaw Trading House for one years trade commencing on the 1st October 1818," in Gaines to Mason, 13 June 1818, Chaktaw Trading House near Ft. Confederation, A. T. [Alabama Territory], ibid., 24–26.

8. "Bartered with Indians," 10 May 1814, CTH: Indian Trade, 5:13.

9. "Gaines' Reminiscences," 147–48; Gaines to J. T. Gaines, St. Stephens, M. T. [Mississippi Territory], 5 March 1809, "Letters from George Strother Gaines," 186–88; "Memorial to the Governor of West Florida," [Judge Toulmin, 21 February 1809], *Territorial Papers*, 5:710; Governor of West Florida to Toulmin, Panzacola, 28 February 1809, ibid., 711; Gaines to Mason, Indian Trade Office, Georgetown, 17 June 1809, ibid., 748; Ora Brooks Peake, *A History of the United States Indian Factory System, 1795–1822* (Greeley, Colo.: Sage Books, 1954), 156.

10. "Conversation with Geo. S. Gaines," Pickett Papers, 24–29; Silver, *Edmund Pendleton Gaines*, 12–17. Also see Albert James Pickett, *History of Alabama and Incidentally of Georgia and Mississippi, from the Earliest Period* (1851; reprint, Birmingham: Birmingham Book and Magazine Co., 1962), 124–25, 518.

11. "Gaines' Reminiscences," 149, 154–56; "2nd Conversation with Geo. S. Gaines," Pickett Papers, 3–6; Secretary of War to E. P. Gaines, 31 July 1807, *Territorial Papers*, 5:558; Silver, *Edmund Pendleton Gaines*, 19–20.

12. Armstrong, *Notable Southern Families*, 1 & 2:88–96; Calvin E. Sutherd, *A Compilation of Gaines Family Data with Special Emphasis on the Lineage of William and Isabella (Pendleton) Gaines* (1969; reprint, Fort Lauderdale: n.p., 1972), 328–33; Ben and Jean Strickland, comps., *Washington County, Mississippi Territory, 1803–1816 Tax Rolls* (1980; reprint, Moss Point, Miss.: n.p., 1987), 5, 8, 14, 30, 35, 61, 72; George Strother Gaines Family Genealogy Materials, Mrs. Chebie Gaines Bateman, Columbus, Mississippi (hereafter cited as Bateman:

Gaines Family Genealogy); Ben and Jean Strickland, comps., *Records of Perry County, Mississippi: 1820–1830 Tax Records, Birth and Death Schedules 1822–1823* (n.p., 1979), 27; Jean Strickland and Patricia N. Edwards, comps., *Who Lived Where: Perry County, Mississippi Book of Original Entry* (n.p., 1992), 12, 13, 14; Ben and Jean Strickland, comps., *Records of Perry County, Mississippi: Tax Rolls 1831–1840* (n.p., 1979), 4, 12, 29, 39, 49.

13. "Gaines' Reminiscences," 160, 175–77; Sutherd, *Gaines Family,* 329–33. The other children were Helen (1819–97), James J. (1821–ca. 1876), Mary Amelia (1823–93), Francis Young (1825–73), Henry Lawrence (1827–?), Abner Strother (1832–1905), and Jonathan Emanuel (1835–ca. 1884). George Washington Gaines died in 1853.

14. "Gaines' Reminiscences," 176–77; Secretary of War to Gaines, War Department, 14 August 1815, *Territorial Papers,* 4:548; Dinsmoor to Crawford, 4 August 1813, ibid., 392; Aloysius Plaisance, "The Choctaw Trading House, 1803–1822," *Alabama Historical Quarterly* 16 (Fall–Winter 1954): 414–15.

15. "Gaines' Reminiscences," 176–78; "The Convention for the Cession of the use of a site for a trading house and military post," Chaktaw Agency, 11–16 December 1815, Records of the Office of the Secretary of War Relating to Indian Affairs, Letters Received, National Archives, Washington, D.C. (microfilm, 6 rolls), 1:1172–78; Gaines to Mason, Chaktaw Trading House, St. Stephens, 25 January 1816, Records of the Superintendent of Indian Trade, 1806–1824, Letters Received, National Archives, Washington D.C. (microfilm, 1 roll), 320–22 (hereafter cited as Letters Received: Indian Trade); Gaines to Mason, Chaktaw Trading House, James' Spring's near Ft. Confederation, 10 June 1816, ibid., 323–24; Receipt to Adam James, Chaktaw Trading House, 20 March 1816, Records of the Office Indian Trade, Choctaw Factory, Miscellaneous Accounts, 1803–25, National Archives, Washington, D.C. (hereafter cited as Choctaw Factory: Miscellaneous Accounts).

16. "Gaines' Reminiscences," 178; "Receipt . . . Chacktaw Trading House to John Cox Porter . . . $75 in full for the above account," 30 December 1816, CTH: Indian Trade, 3:24; Gaines to Mason, 25 January 1816, Chaktaw Trading House, St. Stephens, Letters Received: Indian Trade, 320–22; Gaines to Mason, Chaktaw Trading House, James' Spring's near Ft. Confederation, 10 June 1816, ibid., 323–24; "The annexed plat represents a tract of land ceded by the chiefs of the Chaktaw nation for the factory and military post at James Springs near Fort Confederation," in Gaines to Mason, Chaktaw Trading House, near old Fort Confederation, 25 July 1816, Letters Received: Indian Trade, 327.

17. "Gaines' Reminiscences," 178; Gaines to Mason, Chaktaw Trading House, James' Spring's near Ft. Confederation, 10 June 1816, Letters Received: Indian Trade, 323–24; "Inventory of contingent articles on hand at the Chacktaw Trading House 30th June 1817 estimated at their present value," in Gaines to McKenney, Chaktaw Trading House near Ft. Confederation, A. T., 30 June 1817, Choctaw Factory: Miscellaneous Accounts; Plaisance, "The Choctaw Trading House," 418.

Indian countrymen were white men who lived among the Indians with their Indian wives and offsprings.

18. Postmaster General to Lyon, 29 October 1816, *Territorial Papers*, 4:707; "An a/c of the contingent expenses of the Chaktaw Trading House the qr year ending 30th June 1817," in Gaines to Mason, Chaktaw Trading House, 30 June 1817, Choctaw Factory: Miscellaneous Accounts; Armstrong, *Notable Southern Families*, 1 & 2:89.

19. "Gaines' Reminiscences," 179-80; McKee to Crawford, Chaktaw Agency, 1 July 1816, Letters Received: Indian Trade, 1191-93; McKee to Crawford, Mount [Lawrence], Chaktaw Trading House, 13 July 1816, ibid., 1195; Treaty with the Choctaws, Choctaw Trading House, 24 October 1816, *American State Papers: Documents, Legislative and Executive,* 38 vols. (Washington, D.C.: Gales & Seaton, 1832-61), *Indian Affairs,* 2 vols., 2:95 (hereafter cited as *ASP: Indian Affairs*).

20. "Gaines' Reminiscences," 184-86, 188-89; Gaines to J. T. Gaines, St. Stephens, M. T., 8 February 1814, "Letters from George Strother Gaines," 188-89; Winston Smith, "Early History of Demopolis," *Alabama Review* 18 (April 1965): 85-86; Winston Smith, *Days of Exile: The Story of the Vine and Olive Colony in Alabama* (Tuscaloosa: W. B. Drake & Sons, 1967), 23-30, 35-39; Gaius Whitfield, "The French Grant in Alabama: A History of the Founding of Demopolis," *Transactions of the Alabama Historical Society, 1899-1903* 4 (1901): 325-32, 340; Thomas W. Martin, *French Military Adventurers in Alabama, 1818-1828* (Birmingham: Birmingham Publishing Company, 1949), 18-20.

21. "Gaines' Reminiscences," 186-87; Gaines to McKenney, Chaktaw Trading House, 30 September 1819, Letters Received: Indian Trade, 354-56; Everett to McKenney, Chaktaw Trading House, 16 December 1819, ibid., 358; McKenney to Gaines, Office of Indian Trade, 15 August 1818, *Territorial Papers*, 18:399; McKenney to Gaines, Office of Indian Trade, Georgetown, 12 October 1818, ibid., 435; McKenney to Hersey, Office of Indian Trade, Georgetown, 13 October 1819, ibid., 713-17.

22. "Gaines' Reminiscences," 188-90, 193-98; "Abstract of Property of various kinds received by Henry Randall agent for winding up the concerns of the Chaktaw Factory as per his receipts to John Hersey late factor dated 1st Oct. 1822," Letters Received: Indian Trade, 429; Smith, "Early History of Demopolis," 87-88; Gaines to Pickett, Spring Hill, 27 July 1847, Pickett Papers.

23. Sutherd, *Gaines Family,* 329-30; Bateman: Gaines Family Genealogy; Pauline Jones Gandrud, comp., *Alabama Records,* vol. 29, *Marengo County Wills and Estates, Deeds, Tombstone Inscriptions, Marriages, Chancery Records* (Easley, S.C.: Southern Historical Press, 1979), 28; Pauline Jones Gandrud, comp., *Alabama Records,* vol. 39, *Marengo County, Marriages, Deeds, Wills, Rev. Pensions, 1812 Pensions, Miscellaneous* (Easley, S.C.: Southern Historical Press, 1980), 98.

24. "Gaines' Reminiscences," 180-81; William H. Brantley, *Three Capitals of Alabama: St. Stephens, Huntsville, and Cahawba* (Boston: Merrymount Press,

1947), 165-66, 174-75, 193-94; William Warren Rogers et al., *Alabama: The History of a Deep South State* (Tuscaloosa: University of Alabama Press, 1994), 82-87.

25. "Gaines' Reminiscences," 198-201; "Treaty with the Choctaw, 1830," in Charles J. Kappler, comp. and ed., *Indian Affairs, Laws and Treaties*, 7 vols. (Washington, D.C.: Government Printing Office, 1904-79), 2:310-19; Dillard, "Treaty of Dancing Rabbit Creek," 100-106; Coffee to Jackson, Choctaw Agency, 29 September 1830, John Spencer Bassett, ed., *The Correspondence of Andrew Jackson*, 6 vols. (1926-35; reprint, New York: Kraus Reprint Co., 1969), 4:180; Henry Sale Halbert, "The Story of the Treaty of Dancing Rabbit," *Publications of the Mississippi Historical Society* 6 (1902): 375-402.

26. Jackson to Coffee, Washington, 19 January 1831, Bassett, ed., *Correspondence of Andrew Jackson*, 4:224; Gaines to Dillard, Peachwood, 8 August 1857, Gaines Collection; "Gaines' Reminiscences," 200-202.

27. Gaines to Dillard, Peachwood, 8 August 1857, Gaines Collection; "Gaines' Reminiscences," 202-3; Grant Foreman, *Indian Removal: The Emigration of the Five Civilized Tribes of Indians* (1932; new ed., 1953; Norman: University of Oklahoma Press, 1972), 32 n. 5, 33; Arthur H. DeRosier, Jr., *The Removal of the Choctaw Indians* (Knoxville: University of Tennessee Press, 1970), 133, 134 n. 18.

28. Gaines to Dillard, Peachwood, 8 August 1857, Gaines Collection; "Gaines' Reminiscences," 203-9; James L. Dawson, "Report of J. L. Dawson on His Escort of Choctaw and Chickasaw Delegates in Indian Territory, Dec. 1830-Jan. 1831," in James Henry Gardner, "The Lost Captain: J. L. Dawson of Old Fort Gibson," *Chronicles of Oklahoma* 21 (September 1943): 241-49; Foreman, *Indian Removal*, 33-38. It appears that Gaines Creek of the Canadian River in Pittsburg County, Oklahoma, was named in honor of Gaines, and Gaines County of the Choctaw Nation, Indian Territory, was also named for their old factor. See Muriel H. Wright, "Organizations of Counties in the Chickasaw and Choctaw Nations," *Chronicles of Oklahoma* 8 (September 1930): 319-20.

29. Gaines to Dillard, Peachwood, 8 August 1857, Gaines Collection; "Gaines' Reminiscences," 209-13; "Indian Delegation," *Mobile Commercial Register*, 7 March 1831; Gaines and Reynolds to Eaton, [Washington, A. T.], 7 February 1831, Records of the Bureau of Indian Affairs, Office of the Commissary General of Subsistence, Letters Received 1831-36, National Archives, Washington, D.C.

30. Gaines to Dillard, Peachwood, 8 August 1857, Gaines Collection; Bertram Wallace Korn, *The Jews of Mobile, Alabama, 1763-1841* (Cincinnati: Hebrew Union College Press, 1970), 37.

31. Gaines to Dillard, Peachwood, 8 August 1857, Gaines Collection; "Gaines' Reminiscences," 213-14; Foreman, *Indian Removal*, 44-47; Carolyn Thomas Foreman, "The Armstrongs of Indian Territory," *Chronicles of Oklahoma* 30 (Summer 1952): 294-95; Donald B. Cole, *The Presidency of Andrew Jackson* (Lawrence: University Press of Kansas, 1993), 34-39, 83-86.

32. Gaines to Dillard, Peachwood, 8 August 1857, Gaines Collection; "Gaines'

Reminiscences," 214-15; "Choctaw Emigration," *Mobile Commercial Register,* 12 November 1831; Foreman, *Indian Removal,* 47-48; DeRosier, *Removal of the Choctaw,* 137-41; Muriel H. Wright, "The Removal of the Choctaws to Indian Territory," *Chronicles of Oklahoma* 6 (June 1928): 111-14.

33. Gaines to Dillard, Peachwood, 8 August 1857, Gaines Collection; "Gaines' Reminiscences," 215; "Choctaw Emigration," *Mobile Commercial Register,* 12 November, 24 December 1831; Foreman, *Indian Removal,* 49-68; DeRosier, *Removal of the Choctaw,* 142-47; Wright, "Removal of the Choctaws," 114-19.

34. "Choctaw Emigration," *Mobile Commercial Register,* 24 December 1831; Gaines to Dillard, Peachwood, 8 August 1857, Gaines Collection.

35. Gaines to Dillard, Peachwood, 8 August 1857, Gaines Collection; Foreman, *Indian Removal,* 90; DeRosier, *Removal of the Choctaw,* 148-49; Jesse O. McKee and Jon A. Schlenker, *The Choctaws: Cultural Evolution of a Native American Tribe* (Jackson: University Press of Mississippi, 1980), 78; Gibson to Gaines, [Washington, D.C.], 27 April 1832, Records of the Bureau of Indian Affairs, Officer of the Commissary General of Subsistence, Letters Sent 1830-36, National Archives, Washington, D.C.

36. Gaines to Dillard, Peachwood, 8 August 1857; "Gaines' Reminiscences," 217-18; William H. Brantley, *Banking in Alabama,* 2 vols. (Birmingham: Birmingham Printing Company, 1961-67), 1:253-58, 265.

37. Gaines to Dillard, Peachwood, 8 August 1857; "Gaines' Reminiscences," 218-19.

38. Gaines to Dillard, Peachwood, 8 August 1857; "Gaines' Reminiscences," 219.

39. "Gaines' Reminiscences," 219-23; Brantley, *Banking in Alabama,* 1:265-68; Raymond Walters, Jr., *Albert Gallatin: Jeffersonian Financier and Diplomat* (New York: Macmillan, 1957), 347.

40. Brantley, *Banking in Alabama,* 1:268-73, 465 n. 3.

41. Ibid., 269-70, 296-99, 316-17; "Abstract of Commissioners' Report on the Branch Bank of the State of Alabama at Mobile," 1 October 1834, ibid., 373-74; "Report on the Branch of the Bank of the State of Alabama at Mobile," 5 November 1834, ibid., 374-75; "Report of the President and Cashier of the Branch of the Bank of the State of Alabama at Mobile," 7 November 1835, ibid., 390-94.

42. Caldwell Delaney, ed., *Craighead's Mobile: Being Furtive Writings of Erwin S. Craighead and Frank Craighead* (Mobile: The Haunted Bookstore, 1968), 16, 189; Mary Morgan Ward Glass, ed., *Connecticut Yankee in Early Alabama: Juliet Bestor Coleman, 1833-1850,* National Society of the Colonial Dames of America in the State of Alabama (n.p., 1980), 38; Thomas L. McKenney and James Hall, *The Indian Tribes of North America; With Biographical Sketches and Anecdotes of the Principal Chiefs,* 3 vols. (vol. 1, Philadelphia: Edward C. Biddle, 1837; vols. 2 and 3, Philadelphia: Daniel Rice & James G. Clark, 1842-44), 3:[sub-

scription page]; P. Catlin to F. Catlin, Great Bend, Pennsylvania, 1 January 1835, in Marjorie Catlin Roehm, *The Letters of George Catlin and His Family: A Chronicle of the American West* (Berkeley: University of California Press, 1966), 75–76, 81; Marvin C. Ross, ed., *George Catlin: Episodes from "Life among the Indians" and "Last Rambles"* (Norman: University of Oklahoma, 1959), xix; *Alabama Portraits Prior to 1870,* National Society of the Colonial Dames of America in the State of Alabama (Mobile: Gill Printing and Stationary Co., 1969), 401–2; Thomas McAdory Owens, *History of Alabama and Dictionary of Alabama Biography,* 4 vols. (Chicago: S. J. Clarke Publishing Company, 1921), 2:1005.

43. Brantley, *Banking in Alabama,* 1:285, 288, 304, 318, 323–25, 330–37, 379, 409; Minute Book, 1833–36, Branch Bank of the State of Alabama in Mobile, Alabama Department of Archives and History, Montgomery, Alabama, 8off. (hereafter cited as Branch Bank: Minute Book); Branch Bank: Minute Book, 1836–41, pp. 240–62.

44. Brantley, *Banking in Alabama,* 1:330–40, 355–58, 2:26, 34.

45. "Gaines' Reminiscences," 223–24; Branch Bank: Minute Book, 1836–41, pp. 262; Brantley, *Banking in Alabama,* 2:75; Kane to President of the Senate, Mobile, 26 November 1838, ibid., 306.

46. "Gaines' Reminiscences," 223–24; William Garrett, *Reminiscences of Public Men in Alabama, for Thirty Years* (Atlanta: Plantation Publishing Company's Press, 1872), 79.

47. "A List of the Liabilities of the President & Directors of the Branch Bank of the State of Alabama at Mobile on the 1st November 1835," Brantley, *Banking in Alabama,* 1:393; "Report of Commissioners Garrow and Goldthwaite on the Branch of the Bank of the State of Alabama at Mobile," 21 November 1835, ibid., 403; "Abstract of Report of the Commissioners to Examine the Branch of the Bank of the State of Alabama at Mobile [7 November 1836]," ibid., 420; "Statement of Liabilities of Directors, Mobile Branch Bank [19 November 1838]," ibid., 319. Henry Lazarus named his first son George Gaines Lazarus, born 23 July 1836 in Philadelphia, in honor of his former employer.

48. "Gaines' Reminiscences," 224; *Dictionary of American Biography,* 11 vols. (subscription ed.) (New York: Scribner, 1946–58), 8:94–95.

49. "Gaines' Reminiscences," 224–28; Ben Perley Poore, *Perley's Reminiscences of Sixty Years in the National Metropolis,* 2 vols. (Philadelphia: Hubbard Brothers Publishers, 1886), 1:482–83; Robert M. Kvasnicka and Herman J. Viola, eds., *The Commissioners of Indian Affairs, 1824–1977* (Lincoln: University of Nebraska Press, 1979), 23–27.

50. Records of the Bureau of Indian Affairs, Records of the Commission of Claiborne, Graves, Tyler, Gaines, and Rush, Journals of Proceedings, 1842–45, 8 vols., National Archives, Washington, D.C., 1:27ff., 150–52 (hereafter cited as Journals of Proceedings: Indian Affairs); ibid., vol. 3: 21 July 1843–30 April 1844; Clara Sue Kidwell, *Choctaws and Missionaries in Mississippi, 1818–1918* (Nor-

man: University of Oklahoma Press, 1995), 167–68; Mary Elizabeth Young, *Redskins, Ruffleshirts, and Rednecks: Indian Allotments in Alabama and Mississippi, 1830–1850* (Norman: University of Oklahoma Press, 1961), 51–64.

51. [George S. Gaines Resolutions], 30 April 1844, Louisville, Mississippi, Journals of Proceedings: Indian Affairs, vol. 3; [Final Commission Report], 17 June 1845, [Washington, D.C.], ibid., 4:1–163; Kidwell, *Choctaws and Missionaries*, 168–69; Young, *Redskins, Ruffleshirts, and Rednecks*, 64–65.

52. Gaines to Pickett, Spring Hill, 27 July, 28 September 1847, Pickett Papers. Pickett's marginal note on the first page of his first "Conversation" with Gaines reads, "Notes taken from the lips of Geo. S. Gaines at his home at Spring Hill near Mobile."

53. Robert W. Johannsen, *Stephen A. Douglas* (New York: Oxford University Press, 1973), 310–13; Peter Joseph Hamilton, *Mobile under Five Flags: The Story of the River Basin and Coast about Mobile from the Earliest Times to the Present* (Mobile: Gill Printing Co., 1913), 248–51; Harriet E. Amos, *Cotton City: Urban Development in Antebellum Mobile* (University: University of Alabama Press, 1985), 196–203; Grace Lewis Miller, "The Mobile and Ohio Railroad in Ante Bellum Times," *Alabama Historical Quarterly* 7 (Spring 1945): 37–57; Robert S. Cotterill, "Southern Railroads, 1850–1860," *Mississippi Valley Historical Review* 10 (March 1924): 396–400; Leftwich, "Colonel George Strother Gaines," 454; Owens, *History of Alabama*, 2:1015.

54. Gayle to Webster, Mobile, Alabama, 8 September 1850, Records of the Secretary of State, Letters Received, National Archives, Washington, D.C.; Grant Foreman, *The Five Civilized Tribes* (Norman: University of Oklahoma Press, 1934), 75.

55. U.S. Bureau of the Census, *Fourth Census* [1820; Washington County, Ala.]; ibid., [1820; Perry County, Miss.], 98; *Fifth Census* [1830; Marengo County, Ala.], 428; *Sixth Census* [1840; Mobile County, Ala.], 91; *Seventh Census* [Perry County, Miss.], 432; *Seventh Census: Slave Schedule* [Perry County, Miss.], 461 (preceding census information all found in microfilm at Alabama Department of Archives and History, Montgomery, and the Mississippi Department of Archives and History, Jackson); *Returns of the Census of Perry County by the Sheriff of Perry County for the Year AD 1853*, Mississippi Territorial and State Census Records, Record Group 28 (microfilm copy), Mississippi Department of Archives and History, Jackson, Mississippi, roll 547, p. 2; George Stark Gaines to [Farrell], 2 August 1947, Bateman: Gaines Family Genealogy; Strickland and Strickland, comps., *Records of Perry County: 1820–1830 Tax Records*, 38; Ben and Jean Strickland, comps., *Records of Perry County, Mississippi: 1841–1847 Tax Rolls, 1845 & 1853 State Census* (n.p., 1982), 26, 43, 52, 61.

56. Gaines to Dillard, 8 August 1857, Gaines Collection; Jean and Ben Strickland, comps., *Records of Wayne County, Mississippi: State Census 1816, 1820, 1841, 1845, 1853, 1866* (Milton, Fla.: n.p., 1981), 43; Gaines, Coles & Co., *Catalogue of Peachwood Nurseries, State Line, Wayne County, Mississippi* (Mobile:

Daily Register Steam Print, 1887); Willis Brewer, *Alabama: Her History, Resources, War Record, and Public Men, from 1540–1872* (Montgomery: Barrett & Brown, 1872), 393–94; Leftwich, "Colonel George Strother Gaines," 454; *Eighth Census* [1860; Wayne County, Miss.], Free Population Schedule and Slave Population Schedule.

57. Gaines to Dillard, Peachwood, 8 August 1857, Gaines Collection; Journal of the House of Representatives of the State of Mississippi (microfilm, 27 rolls), Mississippi Department of Archives and History, Jackson, Mississippi, roll 17 (1861–63), pp. 1672ff.; *Eastern Clarion* [Paulding, Miss.], 28 June 1861, Works Progress Administration, Wayne County, Mississippi, Mississippi Department of Archives and Mississippi, Jackson, Mississippi (hereafter cited as WPA: Wayne County); "Civil War," ibid.

58. *Eastern Clarion* [Paulding, Miss.], 15 October 1861, WPA: Wayne County; "Civil War," ibid.; J. E. Gaines to [Abner S. Gaines], Peachwood, 7 September 1863, Bateman: Gaines Family Genealogy; Sutherd, *Gaines Family*, 332; Owens, *History of Alabama*, 3:628.

59. *Ninth Census* [1870; Wayne County, Miss.; Township Six], 2; Jean Strickland and Patricia N. Edwards, comps., *Wayne County, Mississippi, 1831–1844 Tax Rolls and Agricultural Census* (n.p., 1991), 109, 145; *Catalogue of Peachwood Nurseries.*

60. While preparing this introduction I benefited from the assistance of Mrs. Chebie Gaines Bateman, great-granddaughter of George Strother Gaines, who provided access to her Gaines genealogical materials, and Professor David M. Taylor of the University of West Alabama, who read this introduction and made several helpful suggestions for its improvement.

INTRODUCTION FROM THE *MOBILE REGISTER*, JUNE 19, 1872

1. *Mobile Register*, 19 June 1872. The first installment was titled "Notes on the Early Days of South Alabama," and the next four installments (i.e., 27 June and 3, 10, 17 July 1872) were issued with the title "Reminiscences of Early Times in the Mississippi Territory." These five installments are referred to as the "first series."

2. Percy Walker (1812–80) was a lawyer, state legislator, and U.S. congressman from Mobile. The Franklin Society served as a cultural center for Mobile, and its meetings featured discussions of literary and scientific subjects, with lectures by distinguished men "from distant parts." According to a correspondent, "J. S.," writing for the *New Orleans Observer* in 1835, the society had a reading room with a "good" library and had started an archeological collection. Delaney, ed., *Craighead's Mobile*, 49.

3. The manuscript copy of the "first series" has been lost or destroyed.

4. Mobile was seized from British control by Bernardo de Galvez, Spanish governor and military commander of Louisiana, on 14 March 1780 and remained a

Spanish port until its surrender to General James Wilkinson on 15 April 1813. Peter J. Hamilton, *Colonial Mobile,* ed. Charles G. Summersell (1897; reprint, University: University of Alabama Press, 1976), 315, 409–13.

5. Mississippi Territory was organized by the federal government in 1798, with Winthrop Sargent (1753–1820), a B.A. and M.A. graduate of Harvard College and native of Gloucester, Massachusetts, appointed territorial governor (1798–1801) by President John Adams. *Territorial Papers,* 5:18–22, 27–29.

6. Following the Revolutionary War, Gaines' father, Captain James Gaines, moved his family from Culpepper County, Virginia, to Surry County, North Carolina, which was later divided into two counties, Surry and Stokes. The youngest three children of the twelve born to his second wife, Elizabeth Strother, were born in North Carolina: George Strother, Patsey, and Sarah. Armstrong, *Notable Southern Families,* 1 & 2:88–89.

7. Gaines was appointed assistant factor in 1805 and factor in 1807, replacing Joseph Chambers of Salisbury, North Carolina, who was appointed factor of the Choctaw factory known as the Choctaw Trading House in 1802. Plaisance, "The Choctaw Trading House," 395–96.

8. Marshall J. D. Baldwyn was responsible for planning and pushing forward the building of the Mobile and Ohio Railroad. Amos, *Cotton City,* 196.

9. Gaines served as president of the Mobile branch of the State Bank of Alabama from 1832 through 1838, and played an important role in promoting the Mobile and Ohio Railroad and raising money for its construction in Alabama and Mississippi. Brantley, *Banking in Alabama,* 1:285, 304, 379, 409 and 2:34; Hamilton, *Mobile under Five Flags,* 248–51.

NOTES ON THE EARLY DAYS OF SOUTH ALABAMA

1. Gaines started dictating his "Reminiscences" to his friend and business partner Albert C. Coles in the summer of 1871 at the urging of his friend Percy Walker, who deposited the transcripts with the Franklin Society in Mobile in 1872. See Leftwich, "Colonel George Strother Gaines," 443 nn. 2, 3. The first installment appeared in the 19 June 1872 issue of the *Mobile Register* as "Notes on the Early Days of South Alabama."

2. The factory system was started during President George Washington's administration by Secretary of War Henry Knox in 1795, with the Creek factory at Coleraine on St. Mary's River, Georgia, and the Cherokee factory at Tellico Block House, Hiwassee, Tennessee. Thomas Jefferson's administration added four factories, including the Choctaw factory, in 1802 under Secretary of War Henry Dearborn. Plaisance, "The Choctaw Trading House," 393; Peake, *History of the United States Indian Factory System,* 13–14; and Francis Paul Prucha, *American Indian Policy in the Formative Years: The Indian Trade and Intercourse Acts, 1790–1834* (Lincoln: University of Nebraska Press, 1962), 46, 84–87, 214–15.

3. The correct spelling of "Fort Stoddart" is Stoddert, although many sources

spell it Stoddart or Stoddard. Established in July 1799 at Ward's Bluff (present-day Mount Vernon, Alabama) on the Tombigbee River, the fort was named for Benjamin Stoddert, who was the first secretary of the navy and acting secretary of war when the post was established near the new American boundary with Spanish Florida. Francis Paul Prucha, *The Sword of the Republic: The United States Army on the Frontier, 1783–1846* (New York: Macmillan, 1969), 56; Jack D. L. Holmes, ed., "Fort Stoddart in 1799: Seven Letters of Captain Bartholomew," *Alabama Historical Quarterly* 26 (Fall–Winter 1964): 231–52.

4. Silas Dinsmoor (Dinsmore), a native of New Hampshire and graduate of Dartmouth College, was appointed U.S. agent to the Choctaw on March 12, 1802. His name is spelled Dinsmoor in official correspondence with the War Department. *Territorial Papers,* 5:146–49, 154, 189, 190, 214, 624, 675–78, 730, 739, 747; Kappler, comp., *Indian Affairs, Laws and Treaties,* 2:87.

5. James Robertson (1742–1814), a native of Virginia, was a cofounder of Nashville, Tennessee, and served as agent to the Chickasaw (1792–97; 1812–14) and as a commissioner to the Chickasaw and Choctaw (1802–5). Robert S. Cotterill, *The Southern Indians: The Story of the Civilized Tribes before Removal* (Norman: University of Oklahoma Press, 1954), 92, 120, 141, 146, 176, 190; Harriette Simpson Arnow, *Seedtime on the Cumberland* (1960; reprint, Lexington: University of Kentucky Press, 1983), 211–17.

6. San Esteban de Tombecbé (or St. Etienne), located on Hoe Buckintoopa Bluff north of Mobile and north of Ellicott's Line, was evacuated by the Spanish on 5 February 1799. *Territorial Papers,* 5:363; Prucha, *The Sword of the Republic,* 56.

7. James Robertson and Silas Dinsmoor negotiated and signed the Treaty of Mount Dexter with the Choctaw on 16 November 1805. One authority places the site of the Mount Dexter near Starnes' Ferry, a crossing on the Noxubee River near Macon, Mississippi. Kappler, comp., *Indian Affairs, Laws and Treaties,* 2:87–88; William A. Love, "Historic Localities on Noxubee River," *Publications of the Mississippi Historical Society* 9 (1906): 320.

8. Great medal chiefs were the principal chiefs of each nation, and they received medals as a sign of office. The French, Spanish, English, and Americans gave silver medals with the head of the reigning monarch (or president) (i.e., Louis XIV, Charles III, George III, or George Washington) to those chiefs who swore allegiance to their sovereign or nation. The medals were generally solid silver and cast in two or three sizes to recognize the most important chiefs, captains, or warriors (i.e., great medal chief or small medal chief). The Choctaw Nation was generally divided into three districts—Northern, Southern, and Western—by the early nineteenth century. Homastubbee was chief of the Northern District, or Okla Tannap, Pushmataha was chief of the Southern District, or Okla Hannali, and Puckshenubbee was chief of the Western District, or Okla Falaya. Herman J. Viola, *The Indian Legacy of Charles Bird King* (Washington, D.C.: Smithsonian Institution Press, 1976), 28; Richard White, *The Roots of Dependency: Subsistence, Environment,*

and Social Change among the Choctaws, Pawnees, and Navajos (Lincoln: University of Nebraska, 1983), 37.

9. Andrew Ellicott (1754–1820), a surveyor and mathematician from Bucks County, Pennsylvania, surveyed the southern boundary of the United States with Spanish Florida between 1797 and 1800, as provided for in Article II of the Treaty of San Lorenzo in 1795. "Ellicott's line" followed "the thirty first degree of latitude North of the Equator" from the Mississippi River east "to the middle of the River Apalachicola." Samuel Flagg Bemis, *Pinckney's Treaty: America's Advantage from Europe's Distress, 1783–1800* (1926; rev. ed., New Haven: Yale University Press, 1960), 294, 345; Andrew Ellicott, *The Journal of Andrew Ellicott: Late Commissioner on Behalf of the United States* (1803; reprint, Chicago: Quadrangle Books, 1962), 177–238.

10. "Mimms" was Samuel Mims, an Indian countryman who operated a ferry on the Alabama, and the "Lingers" were probably Linders, descendants of John Linder, whom Pickett places in the Tensaw in the 1790s. William and John Pierce were New Englanders, and Pickett gives John Pierce credit for starting the first "American school" in Alabama. Pickett, *History of Alabama,* 416–17, 461, 464, 469, 510.

11. Sampson, Hiram, and John Munger, John Flood McGrew, George Brewer, Josiah Bullock, James Caller, Thomas Bassett, and Jesse, John, and William Womack (Wamack) signed a "Petition to the President by Inhabitants of Washington District [1804]" asking that their rights as citizens be protected and recommending the appointment of "Rodominck H. Gillmer" as judge for Washington District of Mississippi Territory. *Territorial Papers,* 5:353–54.

12. Harry Toulmin (1766–1824), a native of Taunton, Somersetshire, England, immigrated to Virginia in 1793, served as president of Transylvania University and later as Kentucky secretary of state, and was appointed territorial judge by Thomas Jefferson in 1804. Ibid., 262, 320–22.

13. Young Gaines was an early settler who became wealthy in the Indian trade and acquired a Spanish land grant east of the Tombigbee River. "Conversation with George S. Gaines," Pickett Papers; "Petition to Congress by Inhabitants of Tombigbee and Tensaw," [1 August 1799], *Territorial Papers,* 5:69–71.

14. Beginning of second installment in the *Mobile Register* on 27 June 1872, with the title changed to "Reminiscences of Early Times in the Mississippi Territory."

15. According to notes in the Henry Sale Halbert Papers, Alabama Department of Archives and History, Montgomery, Alabama, Pushmataha's village was located at present-day Causeyville, Mississippi, "on the headwaters of Buckatunna" southeast of Meridian, Mississippi.

16. John Pitchlynn (ca. 1764–1835) spelled his name with two "n's" and lived near old Plymouth, Lowndes County, Mississippi, near the mouth of Oktibbeha Creek. Halbert Papers; W. David Baird, *Peter Pitchlynn: Chief of the Choctaws* (1972; rev. ed., Norman: University of Oklahoma Press, 1986), xv.

17. The American Board of Commissioners for Foreign Missions, under the leadership of Cyrus Kingsbury, established several schools in the Choctaw Nation, including Elliot, Mayhew, Bethel, Emmaus, Juzan's, Mushulatubbee's, and, in the Six Towns District, Yokena Chukamah. Kidwell, *Choctaws and Missionaries,* 30–32, 44, 47–48, 50–68.

18. Gaines was very complimentary of Chambers and others who adjudicated the land claims of the early Tombigbee settlers, which included British and Spanish land grants and American land warrants and preemption certificates. "Conversation with George S. Gaines," Pickett Papers; "An Act regulating the grants of land, and providing for the disposal of lands of the United States, south of the state of Tennessee," *Territorial Papers,* 5:192–205.

19. John Mason, a former president of the Bank of Columbia, served as superintendent of Indian trade from 1 October 1807 until his resignation on 1 April 1816 to return to private business. Peake, *History of the United States Factory System,* 39.

20. The lands surveyed and organized into counties in 1807 were acquired from the Choctaw by the treaties of Hoe Buckintoopa in 1803 and Mount Dexter in 1805. Kappler, comp., *Indian Affairs, Laws and Treaties,* 2:69, 87.

21. Lorenzo Dow, a rather eccentric itinerant Methodist preacher from Georgia, arrived in the Tensaw and Tombigbee settlements in 1803 with his wife on their way to Natchez. Dow preached in several of the scattered settlements and reportedly made some ten such visits. Hamilton, *Colonial Mobile,* 386, 393.

22. Colbert's Ferry, located on the Natchez Trace, was operated by George Colbert, the eldest of five influential mixed-blood sons of James Colbert (ca. 1720–84), a Scots trader and Indian countryman in the Chickasaw Nation. "2nd Conversation with Geo. S. Gaines, Spring of 1848," Pickett Papers; Halbert Papers; Dawson A. Phelps, "Stands and Travel Accommodations on the Natchez Trace," *Journal of Mississippi History* 11 (January 1949): 44–45.

23. Edmund Pendleton Gaines (1777–1849), one of Gaines' older brothers, was collector and commandant at Fort Stoddert. Silver, *Edmund Pendleton Gaines,* 11.

24. Gaines traveled overland from St. Stephens to Smithland, Kentucky, at the mouth of the Cumberland River, between 5 November 1810 and 5 January 1811. "For Sundry expenses of a Journey to Smithland and back for which no vouchers could be obtained," St. Stephens, M. T., 31 March 1811, CTH: Indent Book.

25. Fort Massac was located about ten miles below present-day Paducah, Kentucky, on the north bank of the Ohio. Prucha, *The Sword of the Republic,* 35–56, 65, 68, 73.

26. James Caller (1758–1819) was also associated with Reuben Kemper and others in Washington County, Mississippi Territory (1810–11), who plotted to drive the Spanish out of Mobile. Hamilton, *Colonial Mobile,* 399–400.

27. Tandy Walker, an Indian countryman, resided in the West Bend area of the Tombigbee between Coffeeville and Fort Easley in Clarke County, Alabama. He

was seriously wounded in November 1813 while scouting near Burnt Corn Creek. Henry S. Halbert and Timothy H. Ball, *The Creek War of 1813 and 1814,* ed. Frank L. Owsley, Jr. (1895; reprint, University: University of Alabama Press, 1969), 113, 226–28; Timothy H. Ball, *A Glance into the Great Southwest, or Clarke County, Alabama, and Its Surroundings, from 1540 to 1877* (1882; reprint, Grove Hill, Ala.: Clarke County Historical Society, 1973), 525–26.

28. Black Warrior Town was located on the route traveled by Tecumseh in 1811 from the Choctaw Nation to the Upper Creek towns. Oceoche Emathla and many other Creeks responded to his message. Gregory Evans Dowd, *A Spirited Resistance: The North American Indian Struggle for Unity, 1745–1815* (Baltimore: Johns Hopkins University Press, 1993), 140–47, 169–73.

29. Beginning of the third installment of the "first series" in the *Mobile Register* on 3 July 1872.

30. In 1812, the twenty-eight-year-old Gaines married seventeen-year-old Ann Gaines (1795–1868), the daughter of Young Gaines, a longtime resident of the Tombigbee settlements and a prominent landowner. Bateman: Gaines Family Genealogy.

31. Mrs. Crawley was probably captured by Little Warrior, a Creek Red Stick who led a party of Creeks on a visit to Tecumseh's Ohio country and, on their return, attacked a number of Tennessee settlements, killing members of seven families. Benjamin W. Griffith, Jr., *McIntosh and Weatherford, Creek Indian Leaders* (Tuscaloosa: University of Alabama Press, 1988), 84–85.

32. Pitchlynn married into an important Choctaw family and served Gaines and the U.S. government as advisor, subagent, and interpreter. Baird, *Peter Pitchlynn,* 6–12, 15–18.

33. Dick, referred to by Gaines as his "trusted" servant, frequently accompanied Gaines on his travels as noted throughout his "Reminiscences," including this 1813 trip down the Tombigbee.

34. Sam Dale (1772–1841), a noted frontier guide, and Sam Moniac (Manac), a mixed-blood Creek and William Weatherford's brother-in-law, witnessed the arrival of Tecumseh's party at Tuckabatchee and reported hearing Tecumseh's address in the Upper Creek capital. Griffith, *McIntosh and Weatherford,* 71–75.

35. Caller's force of 180 whites, mixed-bloods, and friendly Indians attacked the Red Stick party led by Peter McQueen, High-Head Jim (or Jim Boy), and Josiah Francis (or Hillis Hadjo), the Creek prophet, on the morning of 27 July 1813 at Burnt Corn Creek in Escambia County, Alabama. Griffith, *McIntosh and Weatherford,* 95–97. "Bailey Dix" was probably Dixon Bailey, a mixed-blood, who led a Tensaw company at Burnt Corn Creek.

36. In addition to the four frontier forts listed and the U.S. Army posts, there were many more stockaded posts in the lower Tombigbee: Fort Easley, Fort Pierce, Fort Glass, Fort Sinquefield, Fort White, Landrum's Fort, Mott's Fort, Turner's Fort, Cato's Fort, Rankin's Fort, McGrew's Fort, Fort Carney, Powell's Fort, and Lavier's Fort. Halbert and Ball, *The Creek War,* 106–16.

37. Brigadier General Ferdinand L. Claiborne marched to Fort Stoddert (Mount Vernon) at the head of seven hundred militia volunteers from Mississippi Territory east of the Pearl River. Halbert and Ball, *The Creek War,* 88; John F. H. Claiborne, *Mississippi, As a Province, Territory and State, with Biographical Notices of Eminent Citizens* (1880; reprint, Baton Rouge: Louisiana State University, 1964), 333–34.

38. Gaines' "Capt. Hand" was Obediah Hand. On 30 August 1813 a Creek Red Stick force of seven hundred led by William Weatherford (1765–1824) destroyed Fort Mims. See Halbert and Ball, *The Creek War,* 151–57.

39. Samuel A. Edmondson (ca. 1794–1869), a native of South Carolina, was appointed militia captain by William Wyatt Bibb, governor of Alabama Territory, on 29 March 1818. He later settled in Lowndes County, Mississippi. Halbert Papers; *Territorial Papers,* 18:286.

40. Gaines wrote letters to General Andrew Jackson (1767–1845) and to Willie Blount (1768–1835), governor of Tennessee (1809–15), requesting immediate assistance. *Dictionary of American Biography,* 1:391.

41. Edmondson's route, the "Tennessee Road" or "Big Trading Path" to the Natchez Trace, with the stops noted, was one Gaines had used on several occasions. William Starnes (Starner), a Yankee blacksmith, operated a ferry on the Noxubee River near present-day Macon, Mississippi. Halbert Papers.

42. Major General Thomas Flournoy commanded the Seventh Military District, with headquarters in New Orleans. Griffith, *McIntosh and Weatherford,* 117.

43. Beginning of the fourth installment in the *Mobile Register* on 10 July 1872.

44. Mrs. Gaines' "delicate health" is a reference to her pregnancy with their first child, Elizabeth Ervin Gaines, who was born at St. Stephens in 1813 and died in infancy or early childhood. Sutherd, *Gaines Family,* 329.

45. John Flood McGrew was nominated and recommended to President Thomas Jefferson for appointment to the five-member legislative council for Mississippi Territory in 1808. A prominent landowner in the Tombigbee settlements, he was listed in petitions and memorials from Washington County. *Territorial Papers,* 5:281, 345, 354–55, 643, 693.

46. John McKee (1771–1832), a native of Virginia, was appointed to negotiate a boundary settlement with the Cherokee by Governor William Blount (1749–1800) of Southwest Territory in 1792. In 1794 he served as temporary agent to the Cherokee, and from 1799 until Silas Dinsmoor's appointment in 1802 he served as Choctaw agent. *Dictionary of American Biography,* 6:82–83.

47. McKee, Gaines, and Flood McGrew met at Pitchlynn's, where they discussed raising Chickasaw and Choctaw units to march against the Creeks. Halbert and Ball, *The Creek War,* 213.

48. According to Choctaw tradition, the "Council Ground" was at Kooncheto in Neshoba County, Mississippi. Ibid., 214.

49. Mrs. Nail was probably Molly Nail, the mixed-blood wife of Henry Nail;

their son Joel Nail became a prominent chief in the Southern District prior to removal. Halbert Papers; *Territorial Papers,* 6:444.

50. Gaines describes a ritual followed by the Choctaw from the protohistoric period through the removal era.

51. Pushmataha's speech reflects the Indian policy developed by Washington and his secretary of war, Henry Knox. Prucha, *American Indian Policy in the Formative Years,* 41–49.

52. Pushmataha (ca. 1764–1824) was a nontraditional district chief in that he had gained his position through war exploits; the white beads may have been a symbol of his office. White, *The Roots of Dependency,* 111–12.

53. Pushmataha spoke at the "great council" in 1811 addressed by Tecumseh near old Brooksville Station, Mississippi, and rejected Tecumseh's war message. Halbert and Ball, *The Creek War,* 44–51.

54. A Choctaw company was raised from this council, and some eight hundred Choctaw eventually served during the Creek Indian War of 1813–14 or with Jackson's forces at the Battle of New Orleans. *Territorial Papers,* 6:686–87.

55. Gaines' advice on the "election" of officers was contrary to Choctaw tradition regarding war companies.

56. While the meal prepared by Mrs. Nail featured traditional Choctaw food, such as the corn pounded with pestles and mortars, the "butchering of pigs and a beef" gives a clear indication of the changes to the traditional Choctaw economy brought about by the mixed-bloods, the Indian countrymen, and the civilizing program pushed since the Washington administration. White, *The Roots of Dependency,* 99–104.

57. Gaines refers to a "Fort Republic" and later to a "Citizen's Fort" at St. Stephens; the reference to "the men of the two forts" seems to indicate that there were two makeshift stockades at St. Stephens.

58. Gaines' statement, despite its immodesty, is factual. Not only had he traveled the route taken by Samuel A. Edmondson, he had cultivated the contacts and friendships that made his historic ride successful.

59. Gaines is apparently referring to the engagements at Tallushatchee and Talladega on 3 and 9 November 1813. Robert V. Remini, *Andrew Jackson and the Course of American Empire, 1767–1821* (New York: Harper & Row, 1977), 193–97.

60. Beginning of the fifth and final installment in the "first series," published in the *Mobile Register* on 17 July 1872.

61. Jackson was recovering from wounds to his left arm received in a gunfight with Thomas Hart Benton and his brother, Jesse Benton, at the City Hotel in Nashville, Tennessee, in early September 1813. Remini, *Andrew Jackson and the Course of American Empire,* 184–85, 199.

62. Jackson took command of his Tennessee forces at Fayetteville, Tennessee, on 7 October 1813. Ibid., 192.

63. Pushmataha led the first body of 135 Choctaw volunteers to St. Stephens, where he was commissioned a lieutenant colonel and others were appointed commissioned officers, noncommissioned officers, and privates. Halbert and Ball, *The Creek War,* 215.

64. Mushulatubbee (ca. 1770–1838), district chief of the Northern District, lived on the "Tennessee Road" or "Big Trading Path" about four miles northwest of old Brooksville Station, Noxubee County, Mississippi. Halbert Papers.

65. McKee and Pitchlynn led approximately six hundred Chickasaw and Choctaw to Oceoche Emathla's Black Warrior Town on 7 January 1814. Cotterill, *The Southern Indians,* 183.

66. Mushulatubbee's Northern District and Puckshenubbee's Western District mobilized several groups. Halbert and Ball, *The Creek War,* 286; Bassett, ed., *Correspondence of Andrew Jackson,* 1:380–81.

67. Colonel William McGrew was killed near Wood's Bluff on Bashi Creek in October 1813; Captain William Bradberry, who fought at Burnt Corn Creek, was mortally wounded "on the old Coffeeville and Wood's Bluff river road." Halbert and Ball, *The Creek War,* 219–21.

68. Captain Samuel Dale, Lieutenant Jeremiah Austill (1794–1879), and Lieutenant James Smith killed nine Creek Indians in the now famous "Canoe Fight" on the Alabama River on 12 November 1813. Ibid., 229–37; Pickett, *History of Alabama,* 562–70.

69. Walker, George Foster, and a "mulatto named Evans" were attacked in early November 1813 while scouting for Creeks near Burnt Corn Creek. Foster escaped unharmed, Evans was killed, and Walker's arm was broken "by several balls." Halbert and Ball, *The Creek War,* 226–28.

70. Brigadier General Ferdinand L. Claiborne established Fort Claiborne in November 1813 on the Alabama River in present-day Monroe County, Alabama. Pickett describes it as "a strong stockade, two hundred feet square, defended by three block-houses and a half-moon battery, which commanded the river." Pickett, *History of Alabama,* 572.

71. According to a letter from General Claiborne to David Holmes, governor of Mississippi Territory (1809–17), Pushmataha led fifty-one Choctaw in a raid along the Pensacola road to disrupt communication with the Creeks. Halbert and Ball, *The Creek War,* 242.

72. Colonel Gilbert C. Russell marched his regiment from Mount Vernon to Fort Claiborne on 28 November 1813. Ibid., 243.

73. In 1807, Dinsmoor moved the Choctaw agency from the Chickasawhay River valley near present-day Quitman, Mississippi, to the Pearl River valley "on the main wilderness road from Natchez to Nashville" near present-day Clinton, Mississippi. Cotterill, *The Southern Indians,* 142 n; *Territorial Papers,* 6:425.

74. It is not clear whether Gaines is referring to Charles Murrells, who was given the death sentence for "stealing a negro" and subsequently pardoned by Gov-

ernor David Holmes on 20 November 1810, or to John A. Murrell, "the Great
Western Land Pirate," who operated along the Natchez Trace in the 1820s and
1830s. *Territorial Papers,* 6:133–35; Jonathan Daniels, *The Devil's Backbone: The
Story of the Natchez Trace* (New York: McGraw-Hill, 1962), 240–45.

75. Dinsmoor came under scrutiny in 1805 for purchasing "articles of the
highest luxury, such as . . . delicate spices, anchovies, raisins, almonds, hyson tea,
coffee, mustard, preserves, English cheese, segars, brandy, wine, etc. . . . for an Indian treaty." However, he also had supporters who wrote letters to the secretary
of war praising his work. Cotterill, *The Southern Indians,* 147 n; W. Lattimore to
Secretary of War, House of Representatives, 9 March 1814, *Territorial Papers,*
6:424–25.

76. Claiborne's forces, which included Colonel Gilbert C. Russell's regiment
and Pushmataha's Choctaw auxiliaries, destroyed the Creek town of Ecunchate,
or the "Holy Ground," on 23 December 1813. Cotterill, *The Southern Indians,*
185–86.

77. Following the Treaty of Fort Jackson with the Creeks, signed on 9 August
1814, Jackson marched to Mobile, arriving on 22 August, where he planned to
check the Spanish in Florida and to oppose the imminent British invasion of the
Gulf. Kappler, comp., *Indian Affairs, Laws and Treaties,* 2:107–10; Remini, *Andrew Jackson and the Course of American Empire,* 230–31, 235–37.

78. Although the Creek War of 1813–14 was fought across two military districts—Major General Thomas Pinckney's Sixth District, with headquarters at
Charleston, South Carolina, and Major General Thomas Flournoy's Seventh District, with headquarters at New Orleans—Pinckney exercised direct command
during the war, and Flournoy directed the limited military action in South Alabama. Remini, *Andrew Jackson and the Course of American Empire,* 192, 234.

79. Alexander Arbuthnot, a Scots trader, was hanged from the yardarm of his
ship, and Robert Ambrister, a former lieutenant of the Royal Marines, was executed by a firing squad on 29 April 1818. Both British subjects were found guilty
of aiding the enemy by a military court presided over by General Edmund Pendleton Gaines at St. Marks, Spanish Florida. Ibid., 352–59.

80. Brigadier General John Coffee (1772–1833), a Tennessean and a close
friend of Jackson's, marched two thousand cavalry down from West Tennessee and
added other forces before he reached St. Stephens. Ibid., 240.

81. The prominent citizen falsely charged with conducting a secret correspon-
dence with the British fleet was Judge Harry Toulmin. Gaines also acknowledges
that he is serving as postmaster (ca. 1809–15) at St. Stephens. Gaines to Adjutant
General [Robert] Butler, St. Stephens, M. T., 2 October 1814, Gaines Collection;
Gaines to James T. Gaines, St. Stephens, M. T., 5 March 1809, 11 June 1814,
"Letters from George Strother Gaines," 186–88, 189–92.

82. Gaines spent the night at the home of Thomas Bates, who owned land on
Bates' Creek.

83. Jackson arrived in Mobile on 22 August 1814 and remained there until late

October to oppose a British invasion. Remini, *Andrew Jackson and the Course of American Empire,* 236–38.

84. Gaines' meeting with Jackson in Mobile probably occurred in October 1814, after his letter of 2 October to Jackson's adjutant general Robert Butler and prior to Jackson's withdrawal from Mobile on 25 October.

85. The Shawnee Prophet, Tenskwatawa, was Tecumseh's brother. R. David Edmunds, *The Shawnee Prophet* (Lincoln: University of Nebraska Press, 1983), 28–32.

86. Jackson marched overland from Pensacola on 18 November 1814, arrived at New Orleans on 1 December 1814, and defeated the British forces commanded by Lieutenant General Sir Edward Michael Pakenham in the Battle of New Orleans on 8 January 1815. Remini, *Andrew Jackson and the Course of American Empire,* 244–45, 255–86.

REMINISCENCES OF EARLY TIMES IN MISSISSIPPI TERRITORY

1. Beginning of the "second series" presented to the Alabama Department of Archives and History, Montgomery, Alabama, by Dr. Vivian Pendleton Gaines (George Strother Gaines grandson) of Mobile, Alabama, on 4 April 1908. This part of Gaines' "Reminiscences" is handwritten on ruled paper measuring 8 1/2 x 14 inches, with a cover sheet labeled "2nd Series—Reminiscences of Early Times in the Mississippi Territory By Col. Geo. S. Gaines." The first page of the manuscript bears the title "Reminiscences of Early Times in Mississippi Territory." It appears that this manuscript is a later (or "clean") copy of the original transcription made by Albert C. Coles in 1871.

2. Silas Dinsmoor was dismissed as Choctaw agent and replaced on 28 June 1814 by John McKee, who served until his resignation in 1821. Cotterill, *The Southern Indians,* 189–90, 211 n; *Territorial Papers,* 6:440–42.

3. Gaines and his "family" left St. Stephens in May 1815 on a "furlough" to Tennessee—a trip he had planned on taking in the summer of 1814. Gaines to J. T. Gaines, St. Stephens, M. T., 11 June 1814, "Letters from George Strother Gaines," 189–92.

4. The "trading path" used by Gaines was a route he had used often to reach Colbert's Ferry on the Tennessee via John Pitchlynn's on Oktibbeha Creek, the route referred to as the "Tennessee Road" or "Big Trading Path," and the route used by Samuel A. Edmondson in September 1813 after the destruction of Fort Mims. The route led out of St. Stephens to Landrum's, to Tinnan's, to Juzan's, to Starnes', to Pitchlynn's, to Miatubbee's, to James Colbert's on the Natchez Trace and up to Colbert's Ferry on the Tennessee River. "For Sundry expenses of a Journey to Smithland and back for which no vouchers could be obtained," St. Stephens, M. T., 31 March 1811, CTH: Indent Book.

5. Gaines' party encountered Major General Andrew Jackson, Mrs. Jackson, and Andrew Jackson, Jr., on their journey from New Orleans to Nashville. Jackson

had relinquished his command to Brigadier General Edmund Pendleton Gaines on 6 April 1815 and arrived to a hero's welcome in Nashville on 15 May 1815. Thomas McGee of Columbia, Tennessee, was an old friend who later assisted Gaines with the Choctaw removal in 1831. Remini, *Andrew Jackson and the Course of American Empire,* 318; Gandrud, comp., *Alabama Records: Marengo County,* 39:45.

6. Nicholas Perkins of Franklin, Tennessee, served as register of the U.S. Land Office in Washington County (1806–8) and "attorney General for the county and district of Washington [1808–9]." He assisted with the capture of Aaron Burr in 1807 and escorted him to Richmond, Virginia, for his trial. "Conversations with George S. Gaines," Pickett Papers; *Territorial Papers,* 5:453, 537–40, 653–54, 738.

7. William H. Crawford (1772–1834), a native of Virginia, was James Madison's secretary of war and authorized Gaines to negotiate a site "for the purpose of establishing a factory and a military post." *Territorial Papers,* 6:548.

8. The Spanish constructed Fort Confederation (1794–97) on Jones' Bluff on the Tombigbee River to slow the American advance into the lower Mississippi River valley and to use the southern Indians as a buffer to American expansion. They evacuated the fort in March 1797 following the Treaty of San Lorenzo, which established the thirty-first parallel as the boundary between the United States and Spanish Florida. James P. Pate, "The Fort of the Confederation: Spain on the Upper Tombigbee," *Alabama Historical Quarterly* 44 (Fall–Winter 1982): 171–86.

9. Gaines and John McKee, the Choctaw agent, negotiated a cession agreement with the Choctaw on 11–16 December 1815 for a new trading house site near the "old Spanish Fort." "The Convention for the cession of the use of a site for a trading house and military . . . " Chaktaw Agency, 12 December 1815, Letters Received: Indian Affairs, 1172–78.

10. Gaines actually selected a site one mile west of Fort Confederation at James' Springs on a small tributary of the Tombigbee that became known as Factory Creek. He purchased the cabins of a mixed-blood who lived on the site. Gaines to Mason, Chaktaw Trading House, near old Fort Confederation, 25 July 1816, Letters Received: Indian Trade, 325–27.

11. Charles Juzan, a noted French Indian countryman, married a niece of Pushmataha and operated several trading houses in the Choctaw country—at Coosha, Chunky, and Tuscahoma. Halbert Papers; Halbert and Ball, *The Creek War,* 47–48. Halbert provides some notes on the origins of "Etomba-igabee" and the name of the Tombigbee River. Halbert Papers.

12. Gaines complained that the soldiers sent from the Third Military District at New Orleans, who arrived at St. Stephens on 4 February 1816, were old men and sick with influenza. Gaines to Mason, Chaktaw Trading House, James' Springs near Ft. Confederation, 10 June 1816, Letters Received: Indian Trade, 323–24.

13. Hopia-skitteena, or Little Leader, was an important Choctaw subchief (captain) who lived on the south bank of the Sucarnochee River near Narketa, Kemper County, Mississippi, in 1830. Dillard, "Treaty of Dancing Rabbit Creek," 103 n.

14. With the decline of game, especially deer, and the increased presence of white settlers and their livestock, the killing or stealing of livestock became more widespread. White, *The Roots of Dependency,* 109–10.

15. The treaty conference with the Choctaw was convened at the Choctaw Trading House in October 1816, and a treaty of cession was signed by Pushmataha, Mushulatubbee, Puckshenubbee, and ten other Choctaw mingoes and captains. *ASP: Indian Affairs,* 2:95. This treaty is often incorrectly referred to as the Treaty of St. Stephens.

16. The emigrants listed represent many of the founding families of the West Alabama counties of Choctaw, Clarke, Greene, Hale, Marengo, and Sumter.

17. Gaines was a candidate for the Alabama senate from Clarke and Marengo Counties in 1825; one opponent appears to have been Samuel B. Shields, a native of South Carolina. Ball, *Clarke County, Alabama,* 450.

18. Gaines served one two-year term in the Alabama senate (1825–27) and evidently did not seek reelection. Brantley, *Three Capitals of Alabama,* 165–66, 174–75, 193–94.

19. Gaines' comments demonstrate that European-American influences effected radical social and economic changes among the Choctaw. White, *The Roots of Dependency,* 99–138.

20. The story of the "Rain Maker" and his death illustrates the importance of farming among the Choctaw and the traditional role of the town chief in sustaining and protecting his people. Ibid., 41–43.

21. Cyrus Kingsbury (1786–1870), a native of New Hampshire, was a Presbyterian missionary sent by the American Board of Commissioners for Foreign Missions. He established the Elliot school on the Yalobusha River in 1818, and, with the assistance of John Pitchlynn and David Folsom, built the Mayhew school on Oktibbeha Creek in 1822. Angie Debo, *The Rise and Fall of the Choctaw Republic,* 2nd ed. (Norman: University of Oklahoma Press, 1961), 42; Kidwell, *Choctaws and Missionaries,* 29–30; 60.

22. Harry Toulmin (1766–1824) led the Alabama opposition to the Mississippi request to Congress that the "natural boundary" of the Tombigbee and Mobile Rivers should be established as the eastern boundary of the new state of Mississippi. *Territorial Papers,* 18:190–201, 209–14, 268–70, 291–93.

23. General Charles L'Allemand and Charles Villar requested the survey of the four townships in November 1817, and on 10 November 1817 Secretary of the Treasury William H. Crawford issued instructions to Josiah Meigs, commissioner of the General Land Office, to conduct the survey. *Territorial Papers,* 6:811–15.

24. Colonel Nicholas Raoul operated a ferry on French Creek east of Demopo-

lis, emigrated in 1824 to Mexico, where he participated in the revolution, and served as governor of Toulon after returning to France. Whitfield, "The French Grant in Alabama," 352–53.

25. General Charles Lefebre Desnouettes (1773–1823) was the acknowledged leader of the French emigrants. Ibid., 340–41.

26. Desnouettes also attempted to recruit German redemptioners as a labor force to the French grant. Ibid., 341.

27. Despite the hardships associated with settling their grant, the French continued to entertain and to enjoy their books, music, paintings, silver, china, and other luxuries they brought to the American frontier. Anne Bozeman Lyon, "The Bonapartists in Alabama," *Gulf States Historical Magazine* 1 (March 1903): 329–30.

28. Desnouettes served as an aide-de-camp to Napoleon at Marengo, shared his carriage in the retreat from Moscow, supported his return from Elba, and served at Waterloo. Whitfield, "The French Grant in Alabama," 351–52.

29. Desnouettes left Alabama in 1823 to seek refuge in Belgium but lost his life in a shipwreck off the coast of Ireland. Ibid., 352.

30. William Wyatt Bibb (1781–1820), a native of Amelia County, Virginia, served in the U.S. Congress from Georgia (1806–16). President James Monroe appointed him governor of Alabama Territory (1817–19), and he became the state's first governor in 1819. Brewer, *Alabama*, 108.

31. Captain Jack F. Ross, Colonel Thomas H. Herndon (1793–1842), and James G. Lyon served on the board of directors of Tombeckbe Bank at St. Stephens. Ross was the treasurer for Alabama Territory and the first state treasurer (1818–22), and Lyon was Gaines' nephew and the brother of Francis Strother Lyon. Herndon moved to Erie, Greene County, Alabama, where he was a merchant, slave owner, and large landowner. Brantley, *Banking in Alabama,* 1:37–48, 77, 432 n. 28; Armstrong, *Notable Southern Families,* 1 & 2:90.

32. Abner S. Lipscomb (1789–1857), a native of Abbeville, South Carolina, was a lawyer and Tombeckbe Bank director, and he later served as chief justice of the Alabama Supreme Court (1824–35). William Crawford (1784–1849), a native of Louisa County, Virginia, was the first U.S. attorney in Alabama, the second president of Tombeckbe Bank, and the second federal judge in Alabama. Both Hitchcock (1795–1839) and Saffold served on the Alabama Supreme Court and as chief justice, Hitchcock in 1836–39 and Saffold in 1835–36. John Gayle (1792–1859), a native of South Carolina, was elected governor of Alabama in 1831 and again in 1833. George F. Sallee was a noted lawyer in St. Stephens. Brantley, *Banking in Alabama,* 1:431 n. 6, 432 n. 28; Garrett, *Reminiscences,* 91, 118, 458, 587, 775, 789.

33. Thomas Eastin (Easton) established the *Halcyon and Tombecbe Advertiser* in 1815 and served as the first printer for the territory and the state. Brantley, *Banking in Alabama,* 1:47–48, 433 n. 36.

34. Francis Strother Lyon (1800–1882), a native of Stokes County, North

Carolina, was Gaines' nephew and the son of James G. and Behethland (Gaines) Lyon. He came to St. Stephens in 1817 and studied law with William Crawford. Lyon served as secretary of the Alabama senate (1822–30), as state senator and representative, and as U.S. congressman, and was a representative in the Confederate Congress (1862–65). Garrett, *Reminiscences,* 587–88; Armstrong, *Notable Southern Families,* 1 & 2:90.

35. Tombeckbe Bank was chartered in 1818, with Israel Pickens (1780–1827), a native of Mecklenburg County, North Carolina, elected as president and Gaines as cashier. The bank was located on the northwest corner of the intersection of High and Lime Streets. Thomas L. McKenney, superintendent of Indian trade (1816–22), tried to convince Gaines to remain as factor. Brantley, *Banking in Alabama,* 1:37–48; *Territorial Papers,* 18:399–400.

36. Benjamin Everett was also Gaines' brother-in-law and married to his second-youngest sister, Patsey. Armstrong, *Notable Southern Families,* 1 & 2:89.

37. Henry Bright, Silas Dinsmoor, David Files, James Pickens, Daniel B. Ripley, and Benjamin S. Smoot chartered the St. Stephens Steamboat Company in 1818, but the general assembly of Alabama Territory denied their request for the exclusive privilege of navigating the Alabama and Tombigbee Rivers by steam power. A letter written by Benjamin Hatch on June 1818 reported the construction of a steamboat, *The Alabama of St. Stephens,* at a cost of $50,000. B. Hatch to W. Whitfield, St. Stephens, 29 June 1818, Halbert Papers; *Territorial Papers,* 18:294, 354, 457; Jacqueline Anderson Matte, *The History of Washington County: First County in Alabama* (Chatom, Ala.: Washington County Historical Society, 1982), 53 n. 166, 60.

38. The French immigrants founded Demopolis in 1817 on lands they thought were within their grant of four townships, but they subsequently founded the new settlement of Aigleville when surveys revealed that their townships were about one mile further east. *Territorial Papers,* 6:811–12, 18:365, 509–10; Smith, "Early History of Demopolis," 85–86.

39. When the territorial legislature adjourned at St. Stephens in November 1818, the legislators had agreed to build a new capital at the confluence of the Alabama and Cahaba Rivers and selected Huntsville as the new temporary capital for the territory. Pickett, *History of Alabama,* 634.

40. The record is unclear whether the "Demopolis Town Company" and the White Bluff Association were the same land company; Gaines was a partner in the latter organization. Smith, "Early History of Demopolis," 86.

41. Allen Glover (1770–1840), a native of Edgefield District, South Carolina, moved to Demopolis in 1818. He became a wealthy merchant and planter and had more than one hundred slaves before his death in 1840. Ibid., 87–88; Gandrud, comp., *Alabama Records: Marengo County,* 29:28.

42. Desnouettes' visit to St. Stephens came prior to Gaines' resignation as cashier of Tombeckbe Bank and his move to Demopolis in 1822.

43. Dinsmoor moved to St. Stephens after John McKee replaced him as U.S.

agent to the Choctaw in 1814. He became a valued member of the community and was an active member of Masonic Lodge No. 9, but he struggled as a businessman. Matte, *History of Washington County,* 59, 63.

44. Nathan Bryan Whitfield, a native of Lenoir County, North Carolina, developed a plantation near Jefferson, Marengo County, Alabama, in 1837 and purchased Gaines' property near Demopolis in 1842. Whitfield incorporated part of Gaines' double-pen log house into the classical Greek Revival mansion constructed between 1842 and 1861. The mansion was known as Marlmont in the early years, but called Gaineswood by Whitfield in honor of Gaines by 1856. Smith, "Early History of Demopolis," 88; Regina Ulmer Galloway, *Gaineswood and the Whitfields of Demopolis* (Montgomery, Ala.: Skinner Printing Company, 1994), 1–5, 32–33. Gaines' traveling companion, "the son of Mr. Glover, a youth of sixteen or seventeen," was Williamson Allen Glover, the second son of Allen and Sarah Serena Norwood Glover. See Owens, *History of Alabama,* 3:668–69.

45. The act that closed the federal factory system was signed into law on 6 May 1822, and on 22 May, Thomas L. McKenney, superintendent of Indian trade, sent notices to all factors to conduct inventories in preparation for closing all operations. Henry Randall from the Office of Indian Trade settled the accounts of the Choctaw Trading House and sold the property and inventory to Gaines and Glover in October 1822. Peake, *History of the United States Indian Factory System,* 202–3.

46. Gaines managed the trading house, welcomed customers from the Northern and Southern Districts, and purchased goods for the annuity payments.

47. John McKee resigned in 1821 to enter politics, and William Ward was appointed U.S. agent to the Choctaw on 1 March 1821. Edward Hill, *The Office of Indian Affairs, 1824–1880* (New York: Clearwater Publishing Company, 1974), 46.

48. Puckshenubbee (ca. 1739–1824), a member of the 1824 Choctaw delegation to Washington, died from injuries sustained in a fall at Maysville, Kentucky, on 13 October 1824, at the age of eighty-five. Robert Cole, a mixed-blood, replaced Puckshenubbee as chief of the Western District, but he was deposed on 21 June 1826 by Greenwood LeFlore, the twenty-six-year-old son of Louis LeFlore. Grant Foreman, *Indians and Pioneers: The Story of the American Southwest before 1830* (1930; rev. ed., Norman: University of Oklahoma Press, 1936), 157–58; Kidwell, *Choctaws and Missionaries,* 93–94, 111.

49. The Treaty of Doak's Stand was negotiated by treaty commissioners Andrew Jackson and Thomas Hinds and signed by Puckshenubbee, Pushmataha, Mushulatubbee, and the other mingoes and captains of the Choctaw Nation on 18 October 1820. Kappler, comp., *Indian Affairs, Laws and Treaties,* 2:191–95.

50. The Arkansas lands were repurchased by the federal commissioners for twenty annual payments of $6,000, as provided for in Article 1 of the Treaty of Washington in 1825. Ibid., 911–12.

51. Pushmataha probably died of pneumonia at Tennison's Hotel, Washington, D.C., on 24 December 1824. Foreman, *Indians and Pioneers,* 158.

52. John Randolph (1773–1833), a native of Prince George County, Virginia, was a noted orator and statesman and served in the U.S. House of Representatives (1799–1813, 1815–25, 1827–29) and Senate (1825–27). Russell Kirk, *John Randolph of Roanoke: A Study in American Politics* (Chicago: Henry Regnery Company, 1964), 2–8ff.

53. Under charges of intemperance and immorality, Tapenhahamma, Pushmataha's nephew, was replaced in 1826 by John Garland, a mixed-blood. White, *The Roots of Dependency*, 125.

54. Nitakechi (Netuckijah), a member of the 1824 Choctaw delegation, replaced John Garland in 1829 as chief of the Southern District. An eloquent speaker, Nitakechi was quite popular among the whites. Kidwell, *Choctaws and Missionaries*, 136; Gideon Lincecum, "Life of Apushimataha," *Publications of the Mississippi Historical Society* 9 (1906): 482–83.

55. A classic story of Choctaw honor and blood revenge. White, *The Roots of Dependency*, 38, 48, 51, 61–62.

56. The young clerk, William Proctor Gould (1793–1867), and his wife became McKee's white family, while there is some evidence that McKee had a Choctaw wife, and a son from that union. *Dictionary of American Biography*, 6:82; Brewer, *Alabama*, 552.

57. John McKee served three consecutive terms (1823–29) as U.S. congressman from the Tuscaloosa District. McKee's "Hill of Hoath" was located in present-day Boligee, Greene County, Alabama. Garrett, *Reminiscences*, 771; *Dictionary of American Biography*, 6:82.

58. The confrontation described by Gaines occurred in July 1830 and reflected a deep political split between the mixed-bloods led by Greenwood LeFlore and the full-bloods led by Mushulatubbee, who opposed LeFlore's efforts to control the nation. Debo, *Rise and Fall of the Choctaw Republic*, 52–54; Kidwell, *Choctaws and Missionaries*, 134–39.

59. While Mushulatubbee supported the educational efforts of the missionaries, he opposed their religious activities, and the power struggle pitted traditionalists against progressives at a time when the Choctaw Nation desperately needed a strong and unified leadership. Kidwell, *Choctaws and Missionaries*, 140–41.

60. Louis LeFlore (Lafleur), a native of Canada and an Indian countryman, was the father of Greenwood LeFlore and a successful Indian trader and merchant who operated a trading house at LaFleur's Bluff on the Pearl River (now the site of Jackson, Mississippi) and a house of entertainment, LaFleur's Stand (or French Camp), on the Natchez Trace. Phelps, "Stands and Travel Accommodations on the Natchez Trace," 27.

61. The march by Greenwood LeFlore's followers, singing "hymns and spiritual songs," is a clear demonstration of the impact of the Baptist, Methodist, and Presbyterian missionaries on the Western District. Kidwell, *Choctaws and Missionaries*, 117–37.

62. While the Choctaw council at the trading house defused the immediate

confrontation between Greenwood LeFlore and Mushulatubbee, Mushulatubbee's ruse with his resignation clearly demonstrated that the traditionalists had their supporters and that the Nation was careening forward without a strong and unified leadership.

63. Gaines was obviously out of touch with the political factionalism that had brought the Choctaw Nation to the brink of armed conflict and which left the factions deeply divided as federal treaty commissioners journeyed to the Nation in September 1830. Kidwell, *Choctaws and Missionaries,* 134–41.

64. William Ward's visit was in the summer of 1830 and not the "summer of 1829," as the federal treaty commissioners arrived in Mississippi in September 1830. Halbert, "The Story of the Treaty of Dancing Rabbit," 375.

65. Gaines is in error here—John McKee played no role in the negotiations. John H. Eaton, Jackson's secretary of war (1829–31), and John Coffee were the only federal commissioners at Dancing Rabbit Creek. Ibid., 375–99; Kappler, comp., *Indian Affairs, Laws and Treaties,* 2:310, 315.

66. Although Eaton, Coffee, and many of the other participants arrived at the treaty grounds on Dancing Rabbit Creek on 15 September 1830, the treaty conference was formally opened at eleven o'clock on Saturday morning, 18 September, when the two commissioners addressed several thousand Choctaw. Halbert, "The Story of the Treaty of Dancing Rabbit," 378–79; Kappler, comp., *Indian Affairs, Laws and Treaties,* 2:310.

67. Gaines' suggestion was embodied in Article 16 of the Treaty of Dancing Rabbit Creek, which provided the Choctaw would be removed "under the care of discreet and careful persons, who will be kind and brotherly to them." Kappler, comp., *Indian Affairs, Laws and Treaties,* 2:313.

68. In 1829, Mississippi legislators passed legislation extending state law over the Choctaw and Chickasaw. The law became effective on 19 January 1830, granting citizenship to the Indians of Mississippi and abolishing tribal governments. Debo, *Rise and Fall of the Choctaw Republic,* 51.

69. The final discussions and negotiations occurred on 25 and 26 September 1830, and the final draft of the treaty was formally signed on 27 September by the two commissioners, the three district chiefs, and 168 mingoes, chiefs, captains, and warriors of the Choctaw Nation. Halbert, "The Story of the Treaty of Dancing Rabbit," 391–97; Kappler, comp., *Indian Affairs, Laws and Treaties,* 2:315–17.

70. A supplemental treaty was signed on 28 September 1830 by the three district chiefs and fourteen other Choctaw leaders, with four articles designed to make the Treaty of Dancing Rabbit more palatable and to provide for an exploring party to the new lands in the West. Kappler, comp., *Indian Affairs, Laws and Treaties,* 2:317–19.

71. Although Secretary of War Eaton failed to confirm his original commitment to Gaines in writing, Gaines later reported that Eaton provided a written statement during his visit to Washington in 1843. Gaines to Dillard, Peachwood, 8 August 1857, Gaines Collection.

72. Colonel Benjamin Reynolds (1788–1843), a native of Fayette County, Kentucky, served in both houses of the Tennessee legislature. He was wounded at the Battle of Horseshoe Bend on 27 March 1814 and in 1830 was appointed agent to the Chickasaw by President Andrew Jackson. Marie Bankhead Owen and Emmett Kilpatrick, eds., "White Men Associated with Indian Life," *Alabama Historical Quarterly* 13 (1951): 148.

73. Gaines' "three great chiefs of the nation" were the three district chiefs in 1830: Greenwood LeFlore (Western District), Mushulatubbee (Northern District), and Nitakechi (Southern District). Dillard, "The Treaty of Dancing Rabbit Creek," 26–27.

74. The Sucarnochee River flows out of Kemper County, Mississippi, east and southeast through Sumter County, Alabama, into the Tombigbee River. Greenwood LeFlore refused to join Gaines' exploring party and probably sponsored the independent party, led by George W. Harkins and Robert Folsom, to the new Choctaw country in October 1830. Foreman, *Indian Removal*, 32.

75. Montgomery's Point, occupied as a trading post as early as 1766, was strategically located near the mouth of the White River at its confluence with the Mississippi River. *Arkansas: A Guide to the State* (New York: Hastings House, 1941), 36.

76. Led by Heckaton, mixed-blood Bernard Bone, and Delegate Ambrose Sevier, the Quapaw delegation was on its way to Washington to plead for a return of old tribal lands on the Red River. The Quapaw originally claimed the region from the Red River north to the Arkansas River, but ceded most of this territory to the United States in 1818, reducing their holdings to a small reservation on the lower Arkansas. *Territorial Papers*, 21:304–5, 352–57; Muriel H. Wright, *A Guide to the Indian Tribes of Oklahoma* (Norman: University of Oklahoma, 1951), 219–20.

77. Gaines visited John Pope, governor of Arkansas Territory (1829–35), on 18 November 1830. *Territorial Papers*, 21:3, 487.

78. Colonel Matthew Arbuckle was commander (1824–41) of Fort Gibson, located on the Grand River near its confluence with the Verdigris and Arkansas Rivers. Brad Agnew, *Fort Gibson: Terminal on the Trail of Tears* (Norman: University of Oklahoma Press, 1980), 7, 30.

79. Lieutenant James L. Dawson and his father-in-law, Assistant Surgeon James W. Baylor, joined Gaines' party on 20 December 1830 southwest of the Canadian River. Gardner, "The Lost Captain: J. L. Dawson of Old Fort Gibson," 221; Dawson, "Report of J. L. Dawson on His Escort of Choctaw and Chickasaw Delegates," 241–43.

80. Gaines' exploring party now numbered thirty-five: Gaines, Dick, the eighteen Choctaw, Dawson, Baylor, twelve soldiers, and a Delaware guide hired by Dawson to locate the Choctaw and Chickasaw parties. Dawson, "Report of J. L. Dawson on His Escort of Choctaw and Chickasaw Delegates," 242, 248.

81. The Cross Timbers was a dense, nearly impenetrable growth of vegetation,

mostly post oak, blackjack oak, hickory, and shinnery oak, five to thirty miles wide, located in central Oklahoma southwest of the Arkansas to the Arbuckle Mountains. The False Washita River, the present-day Washita River, was located on the western edge of the new Choctaw country explored by Gaines' party. John W. Morris, Charles R. Goins, and Edwin C. McReynolds, *Historical Atlas of Oklahoma* (1965; rev. ed., Norman: University of Oklahoma, 1976), 6, 9.

82. Reynolds' Chickasaw exploring party numbered sixteen and included Levi Colbert, Pitman Colbert, Henry Love, William D. King, and Elaptinkbahtubbe. With the addition of the Chickasaw party, Gaines' party now numbered fifty-one. Foreman, *Indian Removal,* 33.

83. The "L'Eau Bleu" ("Blue Water") is the Blue River, which flows from the northwest to southeast through present-day Johnston and Bryan Counties in Oklahoma and is a tributary of the Red River. Morris, Goins, and McReynolds, *Historical Atlas of Oklahoma,* 6, 13, 21.

84. Reynolds had served as captain of the 39th Tennessee Regiment at the Battle of Horseshoe Bend, and Gaines deferred to his military experience. Owen and Kilpatrick, "White Men Associated with Indian Life," 148.

85. Gaines' party encountered the two trappers, "Mr. Mayes and Mr. Crider," on a small tributary of the Blue River, where they were trapping for beaver. Dawson reports that they lived "on James Fork of Poteau," and Gaines hired Mayes as a guide. Dawson, "Report of J. L. Dawson on His Escort of Choctaw and Chickasaw Delegates," 247.

86. Francis W. Armstrong, Choctaw agent west of the Mississippi, reported an incident in 1832 involving Shawnee living on the Red River who executed a Choctaw woman as a witch. The Shawneetown community near Idabel, McCurtain County, Oklahoma, was probably the original settlement by this group of Absentee Shawnee. Foreman, *Indian Removal,* 66; Wright, *Guide to the Indian Tribes,* 242.

87. According to Dawson's report, the Fort Gibson detachment left Gaines' exploring party on 10 January 1831 after crossing the Blue River; his party included "Ass't Surgeon Baylor, one private soldier in addition to my command, and Capt. King of the Chickasaw delegation." Dawson, "Report of J. L. Dawson on His Escort of Choctaw and Chickasaw Delegates," 248.

88. Fort Towson was established by Major Alexander Cummings in 1824 near the mouth of the Kiamichi River to protect the upper Red River frontier. Agnew, *Fort Gibson,* 29–30.

89. Gaines or his amanuensis should have written the Red River, not the Arkansas.

90. A "hoe cake" was a simple cornmeal cake, water and meal, baked on a makeshift griddle. *Dictionary of American Regional English,* 2 vols. to date (Cambridge, Mass.: Belknap Press of Harvard University Press, 1985–), 2:1032.

91. Tom fuller, or "tuh-fulla," an important national dish of the Choctaw, was hominey made by boiling corn in a lye solution. The fermented hominey became

known as "tom fuller" on the southern frontier. Joseph B. Thoburn, *A Standard History of Oklahoma*, 5 vols. (Chicago: American Historical Society, 1916), 1:262.

92. Gaines' exploring party arrived at the small frontier village of Washington, Hempstead County, Arkansas Territory, on 29 January 1831. Foreman, *Indian Removal*, 37.

93. Gaines' business reputation and personal contacts in Alabama were critical to the successful conclusion of his 1830–31 exploring expedition. The delegations apparently reached Little Rock on or about 9 February 1831. DeRosier, *Removal of the Choctaw*, 135.

94. Gaines stopped off in Little Rock for a second visit with Governor John Pope in early February 1831.

95. The negative reference to the "Indian country man"—a white man who lived with Indians—gives some insight to racial stereotyping on the southern frontier.

96. Gaines and his servant Dick arrived in Mobile on 2 March 1831, and his "Indian Delegation" was reported in the *Mobile Commercial Register* on 7 March 1831.

97. Jackson's cabinet dissolved over the "Peggy Eaton affair" with the resignations of John H. Eaton and Martin Van Buren in April 1831, but Eaton served as territorial governor of Florida (1834–36) before serving as minister to Spain (1836–40). Cole, *The Presidency of Andrew Jackson*, 83–87.

98. Jonathan Emanuel, an English-born merchant, was twenty-eight-years-old in 1831 when he offered Gaines a partnership in his dry goods business. He became a prominent cotton broker and business and civic leader in Mobile. Amos, *Cotton City*, 50–51.

99. Francis W. Armstrong (1783–1835), a native of Virginia, served in Jackson's Tennessee army during the War of 1812, represented Mobile County in the Alabama legislature in 1820–21, and was appointed to conduct the Choctaw census on 26 April 1831. Foreman, "Armstrongs of Indian Territory," 293–94, 306; Garrett, *Reminiscences*, 759.

100. Armstrong started his work with the Choctaw in early July 1831 and completed the census on 7 September 1831. Cheryl Haun Morris, "Choctaw-Chickasaw Indian Agents, 1831–1874," *Chronicles of Oklahoma* 50 (Winter 1972): 417; Wright, "Removal of the Choctaws," 111–19.

101. Brigadier General George Gibson was commissary general of subsistence in the War Department, and his letter of 12 August 1831 confirmed Gaines' appointment as superintendent of the subsistence and removal of the Choctaw. Wright, "Removal of the Choctaws," 111; *Territorial Papers*, 21:336.

102. Gaines stated in his letter to Anthony Winston Dillard on 8 August 1857 that he accepted his appointment "some time in Aug. 1831."

103. Thomas McGee, Dr. Joseph B. Earle, and Sam Dale were old friends. George W. Harkins and Robert M. Jones, both mixed-blood Choctaw, were em-

ployed in Greenwood LeFlore's district to assist with the removal either directly or indirectly through Gaines. Foreman, *Indian Removal*, 48 n. 11.

104. Gaines received some criticism for the late arrival of the steamboats and for failing to charter more, although five steamboats were finally engaged for the 1831 removal party. DeRosier, *Removal of the Choctaw*, 143–44.

105. McGee, assisted by Peter B. Pitchlynn (ca. 1807–81), who replaced Mushulatubbee as district chief on 16 January 1831, led approximately four hundred Choctaw from the Northern District to Memphis, arriving in early November 1831. Baird, *Peter Pitchlynn*, 42; Foreman, *Indian Removal*, 50–51.

106. The two steamboats dispatched "up the Red river"—the *Talma* and *Cleopatra*—embarked with 1,164 emigrants via the Red River to the Ouachita River to Ecore á Fabre (now Camden, Arkansas) in late November 1831. Foreman, *Indian Removal*, 58–59.

107. Gaines and Earle embarked up the Mississippi on the *Walter Scott* with approximately one thousand Choctaw in late November 1831 for Arkansas Post. Ibid., 56–57.

108. Gaines arrived in Mobile on 16 December 1831, and on 24 December the *Mobile Commercial Register* reported on the successful "Choctaw Emigration" of 1831.

109. Henry Lazarus purchased the dry goods business from Gaines and Emanuel in 1835. Korn, *The Jews of Mobile*, 37.

110. Francis W. Armstrong was appointed federal agent to the Choctaw west of the Mississippi on 7 September 1831 and special agent for removal and subsistence west of the Mississippi on 2 July 1832. One of his brothers, Captain William Armstrong, was appointed superintendent of the Choctaw removal east of the Mississippi on 2 July 1832. DeRosier, *Removal of the Choctaw*, 149–50; Foreman, "The Armstrongs of Indian Territory," 298–99; Morris, "Choctaw-Chickasaw Indian Agents," 419.

111. The Alabama legislature enacted legislation in November 1832 to establish branches of the State Bank of Alabama at Decatur, Mobile, and Montgomery. Brantley, *Banking in Alabama*, 1:254–63.

112. John Gayle (1792–1859), a native of South Carolina, was elected governor in 1831 and reelected in 1833. He was a strong advocate for the Mobile branch bank. Garrett, *Reminiscences*, 458.

113. A special convention in South Carolina on 24 November 1832 had declared the tariff acts of 1828 and 1832 "null and void" in the state in defiance of federal law, and Jackson had responded with his Nullification Proclamation on 10 December 1832. James D. Richardson, comp., *A Compilation of the Messages and Papers of the Presidents, 1789–1897*, 10 vols. (Washington, D.C.: Government Printing Office, 1902), 2:640–56.

114. William Rufus King (1786–1853), a native of Sampson County, North Carolina, was U.S. senator from Alabama (1819–44; 1848–52); James Buchanan (1791–1868), a native of Pennsylvania and the fifteenth president of the United

States (1857–61), was a congressman (1820–31) from Pennsylvania. Garrett, *Reminiscences*, 675; *Dictionary of American Biography*, 2:207–11.

115. Gaines stayed at the Mansion House in New York, where he developed a pamphlet printed by "J. & J. Harper" that he used to sell the Alabama bonds. Brantley, *Banking in Alabama*, 1:267.

116. Joshua B. Leavins was appointed to the original board of directors of the Mobile branch bank. Ibid., 263.

117. Albert Gallatin (1761–1849), a native of Geneva, Switzerland, served as secretary of the treasury (1801–12) under Jefferson and Madison and became president of the new National Bank of New York on 1 April 1831. Walters, *Albert Gallatin*, 347.

118. "Mrs. Gallitin" was Albert Gallatin's second wife, Hannah Nicholson Gallatin (1766–1849), a descendant of a prominent eighteenth-century Maryland family. Ibid., 52–56.

119. The Phoenix Bank was one of the premier banking houses in nineteenth-century New York City, with stockholders such as John Jacob Astor. Kenneth Wiggins Porter, *John Jacob Astor: Business Man*, 2 vols. (New York: Russell & Russell, 1966), 2:973–74.

120. Washington Jackson of Philadelphia was identified by the *Mobile Commercial Register* on 11 July 1833 as one of the financial consultants who had advised Gaines to sell the bonds at par. Brantley, *Banking in Alabama*, 1:270, 465 n. 46.

121. Gaines reached an agreement in early April 1833 with J. D. Beers & Company of New York and Thomas Wilson & Company of London to purchase half of the bonds ($1,750,000), with an option to purchase the balance ($1,750,000) by 4 September 1834. Ibid., 267–73.

122. The Mobile branch bank showed a net profit of $99,000 in 1834 and $155,000 in 1836. Ibid., 373–75, 390–94.

123. Gaines was reelected president without opposition from 1833 through 1836, but in December 1837 he was reelected over John B. Norris by a vote of 63 to 59. Norris was elected bank president in December 1838. See Branch Bank: Minute Book for 1833–36 and 1836–41; Brantley, *Banking in Alabama*, 1:330–40, 355–58, 2:26, 34.

124. Guyandotte, located near the mouth of the Guyandotte River on the Ohio River, is a part of present-day Huntington, West Virginia. The White Sulphur Springs Resort was located at the present White Sulphur Springs, West Virginia.

125. Gaines addressed his letter to James Madison Porter (1793–1862), a native of Pennsylvania and interim secretary of war (1843–44) under President John Tyler (1841–45). *Dictionary of American Biography*, 8:94–95.

126. Henry and Joseph C. Willard, natives of Westminister, Vermont, operated the Willard Hotel, located between F Street and Pennsylvania Avenue. Poore, *Perley's Reminiscences*, 1:482–83.

127. Thomas Hartley Crawford, a native of Chambersburg, Pennsylvania,

served in Congress (1829–33) and later as commissioner of Indian affairs (1838–45) in the War Department. Kvasnicka and Viola, eds., *The Commissioners of Indian Affairs,* 23–27; Reports of the Commissioner of Indian Affairs, Secretary of War, National Archives, Washington, D.C.

128. Lewis Cass (1782–1866), a native of Exeter, New Hampshire, served as Jackson's secretary of war (1831–36) after Eaton's resignation over the "Peggy Eaton affair" and is the subject of the interchange between Gaines and Gibson. *Dictionary of American Biography,* 2:562–64.

129. John Tyler (1790–1862), a native of Charles City County, Virginia, was elected vice president of the United States in 1840 and became president following the death of William Henry Harrison on 4 April 1841. Robert Seager, *and Tyler too: A Biography of John & Julia Gardiner Tyler* (New York: McGraw-Hill, 1963), 146–50ff.

130. In his letter to Anthony Winston Dillard on 8 August 1857, Gaines stated that he had petitioned Congress on two separate occasions for additional compensation and that Congress had refused to honor his requests. See Appendix A.

DEATH OF A GOOD MAN FROM THE *HAYNEVILLE EXAMINER*

1. Gaines died at State Line, Mississippi, on 21 January 1873; his obituary was reprinted in Willis Brewer's *Hayneville Examiner.* Sutherd, *Gaines Family,* 328.

APPENDIX A.
GAINES TO DILLARD, 8 AUGUST 1857

1. Gaines' wrote his letter to Judge Anthony Winston Dillard of Sumter County, Alabama, in response to Dillard's request for information about the Treaty of Dancing Rabbit Creek. Owing to his "defective vision," Gaines dictated the letter to one of his sons. The original letter is in the Gaines Collection.

2. It appears from this statement that Gaines had written an earlier letter to Dillard in which he discussed the Treaty of Dancing Rabbit Creek. Dillard, "The Treaty of Dancing Rabbit Creek," 99–100.

3. Nitakechi (Netuckeijah) was the district chief for the Southern District. Foreman, *Indian Removal,* 23–30.

4. Although Gaines and Reynolds operated without written instructions from Secretary of War John H. Eaton, it is obvious from President Andrew Jackson's correspondence that the two agents were expected to reach an agreement to settle the Chickasaw within the Choctaw lands west of the Mississippi. Bassett, ed., *Correspondence of Andrew Jackson,* 4:224.

5. Greenwood LeFlore (Lafleur), a mixed-blood, was the district chief of the Western District. He became a successful planter and slave owner and remained in Mississippi. White, *The Roots of Dependency,* 125, 133, 145.

6. The town of Fort Smith, named for Colonel Thomas A. Smith, developed

around a fort established by Brevet Major Stephen H. Long and Captain William Bradford in 1817 at Belle Point on the Poteau River near its junction with the Arkansas. The fort was abandoned in 1824, reoccupied briefly in 1833–34, and reestablished in 1838. Robert W. Fraser, *Forts of the West: Military Forts and Presidios and Posts Commonly Called Forts West of the Mississippi River to 1898* (Norman: University of Oklahoma Press, 1965), 16–18.

7. Lieutenant James L. Dawson led a mounted escort detachment of thirteen men, including his father-in-law, Assistant Surgeon John W. Walker. Dawson, "Report of J. L. Dawson on His Escort of Choctaw and Chickasaw Delegates," 241–49.

8. Dawson's detachment joined the Choctaw and Chickasaw parties on 20 December 1830 "on a large creek running into the Canadian." Ibid., 243.

9. Benjamin Reynolds, the Chickasaw agent, led an exploring party that numbered sixteen. Foreman, *Indian Removal,* 33.

10. Levi Colbert, a mixed-blood, emerged as the principal leader of the Chickasaw and led the opposition to removal until his death in 1834. Arrell M. Gibson, *The Chickasaws* (Norman: University of Oklahoma Press, 1971), 153, 161, 174, 178.

11. Gaines' "L'Eau bleu" and False Washita are known today as the Blue and Washita Rivers. Morris, Goins, and Reynolds, *Historical Atlas of Oklahoma,* 6.

12. Dawson's forces departed on 10 January 1831 as Gaines' party moved eastward along the Red River. Dawson, "Report of J. L. Dawson on His Escort of Choctaw and Chickasaw Delegates," 248.

13. Gaines and Reynolds' joint report to Secretary of War John H. Eaton was dated 7 February 1831. Foreman, *Indian Removal,* 37–38.

14. Gaines arrived in Mobile on 2 March 1831 and remained there for several days before returning to Demopolis. *Mobile Commercial Register,* 7 March 1831.

15. John H. Eaton resigned as secretary of war on 7 April 1831 when Jackson's cabinet broke up over the "Peggy Eaton affair." He served as minister to Spain in 1836–40. Lewis Cass, governor of Michigan Territory (1813–31) was sworn in as secretary of war (1831–36) on 9 August 1831. Cole, *The Presidency of Andrew Jackson,* 83–87; Francis Paul Prucha, *Indian Policy in the United States: Historical Essays* (Lincoln: University of Nebraska Press, 1981), 76.

16. Because of the turmoil in Jackson's cabinet and his resignation on 7 April 1831, Eaton apparently failed to leave a written record of his commitments to Gaines, to respond to the joint report by Gaines and Reynolds, or to respond to Gaines' correspondence regarding his appointments. Cole, *The Presidency of Andrew Jackson,* 83–87.

17. Though trained as a lawyer, Lewis Cass spent much of his life in the political arena, serving as governor of Michigan Territory (1813–31), secretary of war (1831–36), minister to France (1836), U.S. senator (1845–48; 1851–57), and secretary of state under James Buchanan (1857–60). An old-line Jacksonian Democrat, Cass was defeated by Zachary Taylor in the presidential election of 1848. *Dictionary of American Biography,* 2:562–64.

18. Francis W. Armstrong served in the 24th Infantry Regiment during the War of 1812 (1812–15), became a major before his discharge on 15 June 1815, and served in both houses of the Alabama legislature (1820–21; 1823–25). One of his brothers, General Robert Armstrong, commanded Jackson's artillery during the Creek War of 1813–14 and at the Battle of New Orleans, and Jackson left him a case of pistols and a sword in his last will. Foreman, "The Armstrongs of Indian Territory," 293; Robert V. Remini, *Andrew Jackson and the Course of American Democracy, 1833–1845* (New York: Harper & Row, 1984), 485.

19. William S. Colquhoun was appointed to assist with the Choctaw removal and was directed to Greenwood LeFlore's district on 5 July 1831, after Eaton's resignation and prior to Cass' confirmation. Foreman, *Indian Removal,* 44.

20. Francis W. Armstrong's appointment to conduct a census of the Choctaw in preparation for their removal was made on 26 April 1831, after Eaton's resignation and before Cass became secretary of war on 9 August 1831. Wright, "Removal of the Choctaws," 111; Bassett, ed., *Correspondence of Andrew Jackson,* 4:172; *Territorial Papers,* 21:430 n. 35.

21. Brigadier General George Gibson, commissary general of subsistence in the War Department, wrote Gaines on 12 August 1831 confirming his appointment as superintendent of the subsistence and removal of the Choctaw. Foreman, *Indian Removal,* 46.

22. Gaines was in the process of ending his business partnership with Allen Glover in Demopolis, Alabama, and beginning a new one with Jonathan Emanuel of Mobile in 1830–32.

23. Gaines had employed several old friends as assistants for the Choctaw removal by September 1831: Sam Dale, Thomas McGee, and Dr. Joseph B. Earle.

24. Gaines' emigration numbers were probably closer to about 4,500, since Lieutenant J. R. Stephenson reported issuing rations to 3,749 Choctaw at four stations in the Red River country on 30 April 1832, while Lieutenant G. J. Rains issued rations to another 536 Choctaw near Fort Smith. Foreman, *Indian Removal,* 68; Wright, "Removal of the Choctaws," 119.

25. Gaines' reference to the Washita is the Ouachita River of Arkansas and Louisiana, not the Washita River of Oklahoma, which Gaines also refers to as the False Washita, or Fausse Washita. Foreman, *Indians and Pioneers,* 22 n. 50.

26. Gibson notified Gaines on 27 April 1832 that all of the civilians connected to the first Choctaw removal were now discharged and that all future removals would be directed by the U.S. Army. DeRosier, *Removal of the Choctaw,* 149.

27. On 2 July 1832, Francis W. Armstrong, Choctaw agent west of the Mississippi, was appointed special agent and superintendent for the removal of the Choctaw west of the Mississippi, and one of his brothers, Captain William Armstrong, was appointed special agent and superintendent for the removal of the Choctaw east of the Mississippi. Foreman, "The Armstrongs of Indian Territory," 298–99.

28. Gaines stopped briefly in Washington in April 1833 on his return to Mo-

bile after successfully negotiating the sale of Alabama bonds in New York. Brantley, *Banking in Alabama*, 1:267–68.

29. Martin Van Buren (1782–1862), a native of Kinderhook, New York, served as Jackson's secretary of state (1829–31) and minister to Great Britain (1831–32) and was Jackson's new vice president (1833–37). James C. Curtis, *The Fox at Bay: Martin Van Buren and the Presidency, 1837–1841* (Lexington: University of Kentucky Press, 1970), 6–35.

30. Citing ill health, Gaines declined to run for reelection and was replaced by John B. Norris as president of the Mobile branch bank. Brantley, *Banking in Alabama*, 2:381 n. 49.

31. James Madison Porter was appointed secretary of war on 8 March 1843 by President John Tyler, but the Senate rejected his nomination on 30 January 1844. *Dictionary of American Biography*, 8:94–95.

32. Lewis Cass was the Democratic party's candidate for president in the election of 1848. He lost the election to the Whig candidate, Zachary Taylor.

33. While Gaines gives a very negative view of Cass as an administrator, at least one recent scholar gives him relatively high marks for his Indian policy. See Prucha, *Indian Policy in the United States*, 76–91.

34. While condemning the abolitionists and the partisan politicians, Gaines continued to cling to his faith in the strength and resilience of the American Union to persevere.

Appendix B.
Conversation with George S. Gaines by Albert James Pickett

1. Alabama historian Albert James Pickett interviewed Gaines in 1847 after an exchange of letters in which he asked for Gaines' assistance with Pickett's research for his *History of Alabama*. The first "Conversation" covers twenty-nine handwritten pages, and while some paragraph breaks have been added in the long passages, Pickett's spelling and sentence structure have minimal changes. Pickett added the following marginal note on the first page of the first conversation: "Notes taken from the lips of Geo. S. Gaines at his home at Spring Hill near Mobile." Pickett Papers.

2. The Shawnee chief Tecumseh made a recruiting campaign into Mississippi Territory in the late summer and early fall of 1811 to develop an alliance with the Cherokee, Chickasaw, Choctaw, and Creeks. Glenn Tucker, *Tecumseh: Vision of Glory* (Indianapolis: Bobbs-Merrill, 1956), 195–217.

3. The Black Warrior Town of Oceoche Emathla was located at the falls of the Black Warrior River.

4. Benjamin Hawkins (1754–1816), a native of Bute County, North Carolina, was appointed "the first general or principal agent for all southern nations of Indians" in 1796 by President George Washington, but he served principally as the federal agent to the Creeks for twenty years. See Florette Henri, *The Southern*

Indians and Benjamin Hawkins, 1796–1816 (Norman: University of Oklahoma Press, 1986).

5. The "Tuscaloosa Chief" is Oceoche Emathla, who led the delegation from the Black Warrior Town to the Choctaw Trading House at St. Stephens in 1812.

6. The engagement at Burnt Corn Creek was fought on 13 July 1813, and Fort Mims was destroyed by the Creek Red Sticks on 30 August 1813. Pickett, *History of Alabama*, 523–25, 528–43.

7. Pushmataha, chief of the Southern District of the Choctaw Nation, journeyed to St. Stephens after learning of the destruction of Fort Mims in September 1813. Brigadier General Thomas Flournoy was commander of the Seventh Military District, with headquarters at New Orleans.

8. "Gov. Blunt" was Willie Blount, governor of Tennessee (1809–15), who authorized Jackson to raise volunteer forces to aid the citizens of Mississippi Territory. Remini, *Andrew Jackson and the Course of American Empire*, 191.

9. Samuel A. Edmondson carried Gaines' letters to Governor Blount and General Jackson from St. Stephens via the "Tennessee Road" or "Big Trading Path" to the Natchez Trace north to Nashville, crossing the Tennessee River at Colbert's Ferry. Phelps, "Stands and Travel Accommodations on the Natchez Trace," 45–47.

10. Jackson's encounter with Jesse and Thomas Hart Benton is described in detail in Remini, *Andrew Jackson and the Course of American Empire*, 181–86.

11. Chickasaw agent John McKee and John Pitchlynn met with Gaines and John Flood McGrew at Pitchlynn's residence on Oktibbeha Creek, where they discussed coordinating the Chickasaw and Choctaw volunteers against the Creeks. Halbert and Ball, *The Creek War*, 213.

12. Mushulatubbee was the district chief for the Northern District of the Choctaw Nation and assisted in raising volunteers in his district. William A. Love, "Mingo Moshulitubbee's Prairie Village," *Publications of the Mississippi Historical Society* 7 (1903): 373–78.

13. Mrs. Nail was probably Molly Nail, the mixed-blood wife of Henry Nail. Halbert Papers.

14. In the eighteenth century, most of the southern Indians referred to white Americans from the Atlantic Coast as "Virginians." Henry Sale Halbert claimed that "Virginian" in Choctaw was "Wachina" and credited the Shawnee for developing the term "Virginian." Halbert Papers.

15. According to several sources, Mushulatubbee had two residences and two wives. One home was located near present-day Brooksville, Mississippi, along the Noxubee County and Lowndes County line. This property was purchased by Thomas G. Blewett in 1832. Love, "Mingo Moshulitubbee's Prairie Village," 373–74, 377; Lincecum, "Life of Apushimataha," 418–19.

16. Silas Dinsmoor, the former Choctaw agent (1802–14), was replaced by John McKee on 28 June 1814. Cotterill, *The Southern Indians*, 189–90.

17. Brigadier Ferdinand L. Claiborne, appointed commander of volunteer forces in Mississippi Territory, arrived at Fort Stoddert with seven hundred men on 30 July 1813. Claiborne, *Mississippi*, 333–34.

18. Puckshenubbee served as district chief for the Western District; Pushmataha's district was the Southern (or Six Towns) District, which included the Six Towns, Chickasawhay, and Yowani; and Mushulatubbee's district was generally referred to as the Northern (or Northeastern) District. White, *The Roots of Dependency,* 111.

19. Dinsmoor and Robertson negotiated the Treaty of Mount Dexter, signed by twenty-three Choctaw chiefs and warriors on 16 November 1805. Kappler, comp., *Indian Affairs, Laws and Treaties,* 2:87.

20. Fallectabrenna Oldfield (Fallectabunna in Halbert Papers) was located on the Tombigbee a few miles from Tuscahoma Bluff in the present Choctaw County, Alabama.

21. Clarke County, Alabama, was created in 1812; Wayne County, Mississippi, was created in 1809; and Greene County, Mississippi, was created in 1811. *Territorial Papers,* 6:177, 252.

22. The settlers listed were probably Francis Boykin, James and John Caller (Callier), Joseph and Thomas Bates, John and Daniel Johnson, Adam and William Hollinger, Samuel Mims, Young Gaines, and John Linder. Matte, *History of Washington County,* 9, 12–14, 19–25, 27, 31–33; *Territorial Papers* (see vols. 5, 6, and 18).

23. John Forbes and Company replaced the parent Panton, Leslie and Company as the principal English trading firm in the Spanish Floridas in 1804–5. William S. Coker, "John Forbes & Company and the War of 1812 in the Spanish Borderlands," in *Hispanic-American Essays in Honor of Max Leon Moorhead,* ed. William S. Coker (Pensacola: Perdido Bay Press, 1979), 61–97.

24. Joseph Chambers was appointed register for the land office of Washington County by Ephriam Kirby of Connecticut by authority of President Thomas Jefferson in December 1803. *Territorial Papers,* 5:297, 303, 340, 369–70, 421–22.

25. Ephriam Kirby died at Fort Stoddert on 20 October 1804. Ibid., 356 n. 11, 359.

26. Robert C. Nicholas of Kentucky and Ephriam Kirby of Connecticut were appointed land commissioners of the United States in Washington County, Mississippi Territory, by President Thomas Jefferson in July 1803 to establish land claims east of the Pearl River. Ibid., 222–24, 329–32.

27. The preemption rights for residents of the lands east of the Pearl River were incorporated in an act passed by Congress on 3 March 1803: "An Act regulating the grants of land, and providing for the disposal of lands of the United States, south of the state of Tennessee." Ibid., 192–205.

28. Thomas H. Williams (1780–1840), a native of North Carolina, was appointed register of the land office west of the Pearl River in 1805. He served as secretary of Mississippi Territory (1805–6) and was elected Mississippi's first U.S. senator (1817–29). Ibid., 380 n. 71, 417–18, 532, 744–45.

29. Thomas W. Maury, appointed receiver for the lands east of the Pearl River on 20 December 1805, accepted temporary housing at the factory. He resigned for health reasons on 20 February 1807. Ibid., 425, 492–93, 515–16.

30. Lemuel Henry, a lawyer, was recommended by Thomas H. Williams and James Caller in 1807 to replace Thomas W. Maury as receiver. Williams, while serving as acting governor of Mississippi Territory, later appointed Henry attorney general for Washington County on 5 June 1809. Ibid., 493–94, 542–43, 738.

31. Nicholas Perkins, a native of Virginia, was nominated by Joseph Chambers to serve as register of the land office east of the Pearl River on 12 October 1805. He later served as attorney general for Washington County. Ibid., 421, 453, 738.

32. Isaac Briggs was appointed "Surveyor of the lands of the United States south of the State of Tennessee" on 15 December 1804 by Secretary of the Treasury Albert Gallatin. Ibid., 304, 374, 380, 451–52.

33. Captain Peter Philip Schuyler, a native of New York, was the second commandant following Captain Bartholomew Schaumburgh, founder of Fort Stoddert in July 1799. Fort Stoddert was named for Benjamin Stoddert, first secretary of navy and acting secretary of war when the post was established. Ibid., 304; Prucha, *The Sword of the Republic*, 56.

34. Vinzente Folch was the Spanish governor of West Florida and Captain Cayetano Perez the commandant at Fort Charlotte (Mobile) whom Gaines and other territorial officials debated and corresponded with during this period prior to the seizure of Mobile by General James Wilkinson on 13 April 1813. *Territorial Papers*, 6:138, 142–43, 147–49, 151, 168, 188–89, 362.

35. Henry Dearborn (1751–1829), a native of Hampton, New Hampshire, served as secretary of war (1801–9) in Thomas Jefferson's administration and issued orders to Lieutenant Edmund Pendleton Gaines, U.S. infantry commandant at Fort Stoddert, in 1807 to survey possible routes between Muscle Shoals on the Tennessee and Cotton Gin Port on the Tombigbee. Ibid., 5:558, 598–602.

36. Fort Massac was located on the Illinois shore of the Ohio River about ten miles downriver from Paducah, Kentucky. Prucha, *The Sword of the Republic*, 35–36.

37. Gaines constructed a brick residence and store in 1811 and charged rent to the federal government.

38. Gaines shipped his skins and other trade goods to Joseph Saul at New Orleans, who operated warehouses for the Office of Indian Trade and attempted to market the skins in Europe. Peake, *History of the United States Indian Factory System*, 142, 147, 151–52, 255.

39. Reuben Kemper and Joseph Kennedy were the principal leaders of forces that attempted to seize Mobile in 1810. *Territorial Papers*, 6:79–82, 84–90, 140–43, 152–58.

40. Major William H. Hargrave was a member of Reuben Kemper's filibustering forces and was captured by Spanish forces near Mobile in December 1810. Ibid., 5:157.

41. Nicholas Perkins arrived at Fort Stoddert the morning of 19 February 1807. Silver, *Edmund Pendleton Gaines*, 14.

42. Thomas Malone was assistant factor at the Choctaw trading house, and

Theodore Brightwell served as sheriff of Washington County and later as sheriff of Mobile County. *Territorial Papers,* 6:324.

43. Wakefield was the county seat for Washington County (1804–9). Matte, *History of Washington County,* 29, 50.

44. "Maj. Hinsons" or "Col. Hinsons" appears to be a reference to James Hinson, who lived about eight miles from Wakefield. Silver, *Edmund Pendleton Gaines,* 14–15.

45. Aaron Burr, former vice president of the United States (1801–5), was charged with conspiracy against the U.S. government in warrants issued by Robert Williams, governor of Mississippi Territory, and President Thomas Jefferson. Claiborne, *Mississippi,* 272–84.

46. Gaines intercepted Burr at about 9:00 A.M. on 19 February 1807 a short distance from Major James Hinson's. Silver, *Edmund Pendleton Gaines,* 14–15; Claiborne, *Mississippi,* 288–89.

47. Mrs. Gaines was Frances Toulmin Gaines, the first wife of Edmund Pendleton Gaines and the daughter of Judge Harry Toulmin, who died in 1811. Silver, *Edmund Pendleton Gaines,* 15, 22, 29.

48. Gainesville, Sumter County, Alabama, was founded by Moses Lewis near the mouth of the Noxubee River on the west bank of the Tombigbee River in 1832 and named for George Strother Gaines. Brewer, *Alabama,* 526.

49. The party appointed to conduct Aaron Burr back east for trial included Nicholas Perkins, Thomas Malone, Henry B. Slade, John Mills, John Jay Henry, Samuel McCormack, and John Mertes. Owens, *History of Alabama,* 1:180.

APPENDIX C.
2ND CONVERSATION WITH GEO. S. GAINES, SPRING OF 1848,
BY ALBERT JAMES PICKETT

1. Albert James Pickett conducted his second interview of Gaines at Spring Hill, Alabama, in the spring of 1848. The second "Conversation" covers fourteen handwritten pages and contains a strange break in pagination after the first seven pages—the following page is also numbered "[7]" and the manuscript continues to page thirteen. At the break in pagination, there is a note, "Continuation of the Notes of Hon Geo. S. Gaines." Although there are a number of single pages with additional notes taken from the Gaines interviews in the Pickett Papers, it is not clear when they were taken, and they do not generally add to the "conversations" presented in this volume. Pickett Papers.

2. Hoe Buckintoopa was the Choctaw name for the bluff where the Spanish post San Esteban de Tombecbé (or St. Etienne), was constructed, and Fort Confederation was located on Jones' Bluff on the Tombigbee River near present-day Epes, Sumter County, Alabama. Fort Confederation was evacuated in March 1797, and the Spanish withdrew from San Esteban on 5 February 1799. Pate, "Fort of the Confederation," 186; Lawrence Kinnaird, ed., *Spain in the Mississippi*

Valley, 1765–1794, Annual Report of the American Historical Association for the Year 1945, 3 vols. (Washington, D.C.: Government Printing Office, 1946–49), 3:280, 298.

3. Nanih Waiya is located on the west bank of Nanih Waiya Creek in southern Winston County, Mississippi, and some four hundred yards from the Neshoba County line. Carolyn Keller Reeves, ed., *The Choctaw before Removal* (Jackson: University Press of Mississippi, 1985), 4–5.

4. James Colbert was an Indian countryman who had several children by some three Chickasaw wives. At least two authorities have identified five sons instead of the three listed by Gaines: William, George, Levi, James, and Joseph. Phelps, "Stands and Travel Accommodations on the Natchez Trace," 40–41, 43–48; Samuel Cole Williams, ed., *Adair's History of the American Indians* (1775; reprint, New York: Promontory Press, 1930), 398; Gibson, *The Chickasaws,* 65.

5. George Colbert operated his ferry on the Natchez Trace where it crossed the Tennessee River below the Muscle Shoals from 1801 until 1819, when other roads reduced the traffic and his profits. Gaines probably crossed at Colbert's Ferry in 1810. Phelps, "Stands and Travel Accommodations on the Natchez Trace," 46.

6. Levi Colbert's stand was located on the north bank of Buzzard Roost Creek on the Natchez Trace about nine miles south of Colbert's Ferry and was known as the Buzzard Roost Stand. Ibid., 43.

7. Although the exact location of James Colbert's stand on the Natchez Trace is unknown, it was operated from 1812 to 1821 by Colbert, who was described as "a native of this country who had been baptized, reads and writes, is a man of property; one quarter Indian, is a sober man . . . " Ibid., 40–41.

8. James Brown's stand was located near present-day Tishomingo, Mississippi. Ibid., 42–43.

9. The Chickasaw population is estimated to have been 3,625 in 1817 and 4,715 in 1833, while the Choctaw numbered 19,554 in 1831. John R. Swanton, *The Indian Tribes of North America,* Bureau of American Ethnology *Bulletin 145* (1952; reprint, Washington, D.C.: Smithsonian Institution Press, 1968), 179, 184.

10. Cotton Gin Port was located twenty-five miles south of the mouth of Bear Creek on the Tombigbee River in present-day Monroe County, Mississippi. There is some tradition that the Chickasaw defiantly burned the gin that the federal government built on this site to encourage farming by the Chickasaw. *Territorial Papers,* 5:598–99; W. A. Evans, "Gaines Trace in Monroe County, Mississippi," *Journal of Mississippi History* 1 (April 1939): 102.

11. Gaines is describing the route of the "Tennessee Road" or "Big Trading Path," which led northward from Mobile, struck Jackson's Military Road, crossed William Starnes' ferry on the Noxubee River, and connected to the Natchez Trace below Colbert's Ferry. Love, "Mingo Moshulitubbee's Prairie Village," 374.

12. Oktibbeha Creek was the boundary line between the Choctaw and the Chickasaw.

13. John Pitchlynn (ca. 1764–1835), an Indian countryman, married Rhoda

Folsom, daughter of Nathaniel Folsom, and on her death married her cousin Sophia Folsom, daughter of Ebenezer Folsom. Their son Peter Pitchlynn led the rebirth of the Choctaw Nation in Indian Territory. Halbert Papers; Baird, *Peter Pitchlynn*, xv, 5–19.

14. The Treaty of Doak's Stand was signed by Pushmataha, Puckshenubbee, Mushulatubbee, and the other "mingoes, head men, and warriors of the Choctaw nation" on 18 October 1820. Kappler, comp., *Indian Affairs, Laws and Treaties*, 2:191–95.

15. John H. Eaton and John Coffee (1772–1833), a native of Prince Edward County, Virginia, negotiated a removal treaty with the Chickasaw at Franklin, Tennessee, on 31 August 1830, but this treaty was not ratified by the U.S. Senate. The Treaty of Pontotoc, signed on 20 October 1832 and ratified by the U.S. Senate on 1 March 1833, provided for the cession of Chickasaw lands east of the Mississippi and removal to the West. Kappler, comp., *Indian Affairs, Laws and Treaties*, 2:356–62, 1035–40.

16. "Coonsha towns" may be a reference to Coosha on Lost Horse Creek, Lauderdale County, Mississippi, or Concha (or Kunshak Boluka) in southwest Kemper County, Mississippi. Halbert Papers.

17. Colonel Matthew Arbuckle was the commander (1824–41) at Fort Gibson. Agnew, *Fort Gibson*, 30, 205.

18. Gaines' exploring party began their ascent of the country between the Arkansas and Red Rivers on 6 December 1830 and arrived in Washington, Hempstead County, Arkansas Territory, on 29 January 1831. Gaines to Dillard, Peachwood, 8 August 1857, Gaines Collection; Dawson, "Report of J. L. Dawson on His Escort of Choctaw and Chickasaw Delegates," 241–48.

19. Since he did not trust Lewis Cass and viewed Francis W. Armstrong as a pawn of the secretary of war, Gaines has the sequence of events slightly skewed. The record shows the following: Eaton resigned as secretary of war on 7 April 1831; Francis W. Armstrong was appointed a special agent to the Choctaw on 26 April 1831 to conduct a census in preparation for their removal; Cass was sworn in as secretary on 9 August 1831, and Commissary General George Gibson wrote Gaines' appointment letter on 12 August 1831. Cole, *The Presidency of Andrew Jackson*, 83–87; Prucha, *Indian Policy in the United States*, 76; Wright, "Removal of the Choctaws," 111; Bassett, ed., *Correspondence of Andrew Jackson*, 4:172; Foreman, *Indian Removal*, 46.

20. William Ward was the Choctaw agent who failed to properly enroll the Choctaw who attempted to file land claims to remain in Mississippi as provided for in Article 14 of the Treaty of Dancing Rabbit Creek. Gaines served (1844–46) on the second Choctaw claims commission (1842–46), which validated 1,009 out of 1,093 claims reviewed, but its recommendations, along with those of the first commission (1837), were disregarded. Kidwell, *Choctaws and Missionaries*, 167–69; Young, *Redskins, Ruffleshirts, and Rednecks*, 51–65.

$\mathcal{S}$elected Gaines Bibliography

Armstrong, Zella. *Notable Southern Families.* 6 vols. 1918–33. Reprint (6 vols. in 3), Baltimore: Genealogical Publishing Co., 1974.

Brantley, William Henry. *Banking in Alabama.* 2 vols. Birmingham: Oxmoor Press, 1961–67.

Dawson, James L. "Report of J. L. Dawson on His Escort of Choctaw and Chickasaw Delegates in Indian Territory, Dec. 1830–Jan. 1831." In James Henry Gardner, "The Lost Captain: J. L. Dawson of Old Fort Gibson." *Chronicles of Oklahoma* 21 (September 1943): 241–49.

DeRosier, Arthur H., Jr. *The Removal of the Choctaw Indians.* Knoxville: University of Tennessee Press, 1970.

Dillard, Anthony Winston. "The Treaty of Dancing Rabbit Creek between the United States and the Choctaw Indians in 1830." *Transactions of the Alabama Historical Society, 1898–1899* 3 (1899): 99–106.

Foreman, Grant. *Indian Removal: The Emigration of the Five Civilized Tribes of Indians.* 1932; new ed., 1953. Norman: University of Oklahoma Press, 1972.

Gaines, George Strother. "Extracts from Memoranda of Geo. S. Gaines." *Alabama Historical Reporter* 2 (May 1884): 2–3.

——. "Gaines' Reminiscences." *Alabama Historical Quarterly* 26 (Fall–Winter 1964): 133–229.

——. "George S. Gaines to A. W. Dillard [in reference to the Dancing Rabbit Creek Indian Treaty], Peachwood 8th Aug 1857." *Arrow Points* 11 (September 1925): 25–39.

——. "Letters from George Strother Gaines Relating to Events in South Alabama, 1805–1814." *Transactions of the Alabama Historical Society, 1898–1899* 3 (1899): 184–92.

——. "Notes on the Early Days of South Alabama." *Mobile Register,* 19 June–17 July 1872.

——. "Removal of the Choctaws." In *Dancing Rabbit Creek Treaty.* Historical and Patriotic Series No. 10. State Department of Archives and History. Birmingham: Birmingham Printing Co., 1928.

Halbert, Henry Sale. "The Story of the Treaty of Dancing Rabbit." *Publications of the Mississippi Historical Society* 6 (1902): 375–402.

Leftwich, George J. "Colonel George Strother Gaines and Other Pioneers in Mississippi Territory." *Publications of the Mississippi Historical Society,* centenary ser., 1 (1904): 442–56.

Pickett, Albert James. *History of Alabama and Incidentally of Georgia and Mississippi, from the Earliest Period.* 2 vols. 1851. Reprint (2 vols. in 1), Birmingham: Birmingham Book and Magazine Co., 1962.

Plaisance, Aloysius. "The Choctaw Trading House, 1803–1822." *Alabama Historical Quarterly* 16 (Fall–Winter 1954), 393–423.

Silver, James W. *Edmund Pendleton Gaines: Frontier General.* Baton Rouge: Louisiana State University Press, 1949.

Smith, Winston. *Days of Exile: The Story of the Vine and Olive Colony in Alabama.* Tuscaloosa: W. B. Drake and Sons, 1967.

———. "Early History of Demopolis." *Alabama Review* 18 (April 1965): 83–91.

Sutherd, Calvin E. *A Compilation of Gaines Family Data with Special Emphasis on the Lineage of William and Isabella (Pendleton) Gaines.* 1969. Reprint, Fort Lauderdale: n.p., 1972.

Index

Gaines, Edmund Pendleton (Mobile physician), 80

Gaines, Elizabeth Ervin, 8

Gaines, Elizabeth Strother, 2

Gaines, Esther Lawrence, 6, 29, 161

Gaines, Frances Toulmin, 5, 145, 161

Gaines, Francis (Frank) Young, 31

Gaines, George Stark, 29

GAINES, GEORGE STROTHER, 1–33, 37–39, 131–45, 147–53, 155–67, 178 (n. 1), 187 (n. 1); factor at St. Stephens (1805–16), 3–9, 40, 41, 52, 61, 62, 67, 70, 131–33, 135, 140–41, 142, 144–45, 156, 157, 178 (n. 7), 200 (n. 1); postmaster at St. Stephens, 3, 64, 67, 68; leadership during the Creek War of 1813–14, 7–8, 56–69, 131–36; factor at Fort Confederation (1816–19), 9–12, 73, 74, 76, 78, 79, 80, 81, 188 (nn. 9, 10); postmaster at Fort Confederation, 10; cashier at Tombeckbe Bank (1818–22), 11–12, 80, 82; partnership with Glover (1821–31), 12, 13, 14, 16, 81, 82, 83, 86, 87, 90, 93–94, 100, 102, 107, 119, 122; moves to Demopolis (1822), 81, 82; travels to New York, 20, 82; state senator (1825–27), 13, 75–76, 118, 189 (nn. 17, 18); at Dancing Rabbit Creek treaty conference (1830), 13–14, 91–93, 150, 151; agent for Choctaw exploring party (1830–31), 14–16, 92–93, 94–102, 118, 119–22, 126, 150–52, 155, 157, 165, 195 (n. 80), 209 (n. 18); superintendent for removal and subsistence (1831–32), 14, 17–19, 102, 103–7, 122–26, 155, 158, 161, 165; partnership with Emanuel (1831–35), 16, 19, 21, 24, 25, 107, 123, 124, 125, 160, 202 (n. 22); moves to Spring Hill (1832), 19,

107, 125, 126; state bond salesman (1832–33), 19–21, 107–8, 109–12, 126, 161; president of state branch bank at Mobile (1832–38), 19, 21–24, 107, 112, 118, 126, 178 (n. 9), 199 (n. 123), 203 (n. 30); in Washington (1815, 1832, 1833, 1843, 1849), 8, 20, 25, 28, 71, 108, 113–16, 126, 127–29, 202–3 (n. 28); at White Sulphur Springs (1843), 112–13, 127; Pickett interviews (1847–48), 131–45, 147–53; promoter for Mobile & Ohio Railroad (1847–50), 27, 28, 38, 178 (n. 9); nurseryman (1856–73), 29, 30, 31, 32; Mississippi legislator (1861–63), 31; obituary, 118, 200 (n. 1)

Gaines, George Washington, 8, 12

Gaines, Henry Lawrence, 13

Gaines, James (captain), 2, 3, 178 (n. 6)

Gaines, James Taylor, 11

Gaines, Jonathan Emanuel, 29, 30, 32

Gaines, Mary, 29, 30

Gaines, Vivian P. (Mobile physician), 133, 187 (n. 1)

Gaines, William D. (St. Stephens merchant), 80

Gaines, Young, Sr., 6, 29, 43, 44, 73, 137, 161, 180 (n. 13)

Gaines Invincibles, 31

Gainesville, Sumter County, Alabama, 118, 145, 159, 207 (n. 48)

Gaineswood, Demopolis, Alabama, 82, 167

Gallatin (banker). See Gallatin, Albert

Gallatin, Albert, 20–21, 109–10, 112, 161, 199 (n. 117)

Gallatin, Tennessee, 1, 3, 8, 40, 139

Garrett, William, 24

Scaffolding, ancient custom of, 76

Schuyler (bookkeeper at Emanuel & Gaines), 107

Schuyler, Peter Philip, 140, 206 (n. 33)

Seymour's Bluff, Mobile River, 43

Shawnee, 53, 98–99

Shawnee Prophet, 68, 187 (n. 85)

Shields, Samuel B., 75, 76

Shuquanochie. *See* Sucarnochee River

Six Towns, 7, 103. *See also* Southern District

Skyler (captain). *See* Schuyler, Peter Philip

Slade, Henry B., 145, 207 (n. 49)

Slaves, 6, 10, 12, 29–30, 65, 66, 73, 79, 101, 133, 137, 144, 157, 162

Small medal chiefs. *See* Captains

Smith, James, 158

Smith, Sidney, 27

Smithland, Kentucky, 50, 181 (n. 24)

Smoot, Benjamin S. (captain), 55, 191 (n. 37)

South Carolina, 6, 11, 12, 47, 74, 80, 81, 108, 137, 148, 149, 160, 161

Southeastern District. *See* Southern District

Southern District, 7, 12, 47, 86, 88, 103, 105, 165, 179 (n. 8). *See also* Nitakechi; Pushmataha

Spain, 49, 102, 114, 122, 138, 142, 159

Spanish: at Mobile, 5, 52, 133, 140–41, 142, 156, 206 (n. 34); at Fort Confederation, 72, 147, 188 (n. 8), 207 (n. 2); at Pensacola, 67, 135, 160, 171; at St. Stephens (San Esteban de Tombecbé), 3, 40, 41, 138, 142, 147, 188 (n. 8), 207 (n. 2)

Spanish warrants, 44, 140

Spring Hill, Alabama, 2, 19, 27

Starks (early settlers), 74

Starner, William (blacksmith). *See* Starnes, William

Starnes, William, 57, 149, 150, 183 (n. 41)

State Bank of Alabama: at Decatur, 19, 107; at Mobile, 19, 21–25, 107, 112, 126, 127; at Montgomery, 19, 107

State Line, Mississippi, 2, 29, 158

Steamboats, 16, 17, 18, 81, 91, 100, 101, 102, 105, 106, 107, 124, 125, 150, 158

Stephenson, J. R., 18, 202 (n. 24)

Stokes County, North Carolina, 2, 3, 163, 178 (n. 6)

Strong (St. Stephens physician), 80

Strouds, 83, 142

Sucarnochee River, 14, 73, 76, 94, 162, 195 (n. 74)

Sullivan County, Tennessee, 3

Sumter County, Alabama, 2, 141, 159

Sunflower Bend, Tombigbee River, Washington County, Alabama, 145

Surry County, North Carolina, 2, 3, 178 (n. 6)

Sussex County, Virginia, 157

Swift's place, Spring Hill, Alabama, 107

Talma, 18, 198 (n. 106)

Taney, Roger B., 17

Tapenhahamma, 83, 86, 193 (n. 53)

Taylor, Angus, 31

Taylor, Haynes G., 75

Taylor, Zachary, 28, 156